A GEOGRAPHY OF THE
NEW YORK
METROPOLITAN REGION

EDWARD F. BERGMAN

Herbert H. Lehman College (CUNY)

THOMAS W. POHL

KENDALL/HUNT PUBLISHING COMPANY
Dubuque, Iowa

The authors wish to thank Sylvia Seigel and Barbara Acker
for their assistance in typing from a scarcely legible manu-
script.

Contents

1921601

Prologue:

Defining a Metropolitan Region

Metropolitan Political Fragmentation

The social and economic influence of any large American city extends far beyond the city's legal borders. The borders were first drawn to include the central built-up area plus some surrounding land for future growth, but population dispersal almost inevitably spilled over those margins into suburbs. Some commercial activities followed the population of the central city out, and new enterprises established themselves in the suburbs. The suburban populations, in order to assure themselves public services and, often, to escape annexation by the central city, incorporated as independent municipalities. Thus large metropolitan areas usually cover a considerable number of municipalities, as well as one or more county jurisdictions.

In many cases the suburbs sprawling out from two central cities merged, forming a continuous urban area. So it happened among the suburbs of New York City, Jersey City, Newark, Paterson, Passaic, and several other historic core cities of the New York Metropolitan Region. Of any four suburban neighbors, two may commute to jobs in central cities in different directions, a third may commute to work in another suburb, and the fourth may work in his home suburb! A typical metropolitan pattern is of ubiquitous residential development, but with identifiable principal foci of economic activity—usually the central business districts (CBD) of the older central cities—and secondary foci in the shopping centers and office complexes scattered throughout the suburbs.

Consequent Problems

The political fragmentation of any such metropolitan area causes at least two major problems. One of them is the difficulty of coordinating the many local governments to deal with matters which affect the Region as a whole—matters such as water supplies, solid waste disposal, air and water pollution, and transportation within the Region. No single municipal or county government can solve these problems alone, and metropolitan regions often lack a political framework which covers the whole region and which allows the total population to deal with regional problems together.

A second problem faces anyone who wants to observe and measure the processes of growth and change within a metropolitan region, whether the observer is a beginning student or a professional planner. The many political units within the region are the areal units of record-keeping and statistical analysis, and yet these units may not be the best possible areal units to measure what is really going on. Westchester County, for example, is unquestionably a part of the New York Metropolitan Region. A wide range of statistics are available to measure residential development, industrial development, open space preservation and so forth in that County. Since these measures are taken for the County as a whole, however, they mask important differences between the southern portion of the County, where development is advanced and intensifying, and the North, which is far less developed. Anyone riding through the County can see this, but lack of many important statistical records at a subcounty level frustrates any attempt to measure this.

These two problems—that of Regional mobilization for Regional problem-solving and that of less-than-perfect statistical unit areas—afflict us already when we try to define the limits of the New York Metropolitan Region. We must always look for functional organization, and we learn that different governments differently define the Region for different purposes. Also, since we must always try to measure what we are talking about, we must reconcile ourselves to using certain definitions of the Region as defined by the statistics that are available, however frustratingly inconsistent this may force us to be.

Let us examine, then, a number of definitions of the Region which we will use at various times in this book, beginning with the Region's core and working out (Fig. P-1).

Definitions of the New York Metropolitan Region

THE CENTRAL BUSINESS DISTRICT [CBD]

The principal focus of the Metropolitan Area is unquestionably New York County, which is Manhattan Island. The County supports the extraordinary population density of 1,539,233 people on its 23 square miles, and it also offers the greatest concentration of jobs. The more than two million jobs in Manhattan's Central Business District, that is, the nine and one-third square miles south of 59th Street, clearly make this *the* Central Business District for the entire Region. As we shall see later, some of the specialized activities in Manhattan make it in fact a CBD for the whole nation.

NEW YORK CITY

New York City, as it was politically consolidated in 1898, includes New York County plus four others. Staten Island is Richmond County.* Queens County and Kings County (Brooklyn) are on Long Island, and Bronx County, to the North, is the City's only county on the mainland. The total 1970 population of these five counties was 7,894,862. Whenever in this book we refer to the City, with a capital C, we mean the five counties of New York City.

FEDERAL STATISTICAL DEFINITIONS

To define the wider Metropolitan Region, we shall first turn to various delineations of the Region used by the federal government. Back in 1950 the United States Bureau of the Census first introduced the term *Standard Metropolitan Area* (SMA) in its analysis of America's urban regions. These metropolitan areas consisted of "a county or group of contiguous counties which contains at least one city of 50,000 inhabitants or more...contiguous counties are included ...if...they are essentially metropolitan in character and socially and economically integrated with the central city." At that time the Bureau recognized a broad band of continuous urbanization across New York State and New Jersey as the New York-Northeastern New Jersey Standard Metropolitan Area. The area so defined, however, was too big to be meaningful. Widespread cross-commutation within this SMA did define it functionally as one interrelated Region, and yet analysts of the Region needed statistical subregions of this SMA so that they could better understand its internal dynamics.

In 1960, therefore, the term Standard Metropolitan Area was replaced by *Standard Metropolitan Statistical Area* (SMSA), and the 1950 SMA was broken down into four SMSAs. The New York SMSA included the five counties of the City plus Nassau County, Suffolk County, Westchester County, and Rockland County, all in New York State. A new Paterson-Clifton-

---

*The City officially changed the borough's name to Staten Island in April 1975, but neither the state nor federal government has recognized that change.

Passaic SMSA in New Jersey consisted of Bergen County and Passaic County, focused on the three central cities named. Hudson County in New Jersey was alone named the Jersey City SMSA, and a third New Jersey SMSA, called the Newark SMSA, consisted of Essex County, Morris County and Union County. These four New York and New Jersey SMSAs combined together with Middlesex and Somerset Counties in New Jersey received a new designation as the New York-Northeastern New Jersey *Standard Consolidated Area* (SCA). This was a total of seventeen counties, and this definition of the SCA was maintained through the national censuses of 1960 and 1970. This SCA was in effect the old SMA, but breaking it down into SMSAs proved helpful for sub-Regional analysis. Only one other SCA is recognized in the United States, that of Metropolitan Chicago, which includes more than one SMSA.

In 1972 the Bureau of the Census made a few changes again (Fig. P-2). Nassau and Suffolk Counties were taken out of the New York SMSA to form a separate SMSA. This is the only SMSA in the United States which does not have a central city of at least 50,000 in population. The New York SMSA gained Putnam County in New York State and Bergen County in New Jersey, changing the SMSA name to the New York-New Jersey SMSA. The Newark SMSA gained Somerset County in New Jersey, and Middlesex County in New Jersey became the separate New Brunswick-Perth Amboy-Sayreville SMSA.

Therefore since 1972 the New York-Northeastern New Jersey SCA has included eighteen counties, subdivided into six SMSAs.

So much time has been taken to relate this history because excellent federal statistics are easily obtained and analyzed for the SCA—the eighteen-county Standard Consolidated Area. This SCA is one definition of the Region to be kept in mind throughout this book, for SCA statistics will be introduced periodically. The reader must remember, however, that the SCA is a statistical region only. There is no govern-

mental mechanism at this level planning or providing any public services.

THE PORT DISTRICT

The Port Authority of New York and New Jersey is a bistate agency dedicated to the improvement and promotion of port operations in New York and New Jersey. Its area of jurisdiction radiates about 25 miles from the Statue of Liberty in Upper New York Bay. The Port Authority is not interested in Putnam County, no matter how many Putnam workers might commute to jobs in the City. The Port Authority *is*, however, interested in economic activities in coastal Monmouth County, New Jersey. Therefore the Port Authority's definition of the Metropolitan Region is basically the same as the SCA, except that it *excludes* Putnam County and *includes* Monmouth County. It includes, then, eighteen counties. While the SCA Region is only a statistical unit, albeit defined on the basis of economic and social integration, the Port Authority Region is functionally organized—at least for purposes of port development and regulation.

PLANNING REGIONS

Most definitions of the Region which we have examined so far are used by agencies which wish to analyze or govern certain aspects of the Region as it is today. Their definitions cover the presently built-up areas.

Some agencies exist to plan for the future and, assuming future growth, their definitions of the Region must therefore reach out beyond the developed areas to include areas that are developing or will probably develop on the fringes. Thus these agencies' working definitions of the Region are necessarily much larger.

The Tri-State Planning Region

The first of these agencies is the Tri-State Regional Planning Commission. This Commission is the successor, since 1971, of the Tri-State Transportation Commission formed by the legislatures of Connecticut, New York and New Jersey in 1965. Originally created to plan transportation facilities only, the Commission's new mandate is to define and offer solutions to problems in the development of land, housing, transportation and other public facilities in its Region.

The New York Metropolitan Region as defined by this Commission includes another outer tier of jurisdictions concentric upon Manhattan. It covers twenty-one counties in New York and New Jersey and six planning regions (rather than counties) in Southwest Connecticut.

The Connecticut areas covered bring into consideration the urbanization fringing Long Island Sound and up the Housatonic and Quinnipiac Rivers. This thread of urbanization is contiguous with areas suburban to New York City, and it is an important part of the Northeastern Seaboard Boston-to-Washington corridor (Megalopolis). Its actual social and economic linkages with New York City, however, are less important than are those of closer-in-areas. The federal Bureau of the Census recognizes separate Stamford, Norwalk, Bridgeport, New Haven, Meriden, Waterbury and Danbury SMSAs in the Connecticut portion of the Tri-State Planning Region, but does not include them with the New York-focused SCA. The Tri-State Commission's definition of such an immense 8,000 square mile Region is useful for studying broad trends in the urban Region, but direct functional connections with New York City itself are attenuated in the outer tier areas.

The designated Tri-State Region is a planning Region, rather than a governmental jurisdiction, but the Commission can recommend legislation to the state and local governments, and it does exercise one additional important power: the power to review governmental development programs within the Region. Under the terms of several federal legislative acts, any projects within American metropolitan areas which receive federal financial assistance—roads, waterworks, airports, schools, etc.—must be reviewed by a designated metropolitan planning body. This is the federal government's way of guarding that its financial assistance is not wasted in metropolitan areas because of lack of local intergovernmental cooperation or because of duplication. The Tri-State Regional Planning Commission is the designated review agency for Metropolitan New York. The Commission cannot veto any local project within the Region, but its right to discommend federal financial assistance is a powerful force for Regional intergovernmental coordination. Commissioners representing the three states are appointed by the state governors, and federal representatives are appointed by officers of the Executive branch.

Because the Region defined by the Tri-State Commission does not conform to any other—to the City, the SCA, or the Port Authority Region—the Commission must gather a great deal of statistical data for the Region as the Commission defines it. The Commission is, therefore, an important source of data and data analysis, and we will occasionally refer to Commission-generated data in this book.

The Regional Plan Association

The last and largest definition of the New York Region is that used by the Regional Plan Association. This private civic research group, based in Manhattan, includes thirty-one complete counties in its area of study. The Association has for over fifty years analyzed trends in the Region, and the Association's definition of the Region has expanded outward steadily—always one outer concentric tier ahead of actual contiguous urbanized development. The excellence of the Association's studies of the Region has made them always valuable references, and we will in this book have occasion to refer to Regional Plan Association studies or projections.

And so we have several different answers to the question: What is the New York Metropolitan Region? Different agencies have different answers for different reasons. In some cases the Region as defined is actually politically or administratively organized for one or more purposes: New York County, New York City, the New York-New Jersey Port Authority District, and the Tri-State Regional Planning Region. Some delineations of the Region are for statistical descriptive purposes only: the SMSAs, the SCA, and the Regional Planning Association's Region. Each definition is meaningful. If you ask for one single definition, you should be answered with a question as to why you want to know. This book will draw on all of the definitions, using at any time that definition most appropriate to the purpose of the discussion. The Region will always be identified, so that there should be no confusion. At the same time the discussion of the growth and development of the Region, of the spread of settlement in the Region, and of cross-commutation and other economic and social linkages within and across the Region will help explain how it is bound together as one functioning "place."

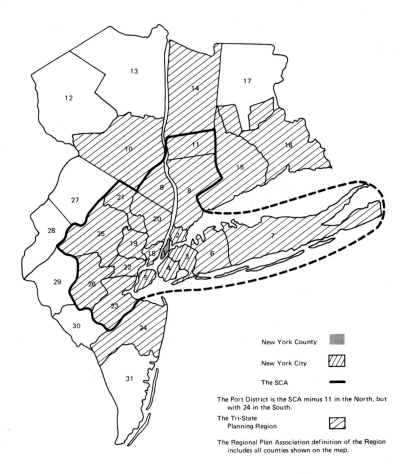

New York County

New York City

The SCA

The Port District is the SCA minus 11 in the North, but
with 24 in the South.

The Tri-State
Planning Region

The Regional Plan Association definition of the Region
includes all counties shown on the map.

Key to Counties Shown on Figure P-1

New York State

1. New York
2. Bronx
3. Queens
4. Kings (Brooklyn)
5. Richmond (Staten Island)
6. Nassau
7. Suffolk
8. Westchester
9. Rockland
10. Orange
11. Putnam

12. Sullivan
13. Ulster
14. Dutchess

Connecticut

15. Fairfield
16. New Haven
17. Litchfield

New Jersey

18. Hudson
19. Essex

20. Bergen
21. Passaic
22. Union
23. Middlesex
24. Monmouth
25. Morris
26. Somerset
27. Sussex
28. Warren
29. Hunterdon
30. Mercer
31. Ocean

Figure P-1. The New York Metropolitan Region.

1. The New York-New Jersey SMSA
   - New York County ⎫
   - Bronx County ⎪
   - Richmond County ⎬ New York City
   - Queens County ⎪
   - Kings County ⎭
   - Rockland County, New York
   - Westchester County, New York
   - Putnam County, New York
   - Bergen County, New Jersey

2. The Nassau-Suffolk SMSA
   - Nassau County, New York
   - Suffolk County, New York

3. The Newark SMSA
   - Essex County, New Jersey
   - Morris County, New Jersey
   - Somerset County, New Jersey
   - Union County, New Jersey

4. The Jersey City SMSA
   - Hudson County, New Jersey

5. The Paterson-Clifton-Passaic SMSA
   - Passaic County, New Jersey

6. The New Brunswick-Perth Amboy-Sayreville SMSA
   - Middlesex County, New Jersey

Figure P-2. The 18-County New York-Northeastern New Jersey Standard Consolidated Area (defined 1972).

Chapter One

1626-1820:
FROM DUTCH COLONY
TO AMERICA'S COMMERCIAL CAPITAL

Exploration and Political Evolution

Today's Metropolitan Region was explored and settled first by the Dutch among Europeans. In 1609 the United East India Company hired Henry Hudson, an Englishman, to search for a Northwest Passage. During his explorations of North America's Atlantic Coast he sailed up the river later named after him. Hudson's discovery was the basis of Dutch claim to the area called the New Netherlands. The New Netherlands included most of what are today the states of New Jersey and New York.

The Hudson River was not the Northwest Passage sought by the Dutch, but it provided an opening into a region rich in furs, and in 1621 the Dutch West India Company was chartered to pursue the fur trade. In 1626 Peter Minuit, director of the Company, paid the Manhattan Indians twenty-four dollars for Manhattan Island at the mouth of the Hudson River, and a fort and trading post were soon built on the southern tip of the island. This was the beginning of the New Amsterdam settlement.

In 1664 the English conquered the New Netherlands and renamed the area New York,

This lovely wash drawing shows the tiny colony of New Amsterdam in 1643, the year in which the church belfry was completed. Note the windmills on the left. (New York Public Library)

for the new proprietor, the Duke of York. He quickly granted the area west of the Hudson River to his good friends Lord Berkeley and Sir George Carteret. They in turn split their grant into the provinces of West Jersey and East Jersey. In 1702 the two provinces were reunited as New Jersey. The Duke of York ceded his rights to the northeastern portion of his grant to the Connecticut colony in return for that colony's retirement from Long Island. Thus today's Region was first split into separate jurisdictions. These jurisdictions were maintained after 1783 when New Jersey, New York and Connecticut became member states of the United States.

Economic Growth and Spreading Settlement

Between 1626 and 1820 the Region changed from a colonial outpost producing raw materials for its mother country into the most important commercial and manufacturing district of the United States. During the same time, New York City became the country's most populous city, its leading seaport, and its most important manufacturing, wholesaling, and financial center. New York City and the surrounding area also developed the first links which laid the basis for the designation of today's Region.

The Region was important to the Dutch and to the English as a supplier of raw materials. At first timber and furs were the principal exports. Later surplus grains became a more important export. Thus most people in the Region either farmed or hunted, and they lived either on farms or in small settlements. People in the Region's principal settlement on Manhattan served as middlemen, exchanging the Region's products for manufactured goods from Europe or for raw material imports, such as sugar, from the West Indies. The mercantilist policy of the English forbade manufacturing. Consequently, the Region's economic activity was limited to producing and exporting raw materials and to importing goods in exchange.

Between 1626 and 1820 these economic activities expanded slowly for two reasons. The carrying capacity of ships was small, and the capacity of European manufactureres to absorb raw materials was limited.

Ships provided the indispensable link between American producers and European consumers. In the 17th and 18th centuries, however, ships were slow, inefficient, and expensive carriers. A trip from New York to London took many weeks, sometimes two or three months. Ships were also small, not much larger than a tractor-trailer truck today. Moreover, ships required many men to hoist sails and to load or unload cargoes. As a result, only the most valuable products of the Region could be economically exported.

Furthermore, Europeans lacked the technology to produce on a large scale. Thus their raw material needs were not great. A limited market for raw materials, in turn, hampered the expansion of Regional production.

The Region's slowly expanding economy directly affected its population growth. The limited agricultural and commercial opportunities in the Region retarded immigration. During the first century of settlement to 1720 an average of only 100 to 200 people migrated to the Region annually. As many as 2,000 arrived in an average year in the 18th Century, but by 1820 there were still fewer than 375,000 people in the Region.

NEW YORK CITY

Rise to Commercial Pre-Eminence

Since 1626 New York City has been the Region's single most important and populous place. Almost all of the Region's commercial activities and, by 1820, about one-third of its population concentrated on Manhattan.

In the 17th Century activities connected with the fur trade and the processing of pelts, lumber, and wheat for export dominated the commercial life of New York City. By 1637 two windmills were already grinding grain into flour and sawing timber into lumber. Other activities

This view of "Ye Flourishing City of New York" dates from the early 1740s. The prospect from Brooklyn Heights includes the Whitehall Battery (erected 1734-41), the important Lutheran Church, and the New Dutch Church on Nassau Street. The number of ships in the harbor must signify some special occasion, unknown to historians. (New York Public Library)

are soon added. Bakers, coopers, ship-outfitters, brewers, butchers, and tanners contributed their skills to the town's economic diversity.

New York City's trade expanded vigorously after the English conquest in 1664. The City's hinterland became the principal granary for the English West Indian colonies, and the City itself became the Region's leading milling and transshipment center. The single wharf of 1648 became one of many later in the 17th and 18th centuries. In 1687 thirty-five vessels cleared the port; in 1772, 700. In 1760 ships sailing from New York employed 3,500 seamen.

New York City's greater participation in the colonial triangular trade and its expanded connections with its own hinterland explain the port's increased activity. In the triangular trade, ships from the West Indies, for example, brought sugar to New York. New York in turn sent flour and livestock to the West Indies. Both New York and the West Indies exported their raw materials to England as well, and in exchange received manufactured goods.

More of the Region surrounding New York City entered its commercial sphere as the City's intercolonial trade multiplied. By the 1750s ships sailed regularly to ports on Long Island Sound, ascended the Hudson River and connected the City with Staten Island and a number of ports in northeastern New Jersey. The ships' cargoes included passengers and mail as well as the products New Yorkers consumed or stored and processed for shipment elsewhere. In 1765 one contemporary observed that New York commanded "all the trade of the western part of Connecticut and that of East Jersey."

Before 1820 almost all of New York's wharves were located along the East River. The water there was calmer than in the Hudson River, and winter ice floes were less frequent. The East River wharves—more correctly called quays since they did not jut out into the river but rather paralleled it—were enormously active. Bales of cotton and wool; barrels of rice, flour, salt, and sugar; chests of tea; casks of rum and wine lined the quays. The noise and bustle of sailors and carters loading and unloading ships stirred the air. Merchants and clerks wove their way among intricately carved ships' bows extending far out over the quays and shuttled between warehouses and coffee houses. They thronged the fronts of coffee houses on Wall Street where the noisy auctioneering of goods took place. Within the coffee houses traders and brokers, underwriters and merchants were busy

This view of the foot of Wall Street was engraved in 1831. Coffee was the principal import at these docks, and several coffee houses in the neighborhood served as meeting places for the financial community. (New York Public Library)

selling, purchasing, and insuring the ship's wares or the ships themselves.

A direct consequence of New York's function as a collector and distributor of raw materials was its emergence as a processor of raw materials. Processing or manufacturing reduced the bulk of raw materials such as grain and made them less expensive to transport. At the same time manufacturing in New York led to lower prices than those commanded by imported manufactured goods. Thus, despite the English ban on manufacturing, New York developed numerous industries already in the 1700s.

New York's important clothing industry originated in the 1750s when New Yorkers themselves began to make beaver hats from pelts brought to the City. In 1768 seventeen distilleries were busy turning imported sugar and molasses into a half million gallons of rum. New York's breweries produced an excellent beer from the Region's grain crops. A local foundry turned ore into kettles and assorted ironware products. Shipbuilding, sugar refining, and the making of paper and candles were also important industries. Some 250 warehouses, distilleries, and small-scale manufacturing plants formed the skyline of New York seen from the East River.

By 1820 New York City had become America's most active port and its leading wholesaling and manufacturing center. In that year about 25 percent of United States foreign trade passed through the City. At the same time New York emerged as the country's finance and insurance center. New Yorkers advanced money for goods not yet produced, insured cargoes against loss, and loaned capital to entrepreneurs. The activity of New York's coffee houses was soon institutionalized with the founding of the New York Stock and Exchange Board in 1812 and the establishment of numerous banking and insurance firms.

The City's Physical Expansion

Between 1626 and 1820 New York City's population increased to about 125,000, and its built-up area expanded steadily northward on Manhattan. The settlement's earliest inhabitants built cabins of bark and later of wood covered with thatch. Already in 1664, however, more than 300 substantial houses and 2,400 people clustered on the island's southern tip. These newer houses were of brick covered with colorful Dutch tiles. Their stepped gables fronted on the twenty or so streets, lanes, and alleys which laced the village. Gardens and orchards surrounded the widely separated houses and lent New York a rural appearance. A stockade built across the island where Wall Street is today protected the settlement from Indians. A few roads penetrated the wall and linked a number of isolated bouweries (farms) to the enclosed village.

Between 1664 and 1776 the village was transformed into a town, and the town into a city. In 1748 New York still had open spaces and numerous shade trees and appeared "quite like a garden." But by 1775, on the eve of the Revolutionary War, the town had become a compact little city of 25,000 inhabitants. The built-up portion of Manhattan extended from the Hudson to the East River and reached one mile northward from its southern tip, the Battery. It covered about one-half square mile of land, much of it artificially created by refuse dumped into the rivers (Fig. 1-1).*

Population density in 1775 was high, because little land was available for private development. The City owned most of the undeveloped land on Manhattan and refused to sell it cheaply. Buyers turned to individual property owners whose houses were surrounded by gardens. These gardens were parceled off into small lots on which developers erected five and six story dwellings. Thus New York was soon transformed from "a garden" to a congested city.

After the Revolutionary War—during which much of New York had been reduced to rubble—the City grew even more vigorously. By 1820 its population was 125,000. The City and private property owners sold large blocks of land, and New York's built-up area expanded another mile northward as far as Houston Street (Fig. 1-2). Most growth, however, was confined

*Figures for the individual chapters are to be found at the end of each respective chapter.

Fortifications on Governors Island historically defended New York. Fort Jay (1798) dominates the northern part of the island. The low round building at the upper left corner is Castle Williams, built together with its companion Castle Clinton over on Manhattan's southern tip (originally off the tip, but since joined by landfill) to fortify the harbor for the War of 1812. The castle's architect, Lt. Col. Jonathan Williams, Benjamin Franklin's nephew, was the man for whom the Williamsburg section of Brooklyn was named. Castle Clinton became Castle Gardens amusement spot early in the nineteenth century, and later served as an immigrant receiving station.

Today Governors Island serves as a U.S. Coast Guard Station. It offers a training center, harbor patrol facilities, a support base for Coast Guard Cutters, and headquarters for several East Coast Coast Guard Commands. It is the coordination point for at-sea rescue off the entire Atlantic Seabord. (Photo courtesy of the Port Authority)

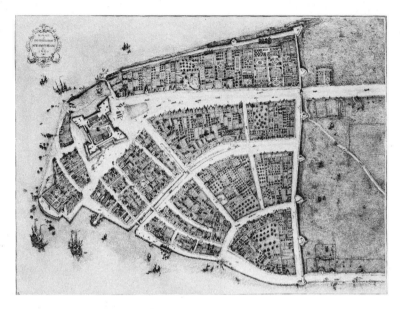

Settlement of the New Amsterdam colony in 1660 was almost entirely confined within the northern defense wall, today's Wall Street. Private gardens and orchards within the City, some of them quite elaborate geometric patterns, guaranteed the City plenty of open space. The wide road is, of course, the Broad-Way. The small canal was a reminder of Amsterdam. (New York Public Library)

to the area east of Broadway, where Manhattan widened considerably. The City's rapidly growing lower and middle classes could move into what is today the Lower East Side once the barrier of Collect Pond had been filled in. This small lake, where municipal and federal buildings now crowd each other between Foley and Chatham Squares, had at first been a recreation spot for New Yorkers. Later it became an open sewer and a dumping site before being filled in and giving way to the notorious Five Corners District. This District served the function today monopolized by the Times Square area. Prostitutes and rip-off artists found plenty of business showing customers a good time.

Residential Quarters

By 1820 a great deal of residential segregation by income had already occurred. The lower and lower-middle classes crowded into smaller, older houses between Broadway and the East River, where they had waterfront jobs. One visitor in 1797 described this section of New York as one where "...the streets are small and crooked....In general the houses are mean, small, and low, built of wood, and a great many of them yet bear the marks of Dutch taste."

The upper and upper-middle classes, on the other hand, built large and elaborate brick houses along Broadway near the Battery and in the area to the west. A view of the Hudson River along with cool, westerly breezes made this a particularly attractive residential area. The townhouses of wealthy merchants have long since been torn down, but the church of the well-to-do, Trinity Church (rebuilt in 1846), still stands and identifies this area of former opulence.

The most affluent residents of the 18th and early 19th centuries occasionally used their in-

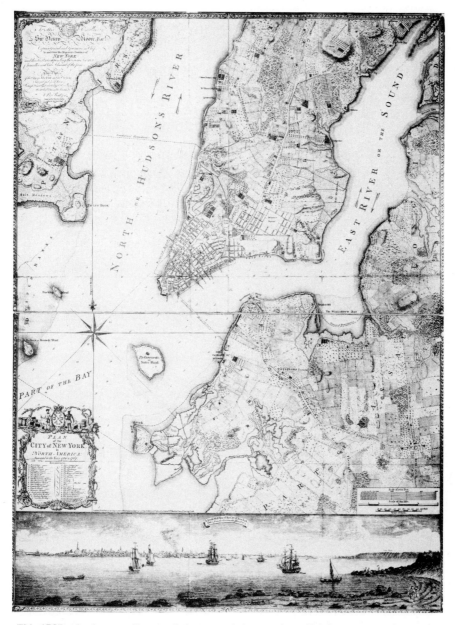

This 1767 print is generally regarded as one of the most beautiful, important, and accurate maps of early New York. The principal roads leading North from New York City were the road to Greenwich and the Bowery Lane, which bifurcated with one branch, the Bloomendale Road, heading up the center of the island, and the other, the Boston Post Road, leading off to Massachusetts. The names of many of the early farms and estates shown here survive as districts of the City today: Delancy Street, Stuyvesant Town, Murray Hill, Kip's Bay, etc. (New York Public Library)

wich Street. In the 18th century it connected the built-up section of New York City with Greenwich Village. One of Manhattan's most important country roads was the Bloomendale Road. It ran up the middle of the island and led to the farming hamlet of Bloomendale, located in the vicinity of today's West 100th Street. Beyond this lay Harlem, a fashionable summer retreat. The Bloomendale Road later became Broadway. Other suburban estates developed along the East River and on Murray Hill. They had access to New York City by way of the Boston Post Road, in part today's Third Avenue. One of these early estates survives as Gracie Mansion (built in 1799), the city mayor's official residence.

Wretched shanty towns such as these could always be found on the frontier of advancing city expansion. These shanties stood on the corner of 5th Avenue and 91st Street in 1898, but they were soon torn down to make way for Andrew Carnegie's mansion, which today houses the Smithsonian Institution's Cooper-Hewitt Museum of American Design. (Museum of the City of New York)

Trinity Church is on Broadway at the head of Wall Street, from which canyon this picture was taken. The Church parish was chartered by King William III in 1697. The Episcopal parish's great land grant from Queen Anne, in 1705, included all the land from Fulton to Christopher Streets, west of Broadway to the Hudson River. Thus missionary activities could be comfortably financed, and the parish established separate chapels elsewhere, including St. Paul's Chapel farther north on Broadway, and St. Augustine's and St. Christopher's Chapels on the Lower East Side. The Church building seen here was constructed in 1846. The parish is still an enormous landowner.

Many famous Americans, including Alexander Hamilton and Robert Fulton, rest in the cemetery on the north side of the Church, to the right in this photograph. (Photo courtesy of the New York Convention and Visitors Bureau)

The very poorest New Yorkers also lived beyond the city's developed area. They built shacks illegally on City land and were known as "squatters." As the City expanded farther northward in subsequent years, the squatters stayed just one step ahead of real estate developers. By the 1850s they occupied what soon became Central Park. The squatters moved on to Harlem and by 1900 into the Bronx. Many squatters today live in City-owned condemned properties, again awaiting eviction before urban renewal.

fluence to obtain land grants from the City to build suburban mansions along the Greenwich and Bloomendale Roads. The Greenwich Road paralleled the Hudson River and is today Green-

By 1820 the population density per square mile approached 50,000 in the City's built area, and only continued northward expansion could relieve congestion. In anticipation of this expansion, the City already in 1811 planned a street grid for most of the rest of the undeveloped area north of Houston Street. By then the City needed money and actively sold land which could, with guaranteed street frontage, command higher prices. Disregarding topography and existing property lines, twelve parallel, broad, and widely spaced avenues swept northward to the Harlem River. These avenues were intersected by more than 150 parallel, narrow, and closely spaced streets. So many more cross-town streets than north-south avenues were provided in order to facilitate access to the Hudson and East Rivers. It was assumed that these rivers would eventually become the City's most important north-south transportation routes.

Ethnic Diversity

As the City's population grew, it became more ethnically diverse, so that already in the 1640s eighteen languages were widely spoken. The Dutch, however, predominated. In 1685 perhaps three-fourths of the City's residents were Dutch; the other one-fourth were largely English and French. By 1705 a significant change occurred. The Dutch proportion of the population declined as large numbers of English immigrants came to the City, while the offspring of many Dutch City residents emigrated to other parts of the Region. The Dutch and English groups each composed about forty percent of the total population. In time, the distinction between these two original groups of settlers faded as intermarriage and time blurred their differences. Together the English and the Dutch came to be thought of as archetypical New Yorkers.

During the 1700s significant numbers of Negroes, Irish, Germans, and French joined the immigrant stream. Between 1720 and 1726 some 800 slaves were imported to relieve the City's labor shortage. In mid-century about 20 percent of the white families owned at least one slave.

Then, however, indentured servants from Ireland replaced those blacks who were household servants. Several thousand Germans and French also arrived to escape political or religious persecution in Germany or in the French West Indies.

Most newcomers to the City in the 18th Century were not foreigners, but came from other places in the Region or from New England. They added not only to the City's numbers, but also to its pool of skill and capital. Together with the Dutch and English, the New Englanders formed the dominant group in New York City until the 1820s, numerically, politically, socially, and economically.

THE NEW JERSEY SECTOR

Settlement

Outside New York City between 1626 and 1820, agriculture expanded and new settlements appeared (Fig. 1-3). By 1820 some two-thirds of the Region's population lived outside the City, but the pattern of expansion and settlement was largely dependent upon connections to the City.

Some of the earliest agricultural settlers responded to the Dutch West India Company's grants of farmsteads "the better to people [our] lands, and to bring [our] country to produce more abundantly." The farmers' products not only fed the City's growing population, but also provided the port with marketable commodities for international trade.

Most settlers chose homesteads close to one of the Region's many rivers and bays for easy water transport to Manhattan. The Region's shorelines in the 17th Century were quite different from what they are today. The immediate shorelines along many of the Region's waterways were too marshy for settlement. In most of the Metropolitan Region such areas have been filled, but some still exist on the west side of Staten Island, on southern Long Island and along the Hackensack and Passaic Rivers in New Jersey. Most early settlements were made as close to the shore as possible, but not always along the water itself. Brooklyn and Jersey City

These Great Falls of the Passaic River powered the early industrialization of Paterson, New Jersey. Today the historic district surrounding the falls includes the old mills shown below. The sandstone building with the pipe on the roof in the center of this picture is the "Gun Mill." Sam Colt first manufactured his famous handguns there.

occupied fortunate positions on heights far above the water level. Gowanus, Flatbush, and Jamaica, on the other hand, had to be founded a little farther inland (Fig. 1-4).

New Jersey's population grew more rapidly than that of other areas of the Region partly because more navigable waterways penetrated its interior. The Dutch first crossed the Hudson, and from their initial farming settlement at Paulus Hook (now part of Jersey City), they migrated up the valleys of the Hackensack, Passaic, and Raritan Rivers. There they established farms and villages. Wheat was collected at Jersey City and thence ferried across to New York City. Dutch out-migration from New York contributed to a substantial Dutch population in New Jersey, even though Dutch immigration from Europe came to a virtual standstill after 1664. At the end of the 18th Century almost twenty percent of New Jersey's settlers were of Dutch ancestry.

The New England Puritans were even more numerous in New Jersey than the Dutch, although they arrived somewhat later. They established communal settlements, following New England models, at Newark, Woodbridge, Piscataway, and elsewhere. The New Englanders, like the Dutch, were chiefly farmers. Newark grew at an especially favored site on a relatively large and productive plain. By 1820 it was already the chief commercial center on the New Jersey side of the Hudson River, as well as a minor manufacturing center.

A large contingent of Scots arrived in northern New Jersey just before 1700. They settled chiefly in Union and Middlesex counties. By 1820 they had founded more than sixty villages, among them Scotch Plains and Perth Amboy. The Scots were New Jersey's most numerous immigrant group. English immigrants, too, settled in New Jersey and founded a number of villages, the most important one being Elizabeth.

Early Industry

New Jersey had timber and iron ore resources as well as productive agricultural land. Iron furnaces drawing on these two materials were built in Monmouth County, in Morris County at Morristown, and in Passaic County at Ringwood. Ironmaking was New Jersey's first important industry, though the timber was soon exhausted and most iron furnaces were abandoned.

The founding of Paterson involved New Jersey's most significant industrial development prior to 1820. After the Revolutionary War Federalist policy was to gain United States independence of English manufactures by fostering industrial self-sufficiency. Accordingly, the government organized the Society for Establishing Useful Manufactures (S.U.M.) in 1791. S.U.M. bought six square miles of land adjacent to the Great Falls of the Passaic River. It hoped to harness the Falls as a source of

power for a number of industries. S.U.M. failed to achieve its goals and the Society soon folded, but the city of Paterson had been established, and it grew without federal assistance. By 1825 eighteen textile mills employed the town's 4,000 people.

Links with New York

Most of New Jersey's trade was waterborne, but a number of good roads also connected the important settlements. They improved the links between New Jersey and New York, so that New York peddlers were soon selling their wares to New Jersey customers. A number of stage lines provided direct access from New York City to Newark, New Brunswick, and Paterson as soon as bridges spanning the Hackensack, Passaic, and Raritan Rivers replaced ferries in the late 18th Century. By 1810 three daily stage coaches delivered commuters from Newark to New York by way of the Hudson ferry crossings at Jersey City.

Hoboken in New Jersey was already a suburb as far back as 1775. Large summer residences, owned by New Yorkers and some tended by upwards of fifty slaves, lined the bluffs overlooking the Hudson. Thus New York contributed not only a substantial number of permanent residents to New Jersey settlement through out-migration, but also a number of residents who commuted across the Hudson. The ease of accessibility back and forth between New York and New Jersey soon knit all economic activity between Newark Bay and upper New York harbor.

THE NEW YORK SECTOR

New York City's influence in the rest of the Region was limited to areas with access to the East or Hudson Rivers. Places closer to the Atlantic Ocean or to Long Island Sound were tied to New England towns, such as New Haven, Newport, and Boston. It was not until after the middle of the 18th Century that improved roads, especially on Long Island, granted access to New York for the products of the island's agricultural and fishing economy. New York City provided an increasingly attractive market for Long Island products because of its growing population and better overseas connections. Thus New York's hinterland grew out on Long Island and up into Westchester County and Connecticut at the expense of the hinterlands of New England communities. In 1824 Brookhaven, on Long Island's South Shore, had 100 ships plying in the trade with New York City.

New York City's early limited commercial influence in Connecticut and on eastern Long Island paralleled its negligible role as a source of migrants to these areas. Settlements at Bridgeport and Southampton, for example, trace their roots to England or New England. Dutch farmers, on the other hand, founded those settlements closest to New York City on Long Island and to the North, just as they established the most proximate settlements in New Jersey. They founded the communities of Brooklyn, Flatbush, and New Utrecht in Kings County, and together with the English, Newtown, Flushing, and Maspeth in Queens County. Numerous Dutch-founded communities also line the banks of the Hudson to the North.

Kings County

Kings County was the first area east of the City to develop close connections with New York. The county was divided into six townships, or towns, all of which were first settled in the mid-17th Century: Brooklyn, Flatbush, Bushwick, New Utrecht, Flatlands, and Gravesend. Each town contained a small village surrounded by fields. A ferry connected Manhattan to Kings County via Brooklyn as early as 1640, but still the growth of population in Kings County was slow.

The high cost of land and a slave economy deterred settlement. An 18th Century observer noted that "the nearness of New York assures a market for all farm products, and...the Dutch families who form such a large part of the population refuse to sell their holdings." Slaves worked many of the farms. At the end of the

18th Century almost two-thirds of all Kings County families had at least one slave, and one-third of the county's population was black. Thus freemen's wage labor was not competitive with Kings County's slave labor, and immigrants avoided the county. By 1820 Kings County still had only 11,000 people.

Eventually nonagricultural settlers moved over to Brooklyn, the Kings County town nearest New York. There they built summer houses on Brooklyn Heights, and they commuted to Manhattan. Steam ferries linked Brooklyn and Manhattan after 1810 and accelerated the dormitory character of Brooklyn. In the thirty years prior to 1820 Brooklyn's population jumped from 1,600 to 7,200. The population of the rest of Kings County increased very little in the same period: from 2,900 to 4,000. In 1828 James Fenimore Cooper described Brooklyn as "a flourishing village which has arisen within the last half dozen years from next to nothing; which from its position and connexion with the city, is in truth no more than a suburb differently governed."

Thus, the foundations of today's Region were laid during the years 1626 to 1820. New York City arose as the Region's commercial hub and the first city of the new nation. It established more and more overseas connections, while multiplying its regional links, and increasing its dominance over an expanding agricultural hinterland. The City began to diversify its initial function as a trading center, and took up manufacturing and finance as well. Its population, augmented by immigration, expanded steadily northward on Manhattan and comprised one-third the total regional population by 1820. It surpassed Philadelphia in population and in economic activity by 1815.

The City's hinterland was also diversifying and growing in population in order to supply the needs of the center. Agricultural settlement expanded, increasing the flow of products to the City and also for export. Some settlements developed more specialized functions: Newark was a market town; Paterson, an industrial locale, and Brooklyn, a commuter suburb.

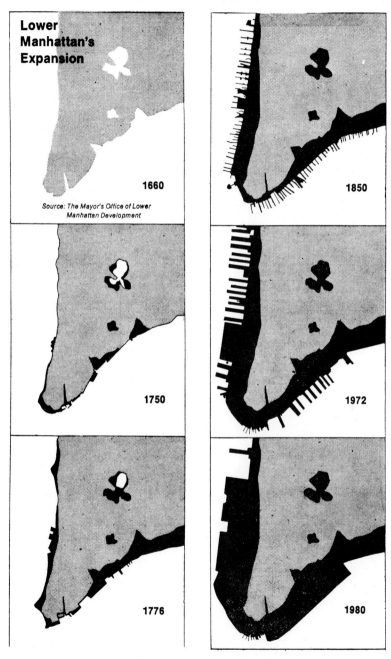

Figure 1.1. The Water Body in the Middle of Lower Manhattan Was the Collect Pond.

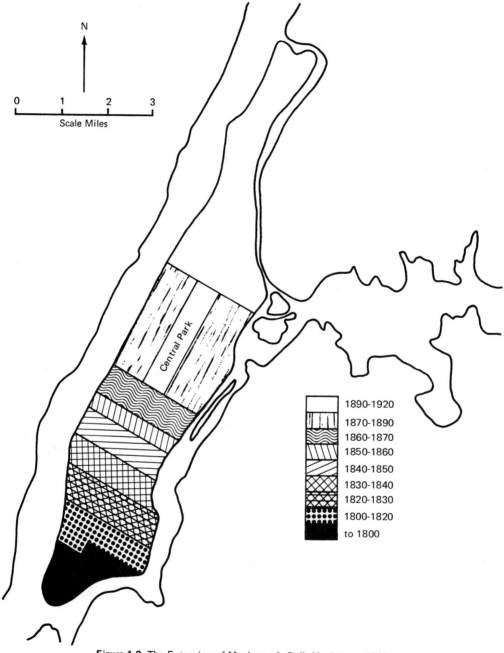

Figure 1-2. The Extension of Manhattan's Built-Up Area to 1920.

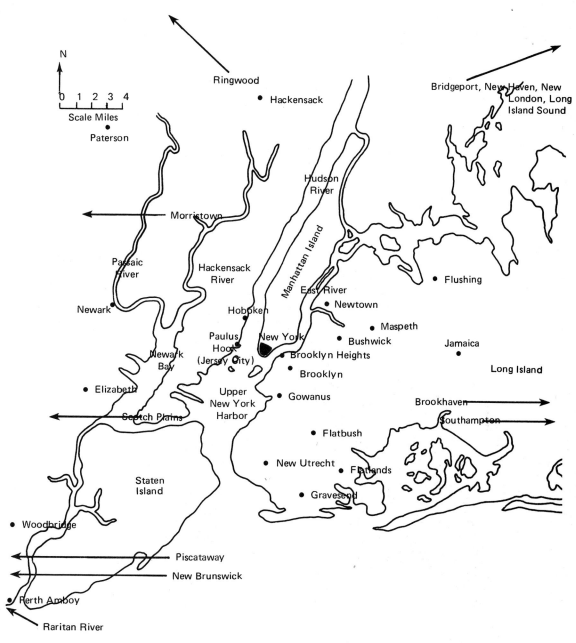

Figure 1-3. Early Settlements in the New York Region.

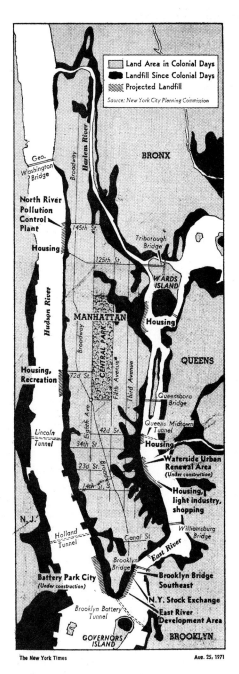

Figure 1-4. Shoreline Fill.

Chapter Two

1820-1920:
EXTERNAL CONNECTIONS,
INDUSTRIALIZATION AND IMMIGRATION

Between 1820 and 1920 four inter-related developments shaped the Region. First, transportation innovations extended the Region's sphere of influence and confirmed New York City's position as America's leading port. Second, industrialization changed the Region's economy and altered the Region's internal form. Third, waves of European immigrants diversified the Region's population and increased it 25-fold. Fourth, population growth and improvements in internal transportation expanded the built-up portions of the Region and led to the coalescence of settled areas and the political consolidation of five counties into Greater New York City in 1898. This chapter examines the first three of these developments, and in Chapter Three we will illustrate the fourth.

New Transport Links

In the period 1820-1920 three new forms of transportation—steam navigation, canals, and railroads—were introduced into the Region. Older forms of transportation were improved, and service was regulated by fixed timetables. The Region thus became more accessible to the outside world by increasing its connections to other regions by cheaper, faster and more reliable transportation. Many of these innovations were inaugurated in the Region before being adopted elsewhere in the United States, and so New York City widened its lead as the na-

tion's most populous city, leading port, and most important manufacturing center.

SHIPPING

Robert Fulton's *Clermont* opened the era of steamboat transportation on the Hudson River in 1807. Steamboats did not, however, take over many of New York's transatlantic or coastwise routes until the 1840s. In 1848 the Cunard Line began regular New York-Liverpool steam service. The steamer's greatest advantage was speed; it achieved a nine-day crossing to Liverpool in 1851. The cost of steam transport, however, remained high, and steamers carried only the best-paying part of oceanic trade: passengers and mail service. Until 1899 steamers on transatlantic crossings continued to be equipped with sails for supplementary power!

Sailing vessels dominated ocean shipping until near the end of the 19th Century. Lower operating costs, design changes, and regularly scheduled runs made them competitive with steamers, especially in the hauling of cargoes and immigrants. Between the 1820s and 1850s the carrying capacity of sailing ships increased three-fold, while the time on the New York-Liverpool run was reduced from an average 39 to 33 days. In addition, more ships sailed according to fixed schedules after 1818, when the Black Ball Line introduced its packet service. New York was the first American city to offer

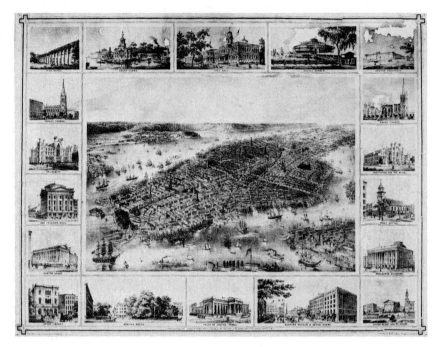

This tourist souvenir of 1850 features several of New York City's most impressive public structures. The panorama of the City in the center is especially interesting for its attractive view of the Palisades in the background. Elysian Fields Park in Hoboken, across the Hudson River in the background, was for many years a favorite resort of New Yorkers. Jersey City is just visible at extreme left, dominated by the First Presbyterian Church spire. Note the train coming down Manhattan Island along what is today Park Avenue. (New York Public Library)

European packet service. One ship sailed each month from New York and one from Liverpool on a specified day and hour. By 1845 52 transatlantic packets sailed the route out of New York, giving the City three regular sailings per week. Packet lines also connected New York with Charleston and New Orleans, and the City soon controlled the carrying of cotton from the South to New York for export or manufacture. On both transatlantic and coastal routes, New York dominated its erstwhile competitors, Boston and Philadelphia, because New York businessmen established more and better international connections. During the period 1820-1860 New York handled 60 percent of all United States imports and 33 percent of all exports.

CANALS

Canals improved the New York Region's inland connections and consolidated its position as the country's leading entrepot. The completion of the 364 mile long Erie Canal between Albany and Buffalo in 1825 was especially significant for the Region (Fig. 2-1). First, the Hudson River-Erie Canal-Great Lakes Route offered the only all-water link between the East Coast and the agriculturally productive Middle West. The Appalachian Mountains prevented the other East Coast cities from reaching the continental interior by an all-water route. Second, the Erie Canal provided the least expensive route for freight movements between the coast and the interior. Transport coasts between Buffalo and New York fell from 100 dollars a ton before the Canal's construction to an average 10 dollars a ton. The Canal's low-cost transportation greatly stimulated trade and encouraged the rapid settlement of the trans-Appalachian Region.

Immigrants crowded inexpensive Erie canalboats and quickly settled Ohio, Indiana, Michigan and Illinois. They soon sent back their agricultural surpluses over the route they themselves had traveled. In 1835 268,000 barrels of flour and wheat were shipped to New York City via the Erie; in 1840 shipments exceeded 1 million barrels; and in 1860, over 4 million barrels. In return manufacturers and wholesalers in the New York Region sent westward products worth 10 million dollars in 1836 and close to 100 million dollars in 1853. Thus New York City early captured a disproportionate share of the trade between East and West from its Baltimore, Philadelphia, and Boston rivals.

In the 1830s two canals were completed across New Jersey, linking the waters of the New York Region with the Delaware River. The 102 mile Morris Canal wound its way through the hills of northern New Jersey before reaching Newark Bay. The Morris carried coal from the anthracite fields of northeastern Pennsylvania to the fuel-short, steam powered industries of the New York Region. South of the Morris, the Delaware and Raritan Canal connected the Delaware River near Philadelphia with the Raritan River at New Brunswick. This waterway afforded a large and well-constructed route from New York to Philadelphia. The three canals together opened up areas previously closed to large-scale freight movements, and thus contributed to the expansion of the Region's hinterland.

RAILROADS

Railroads were first introduced in the early 1830s, although canal barges were cheaper for freight than were the first railroads. In New York State, for example, the total tonnage carried by railroads did not exceed that carried by barges and ships until 1869. Nevertheless, railroads penetrated areas inaccessible to waterways and provided a faster means of transportation. Railroad mileage in the Region grew rapidly in the 1840s. By 1851 the Region had two direct links with Lake Erie: one the forerunner of the New York Central Railroad, the other the Erie Railroad. Shortly thereafter rail connections reached Chicago and the Midwest.

The railroads alone could not handle the tremendous trade expansion between New York and the Midwest. Tonnage carried on the Erie Canal increased despite the railroads' direct competition and did not reach its peak volume until 1880. More and more of the Canal's freight consisted of bulky, low-value commodities such as lumber and grain, while the railroads appropriated passenger traffic and handled high-value perishable products such as livestock.

Commercial Hub

Taken together, the changes in transportation during the 1820-1920 period acted as a centripetal force favoring economic concentration at a few major points, such as New York City. The larger ships in transatlantic service sought out docking facilities which could handle their increased size and larger cargoes. New York City provided such facilities, and thereby captured the trade of smaller ports on Long Island Sound, such as New London, which had previously competed with the City. In 1850 Manhattan appeared to Herman Melville as if "...belted round by wharves as Indian isles by coral reefs—commerce surrounds it with her surf." The fixed canal and river systems which converged on the Region furthered the concentration of commerce and manufacturing. The railroads, in turn, reinforced and then extended the pattern established by canals. The New York Region became the focus of a vast railway network extending north and south and west.

New York City emerged as the focus of the nation's transport systems and its chief link with the outside world. It served as the trade hinge between Europe and the North American interior. New York's port also controlled the Atlantic coastal and West Indian trade. Thus two axes, one East-West, the other North-South, focused on the City and the Region. In 1800 New York City had a 9 percent share in the country's foreign trade. By 1830 New York's share had increased to 37 percent. While New York was increasing its share of the nation's foreign trade, total volume of foreign trade grew tremendously. The country's exports, for example, quadrupled between 1800 and 1830. By 1870 New York port handled 57 percent of the country's foreign trade. Thereafter the total tonnages continued to increase, but New York City's share of foreign trade declined to 37 percent of American exports and 58 percent of its imports in 1913.

The convergence of transportation systems upon the Region and the vast increase in trade volume necessitated the designation of large areas within the Region for the storage and handling of commodities. As trade grew during the period 1820-1920, piers and warehouses came to line the East River in both Manhattan and Brooklyn and to penetrate the Gowanus Canal and Newtown Creek. Docking and storage facilities also transformed the Hudson River's Manhattan and New Jersey shores. By the end of the period, ships' piers had multiplied on Newark Bay, and docking activities extended southward to the waterways between New Jersey and Staten Island.

Railroad yards occupied hundreds of acres of additional space. Terminals were frequently located adjacent to the Region's waterways in order to ease the transfer of cargoes between rail and water carriers. They were especially concentrated on the Hudson River's New Jersey shore, where most rail lines from the West converged. The River prevented direct access to Manhattan until the construction of tunnels in the early 1900s. Jersey City, Weehawken and Hoboken were all dominated by shipping and railroad facilities.

Industrial Growth

The Region's primacy as a transport hub secured its position as the nation's commercial center; trade in turn fostered a wide variety of industries. Accessibility to transport facilities determined the specific locations of industries. Factories grew up adjacent to the waterfront and later sprouted along rail lines. The availability and cost of space and the directness of access to markets and sources of raw materials further influenced industrial location.

Heavy manufactures of iron and steel products for the national market concentrated in New Jersey's cities. These cities had more direct access to raw materials such as coal and iron than did cities east of the Hudson River. They also offered cheaper land for factories requiring large facilities. Processing and manufacturing of

Newark in the 1820s was just a village, with cattle grazing in the main street. The windmill evidences the early Dutch influence. (New York Public Library)

such commodities as foodstuffs and furniture for distribution to the Regional market, on the other hand, developed on Long Island, especially along the Brooklyn waterfront. Light industries which required greater skill and little space and for which the market was national, such as the making of clothing, grew up in Manhattan's loft buildings.

During the 1820-1920 period New York City became the country's most important and diversified manufacturing city. As one European visitor pointed out in 1854, "New York is not merely a commercial city. She is largely engaged in manufactures of various kind,—indeed more so than any other city in America." Even though less than 10 percent of the City's working population was engaged in manufacturing before the Civil War, the City dominated the country's clothing and printing industries and had some share in almost all other manufactures. Already in 1850 the products of New York's industries were valued in excess of 100 million dollars. In twenty years their value tripled. In 1900 the industries of Greater New York City (by then five boroughs) produced almost 1.4 billion dollars worth of goods.

SPECIALIZATION IN NEW JERSEY

New Jersey's cities were more exclusively manufacturing centers than were other cities in the Region. More than 25 percent of Newark's workers, for example, were engaged in manufacturing. As a result, Newark, the country's eleventh largest city in 1860, was its third most important industrial center. Manufacturing in New Jersey's cities was not so diversified as in New York and Brooklyn during the 19th Century, although it was more diversified in Newark than in New Jersey's other cities. Machinery, transportation equipment, food processing, and textile industries predominated in New Jersey.

Many New Jersey cities specialized in one or two products in successive periods through the 19th Century. Boom and bust cycles plagued Paterson throughout its industrial history. Textiles and iron products were its chief industries. The making of machinery early led to specialization in locomotive manufacturing. In 1860 Paterson was already the center of the country's locomotive production. By 1881 one-third of the 17,720 locomotives in the United States had been built in Paterson; that same year Paterson made 457 more. Thereafter production in Paterson declined as the industry relocated to cities more centrally located in the country's interior.

In textiles, cotton first dominated Paterson's economy. In 1840 only Lowell, Massachusetts, produced more cotton goods. This industry gave way to silk manufacturing in mid-19th Century. By 1880 93 silk manufacturers employed 13,000 workers. In 1899 Paterson's mills wove almost one-half of the nation's silk textiles. Even as late as 1925 65 percent of the city's workers were weaving or dying silk, earning Paterson the sobriquet, "The Silk City." Paterson's silk industry subsequently declined, as silk apparel went out of fashion, and synthetic textiles replaced silk.

In 1860 about one-half of New Jersey's factories were located in its three largest cities: Newark, Paterson, and Jersey City. After the Civil War New Jersey industries expanded from these three foci. Industries overflowed from Jersey City into Bayonne to the South and Hoboken to the North. Newark industries spread into the margins of the Hackensack Meadows and westward into the Oranges. While Newark's industrial complex moved up the Passaic River, that of Paterson moved down, and the two coalesced at Passaic.

Some of these New Jersey cities were almost as well known for their specific products as Paterson was for its locomotives and silk. Woolen textiles (from the mills of Julius Forstmann) made Passaic. Soap (William Colgate) and iron products invigorated Jersey City. Wallpaper and rubber dominated New Brunswick. Steam engines vitalized Hoboken (Colonel John Stevens). Sewing machines (Isaac Singer) stimulated Elizabeth. Shoes, shears (Jacob Wiss), beer (Peter Ballantine), thread (Clark Brothers) and forty makers of machinery were

From the village of the 1820s, Newark grew to a considerable industrial city by the time this print was made in 1853. The Passaic River lies in the left background, Newark Bay to the right, and the steeples of New York City in the far distance. (New York Public Library)

Hoboken by 1859 was quite a small city. The docks, where Maxwell House Coffee is imported and roasted today, already carried on some import-export trade, and the terminals in the foreground here provided regular ferry service to New York. The road leading off into the left background (with horsecar service for some distance) went to Newark; the Plank Road to Paterson can be seen extending diagonally across the background. Elysian Park, a popular excursion for New Yorkers, can be seen in the right middle distance. It is interesting to see at so early a period the successful block development in the left foreground. This improvement seems to have been made under the auspices of the Hoboken Land and Improvement Company. (New York Public Library)

just some of the industries which diversified Newark in 1875. Newark was such a strong manufacturing city that it held a "Made in Newark" exhibition in 1872.

In 1890 New Jersey was the nation's fifth most important industrial state, though it ranked 18th in population. By the end of the century New Jersey was called the "Mother of Trusts" because of its lenient corporate laws.

Immigrants

Industrialization attracted millions of European immigrants to the United States. A high proportion chose to remain in the New York Region, their point of entry, rather than continue westward. Figure 2-2 shows the total number of immigrants for each decade between 1820 and 1920 and also indicates the share of migrants contributed by the eight most important areas of origin. Altogether, more than 33 million immigrants came to the United States between 1820 and the 1920s, when restrictive legislation curtailed immigration.

Careful examination of the figure reveals two important aspects of the immigration picture. First, the immigration rate between 1880 and 1920 was substantially higher than in the period 1820-1880. Two-thirds of all immigrants arrived in the forty years after 1880, an average of about 6 million in each decade. Second, the source area of immigrants shifted noticeably in the 1880s. Before that time about 80 percent of all immigrants had come from Ireland, Germany and the United Kingdom. After 1880 the number of immigrants from Italy and the Russian and Austro-Hungarian empires increased

The numerous smokestacks emphasize the industrial character of Jersey City in 1866. The tall church spire in the center of the picture, the only edifice towering over the smokestacks, was that of the First Presbyterian Church. The church was erected on Wall Street in New York City in 1835, but later, in 1844, it was sold to the congregation in Jersey City for $30,000, taken down, and re-erected across the Hudson. The smokestack to the right of the spire is Colgate's Soap and Candle Manufactory. Ferries ply the Hudson between Lower Manhattan and the New Jersey Railroad depot. (New York Public Library)

steadily. These areas accounted for more than 50 percent of total immigration by 1896.

PREDOMINANCE OF IMMIGRANT SETTLEMENT

By far the largest number of all immigrants entered through the port of New York. Castle Garden on the Battery and after 1892 Ellis Island in New York Harbor served as processing points. There, as *The New York Times* described it:

Every immigrant is numbered and tagged, and 240 at a time, in groups of 30, are examined by the men and women inspectors before whom they are compelled to pass and to whom they make their declarations. If any immigrant fails to pass an inspector, . . . he or she is put in the detention pen to await reexamination for his, or her return to the place from which he or she came. Every immigrant who is found ineligible to land is detained on the island and returned to his or her home at the expense of the steamship company that brought him or her here.

Many who were fortunate enough to pass inspection remained in New York or in the Region. One acerbic critic commented in 1883:

Our city has been compared to a filter in which the stream of immigration is purified before it passes westward. Of immigrants from the continent of Europe, 75 per cent, it is estimated, pass westward, and only about 25 per cent remain. Of those from Ireland, 75 per cent remain, and 25 per cent pass on.

In reality, among both the German and the Irish, approximately 20 to 30 percent settled in New York and Brooklyn; the proportion among later immigrants though, was higher.

The Region's cities had a proportionately higher share of foreign-born residents than did other cities in the United States. In 1870 people of foreign birth averaged 34 percent of the total population in America's fifty most populous cities. In 1870 Newark's population was 35 percent foreign-born; Brooklyn's, 36 percent; Paterson's and Jersey City's, 38 percent; and New York City's, 44 percent.

By 1910 the proportion of the nation's population which was foreign-born had declined slightly. Nevertheless, the Region's cities continued to have a proportionately larger foreign-born population. Immigrants averaged 29 percent of the total population in America's 49 cities of over 100,000 people in 1910. In the Region, however, Jersey City's 30 percent, Newark's 32 percent, Paterson's 36 percent, and New York's 41 percent foreign-born population exceeded the national urban average.

Statistics combining the foreign-born population with their offspring born in the United States were first collected in 1890. They reveal even better how "foreign" New York City, for example, had become in the 19th Century. In 1890 71 percent of the population in today's city's five boroughs were first or second generation immigrants (Fig. 2-3). This proportion increased to more than 76 percent in 1900 and to more than 78 percent in 1910. Thereafter it declined slightly, but it remained above 70 percent until after 1930.

MAJOR IMMIGRANT GROUPS

Irish and Germans

The Irish and the Germans were the two largest immigrant groups to arrive in the Region between 1820 and 1890. The Irish arrived in large numbers earlier than did the Germans. They were first attracted to America by jobs available in canal and railroad construction. Consequently already in 1845 New York City had 70,000 Irish residents, about 15 percent of its total population. Then in the late 1840s famines in Ireland added a push factor to the migratory urge of the Irish. This phase of Irish migration peaked in the 1850s, and by 1860 New York City was 25 percent Irish. Thereafter Irish migration leveled off, and the proportion of New York's population born in Ireland fell.

Nevertheless, in 1870 the proportion of Irish residents in all the Region's cities (except

These pens on Ellis Island (circa 1900) were used to sort arriving immigrants. Ellis Island is today being restored as a national park-museum. (New York Public Library)

The Statue of Liberty was a gift of France to the United States, commemorating the two countries' alliance during the American Revolution. Formally presented to the United States on July 4, 1884, the Statue was dedicated at its present site in Upper New York Bay on October 28, 1886. The sculptor was Auguste Bartholdi, and the framework was designed by Alexandre Eiffel. The Statue is 152 feet tall, and it stands on a 150-foot pedestal.

Now a National Monument, the figure of "Liberty Enlightening the World" has greeted generations of newcomers to America. At the base of the Statue is the American Museum of Immigration. (Photo courtesy of the New York Convention and Visitors Bureau)

"Not like the brazen giant of Greek fame, with conquering limbs astride from land to land; here at our sea-washed, sunset gates shall stand a mighty woman with a torch whose flame is the imprisoned lightening, and her name Mother of Exiles. From her beacon-hand glows world-wide welcome; her mild eyes command the air-bridged harbor that twin cities frame. 'Keep ancient lands, your storied pomp!' cries she with silent lips. 'Give me your tired, your poor, your huddled masses yearning to breathe free, the wretched refuse of your teeming shore. Send these, the homeless, tempest-tost to me, I lift my lamp beside the golden door!'"

Emma Lazarus 1883

Newark) was significantly higher than the average Irish share in America's fifty largest cities. In 1870 New York City's population was 21 percent Irish; Newark's, 12 percent; Paterson's, 16 percent; Brooklyn's, 18 percent; Jersey City's, 22 percent. By 1890 the Irish and their children still comprised 28 percent of New York's total population.

German migration increased at a fairly constant rate from the 1830s until the 1880s. Between 1880 and 1890 almost 1.5 million Germans arrived in America. Political and economic crises in the German states acted as expelling forces. Many of the Germans, like the Irish, concentrated in New York City, their chief port of entry. In general, however, German immigrants had greater resources, and proportionately larger numbers moved on to the Middle West.

In 1870 New York City and Newark still had a higher proportion of Germans than the average share of Germans in the country's 50 largest cities. New York was then 17 percent German, and Newark, 15 percent. By 1890 the Germans and their children comprised about 30 percent of New York City's population and constituted its largest ethnic group.

New York by 1900 was a city in which the first and second generation Irish and Germans predominated. The Irish group was not so preponderant as it was in Boston or Providence, and the German population not so numerous proportionately as in Milwaukee or Cincinnati. Nevertheless, there were more Irish and more Germans in New York than in any other American city!

New Immigrants from Southern and Eastern Europe

The huge volume of immigration between 1890 and 1920 brought several million Russians, Italians and Austro-Hungarians to the Region. By emigrating they escaped feudal agricultural conditions in Italy, political and religious upheaval in Austria-Hungary, and religious persecution in Russia. Some 90 percent of Russian immigrants were Jews, then being persecuted by the Russian regime. All of these new immigrants arrived with limited resources, and an extraordinarily high proportion remained in the Region's cities. Most found employment on the mass-production assembly-lines then revolutionizing American industry.

By 1910 the Region's cities had a proportionately high share of these new immigrants than did other large American cities. The combined Russian-, Austro-Hungarian-, and Italian-born populations accounted for 23 per-

Here we look north up Orchard Street from Rivington Street about 1900. This area was by then a principally Jewish neighborhood. Population densities in these five and six story tenements reached astonishing numbers. (New York Public Library)

cent of New York City's population; 18 percent of Newark's and Bridgeport's; 14 percent of Paterson's, and 12 percent of Jersey City's. By 1920 both Italians and Jews were more numerous in New York City than were residents of either German or Irish descent.

The incidence of disease in immigrant ghettos is understandable in view of such communal toilet facilities. Common pumps were many tenements' only source of water. (New York Public Library)

ASPECTS OF IMMIGRANT LIFE

Most immigrants arrived in the Region penniless. They were lucky to find housing of any sort. As early as the 1850s, in fact, cellars housed 29,000 newly arrived immigrants in New York. Other immigrants crowded into blocks adjacent to the expanding commercial and manufacturing districts of cities. These blocks were then being abandoned by more prosperous native residents fleeing to newer and better quarters in the cities' built-up outskirts. Poverty thus segregated immigrant districts from the more prosperous areas of native residents.

Sanitary conditions in immigrant enclaves were appalling. Four cholera epidemics in New York between 1832 and 1855 wiped out thousands of immigrants. Even in the 1850s two-thirds of New York's buildings had no sewerage connections; the proportion of such housing in immigrant districts was still higher. In one such district, a single privy was shared by

78 people. As late as 1870 immigrant districts also lacked running water, even though the Croton Reservoir had been built in 1842. In 1880 about one-half of the City's population was packed into the tenements of the Lower East Side, an area that accounted for about 70 percent of the City's deaths.

The Irish were worse off than were the Germans among early immigrants. Lacking specific skills and unable to improve their earning power, the Irish were relegated to slum life for longer than were the Germans or other European groups who followed. In 1860, 20 percent of all Irish workers in New York City were classified as laborers, as against 3.5 percent of all other immigrant workers. Another 26.4 percent were domestic servants, when only 9.9 percent among other immigrant groups were so classified.

The higher-paying jobs in manufacturing eluded a larger proportion of the Irish than of the Germans. In 1855, when the Irish formed more than 25 percent of New York's population and the Germans 10 percent, the Irish held only 9,100 jobs and Germans 8,300 in the clothing industry, which then employed a total of 20,000 workers. Consequently, the Irish accounted for an extraordinarily high percentage of official paupers (69 percent) and arrests (55 percent) in New York City.

As more and more immigrants from a given source arrived, they joined those who had preceded them. Consequently, immigrant enclaves expanded into adjacent blocks. At the same time, in the late 19th Century, landlords recognized that enormous profits could be made by redeveloping immigrant occupied areas and building tenements. In New York City, Jersey City, and Bayonne, tenements were buildings of five to six stories, one abutting the next, each with at least four two-room apartments per floor and communal kitchen and bathroom facilities. Rents were high in these airless and dark buildings, and often several families crowded into one apartment. Densities in Manhattan's Lower East Side reached 640,000 per square mile in 1900.

Health conditions continued to be atrocious. In 1890 New York City had the country's highest death rate among cities of over 100,000 population, over 30 per 1,000. Unsanitary conditions in Newark and Jersey City were almost as bad. Newark's death rate was second only to that of New York despite its more spacious tenements, partly because Paterson and Newark dumped their raw sewage into the Passaic River. The Passaic was the source for drinking water in Essex and Hudson Counties. Poverty and diseases were thus endemic in immigrant districts.

ETHNIC GHETTOS IN NEW YORK CITY

Poverty, unsanitary housing and high densities were not the only characteristics which differentiated immigrant districts from older residents' middle-class housing. Cultural differences among immigrant groups and between the immigrants and the Region's Anglo-Saxon population furthered segregation. Roman Catholicism set off the English-speaking Irish from the largely Protestant native population. The Protestant Germans were linguistically at odds with both Irish immigrants and the native stock. The Germans' business skills and cultural attitudes, however, helped them gain acceptance among native residents much earlier than the Irish gained that acceptance. The new immigrants—Italians, Russian Jews and a variety of ethnic groups included as Austro-Hungarians—differed on both linguistic and religious grounds from earlier immigrants and from the Region's native stock.

Because immigrants chose to live among others who spoke their language and shared their culture, specific immigrant groups segregated themselves, and smaller ethnic areas developed within the framework of larger immigrant districts. Thus ethnicity as well as slum conditions identified areas of immigrant settlement as ghettos.

These ghettos expanded as new immigrants arrived, and then contracted as the children of immigrants reestablished themselves, again according to ethnicity, in newer neighborhoods farther from the cities' cores. Meanwhile, as some ghettos contracted, adjacent ghettos, enlarged by an influx of new immigrants, expanded into the space vacated by earlier immigrants of a different ethnic affiliation.

Four factors thus conditioned the ethnic population settlement pattern in the Region's cities. First, native Anglo-Saxons grouped themselves by income. They resisted spatial association with immigrants by entrenching themselves in pockets of high land value or by fleeing to the frontiers of urban settlement. Second, new arrivals clustered ethnically in areas abandoned by native residents and adjacent to the cities' cores. Third, ghettos expanded with additions to the immigrant populations, and one immigrant group replaced another. Fourth, more successful immigrant groups moved outward as their economic condition improved; they leaped over fixed islands of other ethnic character settled earlier. As a result, the internal residential structure of the Region's cities became more complex during the 1820-1920 period. Built-up areas expanded outward, which allowed residential segregation according to income as well as ethnicity.

Irish and German Ghettos

Immigrant settlement in New York City illustrates invasion, succession and removal on a large scale. In the early 19th Century, Irish immigrants, the first to arrive in large numbers, concentrated in wards 1 and 2 at the southern tip of Manhattan's East Side. (See Fig. 2-4 for arrangement of Manhattan election wards in the 1870s.) By 1840 the Irish had pre-empted large areas to the north in wards 4, 6, and 7, which included the disreputable Five Corners District. The large Irish immigration in the 1840s and 1850s prompted contiguous expansion of the Irish into wards 10 and 13.

Poverty immobilized the Irish longer than other 19th Century immigrant groups. Between 1860 and 1890, however, many Irish were able to move out of the Lower East Side which comprised wards 4, 6, 7, 10, 11, 13, and 17. Their escape route lay northwestward, beyond the solid barrier of Greenwich Village (ward 9) and the Washington Square area (ward 15). These wards had become an Anglo-Saxon stronghold in the 1840s, and they remained so until the 1880s. The Irish thus leapfrogged to the 20th and 22nd wards on the West Side between 23rd and 59th Streets. This area, known as Hell's Kitchen, also provided employment on the Hudson River docks and in numerous home furnishing and soap factories. By the end of the 19th Century the most successful Irish had moved farther up the West Side to Washington Heights and across the Harlem River into the Bronx. At the same time in Brooklyn the Irish were abandoning "Irishtown," in the vicinity of Jay Street, for Bay Ridge (Fig. 2-5).

The first large German contingent, arriving in the 1840s, shared the 10th ward with the Irish. By 1860, with enormous additions to the German population, "Little Germany" (Kleindeutschland) had developed in wards 11 and 17, the area from south of Houston Street to 14th Street. A German visitor to New York in the late 1850s described Kleindeutschland this way:

> Naturally the Germans were not forced by the authorities, or by law, to settle in this specific area. It just happened. But the location was favorable because of its proximity to the downtown district where the Germans are employed. Moreover, the Germans like to live together; this permits them to speak their own language and live according to their own customs. The cheapness of the apartments also prompted their concentration. As the first Germans came into *Kleindeutschland*, the Irish began to move and the Americans followed because they were ashamed to live among immigrants.

> Life in Kleindeutschland is almost the same as in the Old Country. Bakers, butchers, druggists—all are Germans. There is not a single business which is not run by Germans.... There is even a German lending library where one can get all kinds of German books. The resident of *Kleindeutschland* need not even know English in order to make a liv-

ing, which is a considerable attraction to the immigrant.

The shabby apartments are the only reminder that one is in America....

His description might well apply to any ghetto in New York.

By 1890 German neighborhoods had expanded and dispersed, but they were still well-defined. In 1890 New York City was 27 percent German, and although Germans accounted for at least 10 percent of the population in 23 of the City's 24 wards, 23 percent of all New York Germans lived in *Kleindeutschland.* The story was the same in Brooklyn. Some 35 percent of Brooklyn's German population living in Williamsburg and Bushwick.

The Irish, by contrast, were more scattered. They had arrived earlier and thus diffused sooner than had the Germans. A high percentage of Irish continued to live in as domestic servants among the middle and upper class Anglo-Saxons.

Ghettos of the New Immigrants

The new immigrants who arrived in large numbers in the 1880s moved into areas then being vacated by the Irish and the Germans. Understandably enough, the Italians, Jews, and other new immigrants were more ghettoized in 1890 than were the Germans and the Irish. Among Austro-Hungarian ethnic groups in 1890, 65 percent of all Bohemains in New York City were quartered in ward 19, and 50 percent of Hungarians in ward 11. In 1900 about 6,000 Chinese lived in Manhattan, almost all of them in ward 6. A part of this ward came to be called "Chinatown," which still today contains about 90 percent of New York's 70,000 Chinese. The Italians shared the 6th ward with the Chinese and then expanded rapidly north and west into the 8th and 14th wards. By 1890, 52 percent of all New York City Italians lived in these three wards, known then as "New Italy."

Already, however, clusters of Italians had established themselves beyond the German area of Yorkville in "Little Italy" between East 110th and 116th Streets. (Today the historic "New Italy" is popularly called "Little Italy," and the historic "Little Italy" exists only as a remnant in East Harlem.) Italians also settled to the north of Irish settlement in Hell's Kitchen. Between 1900 and 1920 the more adventurous Italians migrated out to the Fordham section of the Bronx and to the Bushwick section of Brooklyn. The most prosperous penetrated farther into Brooklyn's Borough Park and Bensonhurst districts. Others gravitated toward the communities of Long Island City, Flushing, Corona and Astoria in Queens. By 1928 twenty communities in New York City had populations 50 to 90 percent Italian.

The Russian Jews were at first even more ghettoized than were the Italians. Initially they moved into the 4th and 6th wards, previously Irish, and then advanced north into wards 7, 10 and 13, from the Bowery to the East River. In 1890, 75 percent of all Jews in New York City lived in these wards. The 10th ward became the "Jewish Quarter"; in 1890 it was more than 50 percent Jewish.

The Jewish Quarter expanded northward in the 1890s. One observer remarked shortly after 1900 that the Jews "on the east Side...have pressed up through the Tenth and Thirteenth through the Seventeenth and Eleventh [wards], driving the Germans before them, until it may be said that all of the East Side below 14th Street is a Jewish District."

In the early 1900s many Jews were already on the move. Many had prospered more quickly than had other immigrants as merchants. They followed the German migration up the East Side and into Brooklyn. Jews established colonies between East 97th and 102nd Streets, north of Yorkville and south of "Little Italy," and in South-central Harlem between 110th and 125th Streets, before migrating north into the Bronx in the 1920s. In Brooklyn the Jews followed the Germans into Williamsburg and then farther still into Borough Park and Brownsville.

Jacob Riis, a well-known social reformer, summarized the City's ethnic pattern in his *How The Other Half Lives* (1890). His urban geography is excellent, but the modern reader must beware of his prejudices.

When once I asked the agent of a notorious Fourth Ward alley how many people might be living in it I was told: one hundred and forty families, one hundred Irish, thirty-eight Italian, and two that spoke the German tongue. Barring the agent herself, there was not a native-born individual in the court. The answer was characteristic of the cosmopolitan character of lower New York, very nearly so of the whole of it, wherever it runs to alleys and courts. One may find for the asking an Italian, a German, a French, African, Spanish, Bohemian, Russian, Scandinavian, Jewish, and Chinese colony. Even the Arab, who peddles "holy earth" from the Battery as a direct importation from Jerusalem, has his exclusive preserves at the lower end of Washington Street. The one thing you shall vainly ask for in the chief city of America is a distinctively American community. There is none; certainly not among the tenements.

The Irishman is the true cosmopolitan immigrant. All-pervading, he shares his lodging with perfect impartiality with the Italian, the Greek, and the "Dutchman," yielding only to sheer force of numbers, and objects equally to them all. A map of the city, colored to designate nationalities, would show more stripes than on the skin of a zebra, and more colors than any rainbow. The city on such a map would fall into two great halves, green for the Irish prevailing in the West Side tenement districts, and blue for the Germans on the East Side. But intermingled with these ground colors would be an odd variety of tints that would give the whole the appearance of an extraordinary crazy-quilt. From down in the Sixth Ward, upon the site of the Old Collect Pond... the red of the Italian would be seen forcing its way northward along the line of Mulberry Street to the quarter of the French purple on Bleecker Street and South Fifth Avenue, to lose itself and reappear, after a lapse of miles, in the "Little Italy" of Harlem, east of Second Avenue. Dashes of red, sharply defined, would be seen strung through the Annexed District, northward to the city line. On the West Side the red would be seen overrunning the old Africa of Thompson Street, pushing the black of the negro rapidly uptown, against querulous but unavailing protests, occupying his home, his church, his trade and all, with merciless impartiality. There is a church in Mulberry Street that has stood for two generations as a sort of milestone of these migrations. Built originally for the worship of staid New Yorkers of the "old stock," it was engulfed by the colored tide, when the draft-riots drove the negroes out of reach of Cherry Street and the Five Points. Within the past decade, the advance wave of the Italian onset reached it, and today the arms of United Italy adorn its front. The negroes have made a stand at several points along Seventh and Eighth Avenues; but their main body, still pursued by the Italian foe, is on the march yet, and the black mark will be found overshadowing today many blocks on the East Side, with One Hundredth Street as the centre, where colonies of them have settled recently.

Hardly less aggressive than the Italian, the Russian and Polish Jew, having overrun the district between Rivington and Division Streets, east of the Bowery, to the point of suffocation, is filling the tenements of the old Seventh Ward to the river front, and disputing with the Italian every foot of available space in the back alleys of Mulberry Street. The two races, differing hopelessly in much, have this in common: they carry their slums with them wherever they go, if allowed to do it. Little Italy already rivals its parent, the "Bend," in foulness.... Between the dull gray of the Jew, his favorite color, and the Italian red, would be seen squeezed in on the map a sharp streak of yellow, marking the narrow boundaries of Chinatown. Dovetailed in with the German population, the poor but thrifty Bohemian might be picked out by the sombre hue of his life as of his philosophy....

Down near the Battery the West Side emerald would be soiled by a dirty stain, spreading rapidly like a splash of ink on a sheet of blotting paper, headquarters of the Arab tribe, that in a single year has swelled from the original dozen to twelve hundred, intent, every mother's son, on trade and barter. Dots and dashes of color here and there would show where the Finnish sailors worship their djumala (God), the Greek pedlars the ancient name of their race, and the Swiss the goddess of thrift. And so on to the end of the long register, all toiling together in the galling fetters of the tenement.

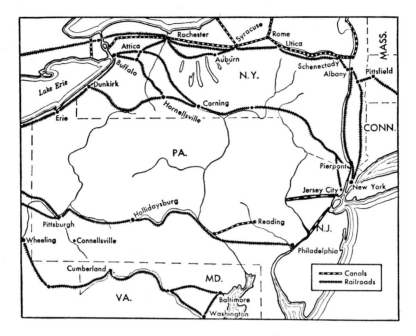

Figure 2-1. Canals and Railroads Before 1855.

	1820-29	1830-39	1840-49	1850-59	1860-69	1870-79	1880-89	1890-99	1900-09	1910-19
Total (in millions)	0.1	0.5	1.4	2.7	2.1	2.7	5.2	3.7	8.2	6.3
Percent of Total from:										
Ireland	40.2	31.7	46.0	36.9	24.4	15.4	12.8	11.0	4.2	2.6
Germany[1]	4.5	23.2	27.0	34.8	35.2	27.4	27.5	15.7	4.0	2.7
United Kingdom[2]	19.5	13.8	15.3	13.5	14.9	21.1	15.5	8.9	5.7	5.8
Scandinavia	0.2	0.4	0.9	0.9	5.5	7.6	12.7	10.5	5.9	3.8
Russia[1]					0.2	1.3	3.5	12.2	18.3	17.4
Austria-Hungary[1]					0.2	2.2	6.0	14.5	24.4	18.2
Italy					0.5	1.7	5.1	16.3	23.5	19.4
All Others[3]	35.6	30.9	10.8	13.9	19.1	23.3	16.9	10.9	14.0	30.1

1. Continental European boundaries prior to 1919 settlement.
2. Includes Scotland, England, and Wales.
3. Includes Canada, France, et al.

Figure 2-2. Decennial Immigration to the United States, 1820-1919

	1890	1900	1910	1920	1930	1940	1950	1960	1970
Total New York City Population	2507.4	3437.2	4766.9	5620.1	6930.4	7455.0	7892.0	7782.0	7894.9
Total Foreign Population	1786.9	2632.1	3747.8	4294.6	5084.1	4831.6	4444.1	3622.9	3306.0
Germany	650.4	784.9	724.7	584.8	600.1	498.3	427.9	323.5	210.0
Ireland	624.9	710.2	676.4	616.6	613.0	518.5	456.4	342.4	220.6
United Kingdom	163.4	210.4	214.4	187.5	254.9	216.7	191.8	142.5	116.3
Italy	68.7	220.4	544.4	802.9	1070.4	1095.4	1029.0	857.7	682.6
Russia/U.S.S.R.	77.6	251.0	733.9	985.7	945.1	926.5	808.2	563.2	393.9
Poland		55.5			458.4	412.5	403.6	389.0	292.3
Austria		133.7	299.0	431.4	289.0	322.6	293.5	219.3	146.0
Czechoslovakia/Bohemia		28.9			72.3	57.6	64.5	58.4	46.0
Hungary		54.4	112.6	123.2	115.1	123.2	114.4	96.7	72.1
Romania			46.0	56.7	93.5	84.7	71.1	62.3	
Sweden	23.4	44.9	55.3	57.8	67.0	55.2	43.8	27.5	
Norway			33.1	40.5	62.9	54.5	50.3	36.8	23.2
Greece					43.8	53.3	56.9	55.6	63.9
Canada			50.6	43.8	85.9	79.7	78.0	64.0	50.1
Cuba									84.2
Other America									375.0
China									56.2
Other Asia									104.5
All Other	178.5	137.8	257.4	363.7	312.7	362.9	364.7	384.0	369.1

Figure 2-3. Area of Origin of Foreign-Born or Native Population of Foreign or Mixed Parentage, Greater New York City 1890-1970 (in thousands).

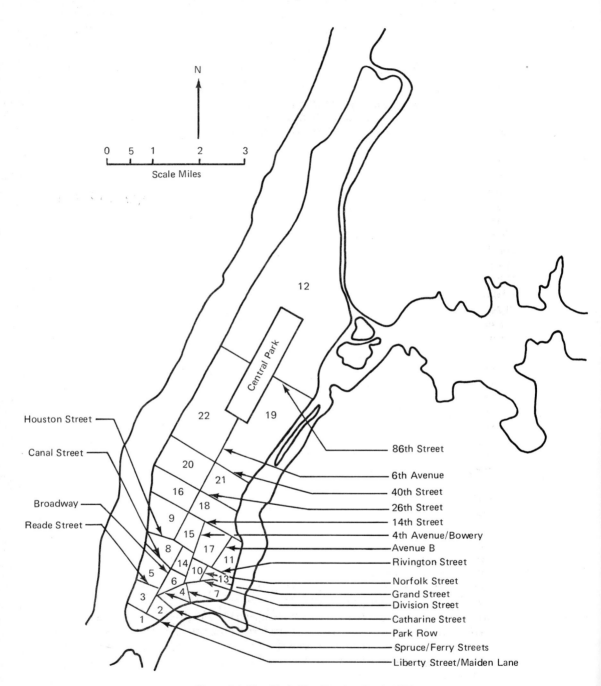

N

0   5   1   2   3

Scale Miles

12

Central Park

Houston Street

Canal Street

Broadway

Reade Street

22   19

20

21

16
18

9

15

8   17   11

14   10
5   13
6
3   4   7
2
1

86th Street

6th Avenue

40th Street

26th Street

14th Street

4th Avenue/Bowery

Avenue B

Rivington Street

Norfolk Street

Grand Street

Division Street

Catharine Street

Park Row

Spruce/Ferry Streets

Liberty Street/Maiden Lane

Figure 2-4. New York City Election Wards 1879.

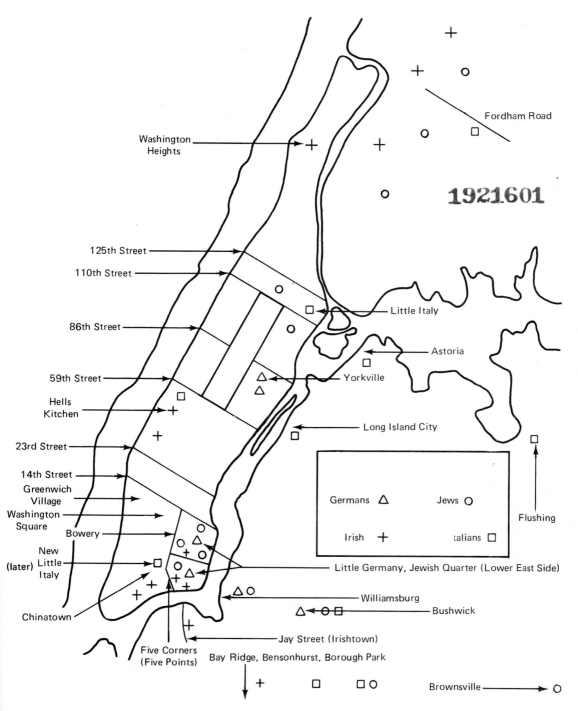

Figure 2-5. Principal Ethnic Settlements.

Chapter Three

1820-1920:
POPULATION EXPANSION
AND REGIONAL CONSOLIDATION

As the Region developed economically and greeted waves of immigrants, the total population swelled, the settled area continued to expand, and by 1920 the Region was clearly recognizable as one interrelated "place." European immigration actually contributed more to the Region's phenomenal population growth between 1820 and 1920 than did natural increase. As Figure 3-1 indicates, the Region's population of about 375,000 in 1820 nearly tripled to more than 1.1 million in 1850, and almost tripled again to 3.1 million in 1880. Between 1880 and 1920 the population again tripled, topping 9.1 million in 1920. In the century from 1820 to 1920 the Region's population increased more than 2,500 percent!

The influx of European immigrants to the Region's central cities and the concurrent expansion of Regional settlement by natives between 1820 and 1920 created a discernable pattern in the Region's population growth. Between 1820 and 1850 the highest growth rates were reached in the Region's four central counties: New York, Kings, Essex, and Hudson. Between 1850 and 1880 these four counties shared the highest rates of growth with four contiguous counties: Queens, Bronx, Passaic, and Union. Between 1880 and 1920 population increases continued to exceed the Regional average increase in seven of these eight counties as well as in four additional counties still farther out: Westchester, Nassau, Bergen, and Middlesex.

This pattern of increasing growth rates over time away from the Region's core reflects European immigration into the Region's industrial cities and native emigration to more rural counties. By 1920 the populations of the four New York counties of New York, Kings, Queens, and Bronx were 100 percent urban. New Jersey's Union, Passaic, Hudson, and Essex counties had become 82 to 97 percent urbanized. Together the twelve highly industrialized, urbanized, and suburbanized counties listed above contained 90 percent of the Region's population in 1920.

Population Growth of the Cities

As Figure 3-2 shows, the populations of the major cities in today's Region increased enormously between 1820 and 1880. The rates of population growth in the early industrial cities of New York, Newark, Brooklyn, Jersey City, and Paterson were especially high in the period before 1880.

In just forty years, between 1840 and 1880, the population of Newark expanded almost 800 percent, while that of Jersey City grew an astounding 3,900 percent. Industrialization and consequent European immigration, rather than natural increase, account for this phenomenal rise in population.

After 1880 the growth rate in these already populous cities declined. Between 1880 and 1920 Newark's population grew about 300 percent, and Jersey City's less than 250 percent. Their populations of about 400,000 and 300,000, respectively, still ranked Newark and Jersey City among the nation's fifty largest cities in 1920. The large additions to these cities' populations between 1880 and 1920 were due almost solely to the enormous volume of European immigration. In the next decade, however, as immigration slowed and outmigration began, their populations peaked and started a decline not yet halted.

Between 1880 and 1920 a new set of cities in the Region began a period of astounding population growth. Some, such as Clifton, Passaic, Bridgeport, and Yonkers, were recently industrialized; others, such as Montclair, New Rochelle, and Mount Vernon, were newly settled residential suburbs. The populations of many of these have continued to grow up to the present.

POPULATION GROWTH AND POLITICAL CONSOLIDATION OF NEW YORK CITY

The population increases of New York City and the city of Brooklyn merit special considera-tion. New York City, with 123,700 people in 1820, the country's most populous city, continued to hold its preeminent position. Between 1820 and 1890 its population increased almost 1,200 percent to a total of 1.4 million.

The city of Brooklyn's population growth rate of 7,600 percent was even more spectacular than was that of New York City during the same period. Brooklyn's population increased from 7,000 in 1820 to 838,000 in 1890. Brooklyn achieved such a rapid rate of growth and such a large total population through the annexation of contiguous towns in Kings County and by attracting both European immigrants and New York City outmigrants and commuters.

Already in 1850 Brooklyn ranked as the country's seventh largest city. By incorporating the Kings County city of Williamsburg and its town of Bushwick, Brooklyn became the country's third largest city in 1860. Later the city of Brooklyn absorbed the remaining Kings County towns (Flatbush, New Lots, and others) and thus became coextensive with Kings County by 1896.

The linkages between New York City and Brooklyn and the spillover of a commuting

Brooklyn by 1845 had a population of about 30,000, and this view emphasizes the important ferry link to Manhattan. These Fulton Street docks soon became the City's fish market, and the district is today a museum/ district of nineteenth century New York, complete with several historic ships at the docks. (New York Public Library)

The Brooklyn Bridge, designed and built by John A. Roebling and his son Washington, opened on May 24, 1883. At the time of its opening it was twice as long as any other bridge in the world. Its opening paved the way for the incorporation of the City of Brooklyn (and the other boroughs) into Greater New York. Many consider it still the most beautiful bridge in the world. The view here is toward Manhattan, and the tall crowned building is the Woolworth Building. (Photo courtesy of the New York Convention and Visitors Bureau)

population into the three adjacent counties of New York State (Queens, Richmond, and Westchester) created a single functioning urban unit spread out over numerous political jurisdictions. Already in the 1850s the State Legislature created Metropolitan Police, Sanitary, and Fire Districts serving both Brooklyn and New York City. A number of official reports urged a common municipal government for an even wider area in the 1860s. In the 1870s and again in the 1890s New York City annexed a number of towns, including Morrisania, West Farms, and Kingsbridge in southern Westchester County. In 1894 a referendum on the extent of metropolitan

government was held in New York, Kings, Queens, Richmond, and Westchester counties.

The vote for political consolidation had the following results:

	For Consolidation	Against Consolidation
	(in selected areas)	
New York (county)	96,938	59,959
Kings (county)	64,744	64,467
Queens (county)	7,712	4,741
Richmond (county)	5,531	1,505
Mt. Vernon (Westchester county)	833	1,603
Westchester (Westchester county)	620	621
Pelham (Westchester county)	251	153

Parts of Queens, including Oyster Bay and Hempstead, voted against consolidation; together these areas formed Nassau County in 1899. The Westchester towns previously annexed by New York City, together with those voting for consolidation, became part of New York County. Not until 1914 did the part of New York County north of the Harlem River become Bronx County. This 1894 referendum led to the creation of Greater New York City in 1898. Today it comprehends five boroughs coextensive with five counties; Manhattan is New York County; Brooklyn is Kings County; the Bronx is Bronx County; Queens is Queens County; and Staten Island is Richmond County.

Expansion of Manhattan Settlement

New York City's settled area continued its expansion northward in the 19th century as its population grew. By 1830 the City's built-up area reached 14th Street, and one observer commented in 1837 that even then "not more than a sixth part of the island of Manhattan is compactly covered with houses, stores, and paved streets. The rest is occupied with farms and gardens." Land speculators in the 1830s hastened the expansion of the settled area by sub-

This anonymous photograph from 1870 looks northwest from the corner of Madison Avenue and 55th Street. The white "chateau" at left, on the northeast corner of 5th Avenue and 57th Street, was the home of the socially prominent Mrs. Mary Mason Jones. The Northwest Reformed Dutch Church was, in 1870, just topping off its tower, to the right. Squatters' shanties occupy the foreground. (Museum of the City of New York)

dividing all of Manhattan into enough building lots to house an eventual population of 2 million, a population achieved in 1900 (Fig. 1-2).

The City's most prosperous residents were in the vanguard of its expansion northward. In the early 1800s they lived near the Battery. In subsequent decades the upper-class residential areas expanded up the island's center, first along West Broadway to Washington Square in the 1840s, then up Fifth and Madison Avenues as far as Central Park in the 1850s and 1860s. Areas adjacent to these Avenues, such as Gramercy Park Square, Madison Square, and Murray Hill, became synonymous with fashionable New York at various times in the 19th Century. An aura of exclusiveness suffuses some of these areas still today (Fig. 3-3).

By 1840 New York's settled area reached 23rd Street; by 1850, 34th Street; and by 1860, 42nd Street. In 1860 more than 50 percent of the City's population already lived north of 14th Street, the limit of settlement in 1830! The area

south of Canal Street actually declined in population after 1850, as it converted to business and commercial uses. One writer in 1855 aptly described the process of conversion:

> The City has not only advanced in magnitude, it has also been rebuilt. The palaces of the last generation were forsaken and turned into boarding houses, then pulled down and replaced by warehouses. He, who erects his magnificent palace on Fifth Avenue today, has only fitted out a future boarding house, and probably occupies the site of a future warehouse.

By 1870 Manhattan's built-up area reached 59th Street, the southern edge of Central Park. The area bounded by 59th and 110th Streets and 5th and 8th Avenues had been set aside in 1853 for future development as a park. Already in 1870 buildings struggled irregularly as far as Harlem village on the East Side. Less continuous construction marked the West Side and stretched northward to "scattered suburban residences of Manhattanville and Washington Heights." New York City's first luxury apartment house, built on West 72nd Street in 1884, was called the Dakota because it was thought as far away as that state. In the late 1880s and in the 1890s Harlem was solidly built up with brownstones, apartment houses, and tenements. By 1920 the remaining neglected pockets of Manhattan, as well as the upper reaches of the island as far as 220th Street, had been developed.

Innovations in Internal Transportation

Through the 17th, 18th, and into the 19th centuries almost everybody walked where he had to go. The populations of places were small, and the distances were short. People lived not only close to each other, but also close to where they worked and shopped. In those days most people worked on or near the waterfront. Building

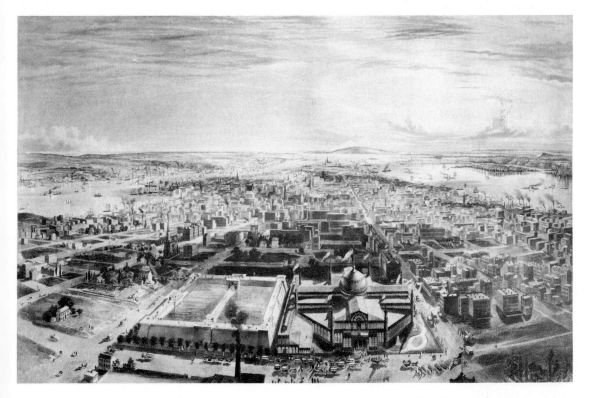

This print reproduces the view of New York in 1855 from the Latting Observatory. Forty-Second Street is shown in the immediate foreground, with the Croton (distributing) Reservoir and the Crystal Palace. Fifth Avenue is to the left. The Croton Reservoir was built from 1839 to 1842 and covered the eastern one-half of the blocks between 5th and 6th Avenues, 40th and 42nd Streets, today the site of the New York Public Library. The site had previously (since 1823) constituted part of the "potter's field." The Reservoir was demolished in 1899-1900 to make way for the library. This print is unusual in showing the undeveloped condition of the City around the Reservoir. Mount Croton Garden occupies the blocks between 5th and Madison Avenues, 39th and 41st Streets. Three houses occupying the block front on the east side of Madison Avenue between 36th and 37th Streets were built in 1853; later J.P. Morgan purchased the properties and built his home there. The Morgan Library today stands at 36th and Madison. The Manhattan skyline is dominated by church spires, all of them lost in the immense forest of skyscrapers today. Kip's Bay in the middle left distance is busy with shipping, and one might notice there, as all around the island, the predominance of sailing ships over steam vessels. Newtown Creek, the boundary between Brooklyn and Queens, empties into the East River. Brooklyn can be identified, but most of Long Island remains rustic, as does most of visible New Jersey. (New York Public Library)

"Society" moved uptown through the nineteenth century and upper 5th Avenue became a row of marble and brick palaces. This picture taken in about 1900 shows the enormous chateau of Commodore Eldridge Gerry at the corner of 61st Street and 5th Avenue. (Museum of the City of New York)

ships, supplying their provisions, and storing their cargoes employed many workers. Since the wharves and docks and slips of the waterfront surrounded New York on three sides, places of work were easily accessible.

New York's main shopping street then was Broadway below Houston Street. Running North-South, it divided the lower part of the island in half, and consequently it was just as accessible to the city's shoppers as the City's wharves were to its workers. In addition, half a dozen markets selling fresh meats and vegetables brought in from the rural districts and numerous small shops selling bread and other groceries were scattered throughout the city. If the men wanted to go to a tavern in the evening, they could have found one at every other street corner. Ladies stayed home at night.

This convenience changed rapidly as the population grew and expanded outward. Lower

Manhattan was increasingly given to business, as people moved either uptown or to fill in the island's eastward bulge, the Lower East Side. One commentator pointed out in 1853 that it was "now no unusual thing for people to reside three, four, or five miles from their places of business." As the distances between residential areas and places of work and shopping increased, many people came to rely on public transportation.

THE OMNIBUS

The second quarter of the 19th Century can be called the omnibus era. Omnibuses were large horse-drawn stage coaches accommodating about a dozen passengers. They ran regularly up and down Broadway and the Bowery and across town where the island was widest. In a letter of 1833 one observer noted that "[one] has only to step to the corner wh[ich] the B[roa]day caravans pass every 5 minutes. From 8 to 10, they are crammed with businessmen, after 10 there is space eno[ugh].... B[roa]dway is such a thoro'fare as to render it hazardous crossing the streets...." By 1850 it seemed a continuous chain of omnibuses crowded Broadway, creating such a "crush of traffic" that "you often have to wait ten minutes before you are able to cross the street." A couple of years later Broadway witnessed 16,000 vehicles pass up and down every hour.

Streets in parts of New York were not only as badly congested then as they are now, but they were also filthy and dangerous. Cars pollute the air today, but horses polluted the ground then, and they and their drivers were a lot less predictable than even today's taxi drivers.

THE HORSECAR

One remedy for the problem of erratic driving was laying tracks in the streets from which coaches could not deviate. This is how the omnibus led to the horsecar, the first urban transit vehicle to make a major impact on New York and other cities in the Region. The horsecar yielded immediate benefits, and soon a number of avenues paralleling Broadway were equipped

This Currier and Ives print of 1875 shows Broadway looking North from just below Fulton Street. Saint Paul's Chapel is on the left; the Post Office is in the center. Broadway is quite exaggerated in width, and shown with apparently no rule of the road—stages, carriages, wagons, and a fire engine all rush about in a tangle. A policeman escorts a lady across Broadway, an activity which was frequently a subject of caricature. (New York Public Library)

The New York Crystal Palace was erected in 1852-53 to house exhibits of the World's Fair of 1853. It stood on the east side of 6th Avenue between 40th and 42nd Streets.

The Latting Observatory, seen here in the left background, was also erected in 1852. It stood near the northwest corner of 5th Avenue and 42nd Street, and was built of timber braced with iron. Standing over three hundred feet high, it was the highest edifice built in America up to that time. A steam elevator took visitors to landings, where telescopes provided an impressive panorama. The observatory was destroyed by fire in 1856; the Crystal Palace by fire in 1858.

Sixth Avenue is shown here as a busy thoroughfare for pedestrians, horsemen, private carriages, omnibuses, and horsecars. The Chinese in the foreground added a note of the exotic to this popular print. (New York Public Library) with fixed-line tracks. Downtown Newark and Brooklyn developed horsecar systems at the same time. The tracks reduced confusion, increased speed and allowed more passengers to be carried per coach. Whereas the omnibus rode directly over the cobblestone streets and made a ride bumpy and slow, the tracked vehicles provided a smoother ride. By reducing friction, the tracks enabled an equal number of horses to pull larger cars, accommodating twenty to thirty people, and at greater speeds. Increased speed and greater carrying capacity in turn brought lower fares and allowed more and more people to live farther and farther away from the developing business sections of New York, Newark, and Brooklyn.

During his visit to New York in 1873 the German geographer Friedrich Ratzel felt that the superiority of New York's transit system over that of large European cities was due to its horsecar network. It not only allowed the increased separation of business and residential areas, but actually encouraged it. Ratzel observed that high rents and population pressure forced more and more New Yorkers to retreat even farther North or to cross one of the rivers over onto Long Island or to New Jersey.

Even omnibuses and horsecars together did not answer Manhattan's transportation needs. In 1867 Mark Twain complained that he could not get a thing done in the city without devoting a whole day to it.

> The distances are too great... you cannot ride... unless you are willing to go in a packed omnibus that labors, and plunges, and struggles along at the rate of three miles in four hours and a half always getting left behind by fast walkers, and always apparently hopelessly tangled up with vehicles that are trying to get to some place or other and can't. Or if you can stomach it, you can ride in a horse-car and stand for three-quarters of an hour, in the midst of a file of men that extends from front to rear (seats all crammed of course),—or you can take one of the platforms... but they are so crowded you will have to hang on by your eye-lashes and your toe-nails....

Mark Twain lived by selling exaggeration and humor, but his criticism was not without foundation. Even the *New York Evening Post*

lamented that "the means of going from one part of the city to the other are so badly contrived that a considerable part of the working population spend one-sixth of their working day on the street cars and omnibuses, and the upper part of the island is made almost useless to persons engaged in daily business in the city."

Manhattan had become a city of almost a million people by 1870, and distances between residence and employment had increased. Horse-drawn surface transportation was not only chaotic, but it was too slow. Still more roads were needed, and something had to replace the horse to make transportation more efficient. But how could roads be put through without eliminating built-up areas, and what could replace the horse as a source of power? Many answers to these questions appeared in the last third of the 19th Century. Some people suggested roads underground, as an alternative to surface roads; others argued that roads above the ground would be better. A new power source remained the chief problem. Compressed air was used to blow New York's mayor through an experimental underground tube in 1870, but further work on this solution was abandoned as impractical. Instead, efforts were concentrated on building tracks elevated above street level for trains pulled by steam-powered locomotives, like those used on railroads.

THE "ELS"

An elevated line built in 1868 marked the first real advance in providing the growing City with a rapid transit facility. By 1880 four major north-south "els" had been completed on Manhattan, and construction into the Bronx was well under way. The els were one of Manhattan's most spectacular sights. At two- to three-minute intervals trains raced overhead at second-story level. Their glittering lights and high speeds added visual excitement to Manhattan which until then had known only lumbering horses and streets badly lit by the flicker of gas lamps.

Nevertheless, even the exciting els had their drawbacks. People criticized them then, as peo-

Looking north along the Bowery from Grand Street in 1895, we can see horses, horse-drawn wagons, the cable cars which were introduced on the Broadway and 3rd Avenue lines in 1891, and elevated trains. (Museum of the City of New York)

ple still do, for ruining perspectives, for decreasing the value of abutting property, and for creating a perpetual twilight zone on the streets underneath. Those unfortunates who lived on the second floors of buildings next to the els had no privacy. A contemporary wrote that the cars careened "so near to the house you might shake hands with the inhabitants and see what they had for dinner." Also, as long as trains were pulled by steam engines, the engines' hissing and shrieking and their smoke and flying cinders polluted the air and assaulted the senses.

Electricity solved some of these problems and brought about the most significant changes in the City's mass transportation history. Electricity was clean (except where generated), it was noiseless, and it could provide power anywhere, underground or overhead. In Brooklyn and in the Bronx, as well as in some New Jersey cities, electric lines had been strung overhead as early as the 1880s. Horsecars thus became trolley cars, and people in Brooklyn came to be called "the dodgers," because they learned to hop out of the way of these fast-moving cars quickly. The els in Manhattan were electrified later, in 1899, and by 1900 the Region's first subway was under construction.

THE SUBWAY

Between 1900 and 1920 New York City financed about 100 miles of subway construction for two private companies, which actually operated the lines. The Interborough Rapid Transit Company and the Brooklyn-Manhattan Transit Corporation are still recalled in parts of today's system as the IRT and BMT lines.

This photograph was taken in 1902 from below 43rd Street, looking north across the triangular plot between Broadway and 7th Avenue. The excavation work shown here was for the foundations of the *Times* building, and the area was soon known as Times Square. Within two years the subway connected Times Square with downtown offices; the electric subways and electric lights defined Broadway's future as "The Great White Way." (Museum of the City of New York)

Another eighty miles of subway were built in the years 1920-1940, many of these by the municipally-owned and operated Independent System (IND). In 1940 the City took over the entire system of more than 250 miles of both elevated and subway lines.

The Spread of Settlement

In the early decades of the 19th Century it became clear that the metropolitan character of New York was not limited to Manhattan. As lower Manhattan was transformed into a business district, and as new immigrants poured into the available housing, increasing numbers of the City's residents moved east and west of the crowded wards—over the East and Hudson Rivers to new homes from which they could easily commute by ferry to the core area.

By the 1830s 86 steam ferries regularly plied the Region's waterways. The steam ferries' reliability and speed compensated for their greater operating costs over sailing vessels. A perceptive observer noted in 1844 that

"Hoboken on the Jersey side, and Brooklyn and Williamsburg on the other side of the East River, considering their short distant [might properly be regarded as portions of New York." In 1857 many people already agreed that northeast New Jersey, Brooklyn, and New York "form but one city in fact, though differing in name."

Expansion Into Brooklyn

Areas as far as 14 miles from the East River waterfront were laid out in lots in the 1830s. East New York in the Kings County town of New Lots was planned in 1835-36 to rival New York City itself, and it soon grew into a small city of 4,000 people. Transportation improvements in the 1830s and 1840s reduced the traveling time to Rockaway from five hours (by horse) in 1834 to two hours (by combining ferry, railroad, and six-horse omnibus). The rich established summer residences near the ocean in Rockaway, Coney Island, and Bay Ridge.

In 1850 New York City health officials commented that "within the last five years nearly 100,000 of our most healthy citizens (viz. of that class who live neatly and comfortably)," have left for Brooklyn and Williamsburg, "since the ferries and avenues of access to our city have become so numerous and easy." In the 1850s ferries between Manhattan and Brooklyn ran every five minutes and could accommodate not only passengers but 12 to 14 carriages and their horses as well. Some 20,000 people commuted daily from Brooklyn to New York in 1865. To Walt Whitman the Brooklyn ferry symbolized the oneness of Brooklyn and New York.

The opening of the Brooklyn Bridge in 1883 more than any other single event hastened the consolidation of New York City and Brooklyn. The Bridge and the transport system which crossed it helped swell Brooklyn's population from about 600,000 in 1880 to nearly 1.2 million in 1900. Coney Island, for example, changed from "a place where the fashionable or aristocratic multitude...congregage; [to] a rather fast, jolly, rollicking place, [which] serves

its purpose well, as the health-breathing lungs of a great city," where on a hot Sunday half a million people on "a wide stretch of silver sand" create a "carpet of heads."

CONNECTIONS WITH WESTCHESTER AND QUEENS

Areas in the New York sector of the Region inaccessible by steam ferry were soon served by railroads. The New York and Harlem Railroad Company laid tracks along what is today Park Avenue in Manhattan. They reached White Plains in 1844. The Hudson River Railroad paralleled this route farther to the west, along the river. Together they opened up what later became the Bronx and Westchester County. One commentator remarked in 1853 that railroads had already brought some areas 10 miles beyond Manhattan "into such intimate union with the city itself as to render them suitable and even economical places of residence for those who spend their hours of business in the densest part of the town." He predicted that by 1900 "a city of cottages...and villas... among cultivated fields" would cover the area in a radius of 25 miles from New York's City Hall. By 1865 some 2,000 commuters traveled to downtown Manhattan every day. In 1873 110 miles of track and 137 daily trains to Manhattan served Westchester County.

Westchester and Queens Counties remained largely rural, however, until about 1900. Only the part of Queens adjacent to the East River towns, such as Long Island City and Newtown, grew rapidly between 1860 and 1890. Despite train service to the rest of Queens County, suburban nuclei developed only in areas within walking distance of railroad stations. Thus Garden City, a model town founded by a rich New York merchant, and Flushing, "a city of gardens and nurseries," served by 22 daily trains to New York in 1875, became suburbs. In much of the rest of Queens, by contrast, "the people are largely engaged in market-gardening and dairying." In 1880 the United States Census Office described the Bronx section of Westchester

County as "an almost purely country district, with hill and dale, upland and meadow, forest and open...."

LINKS TO NEW JERSEY

Steam ferries connected Manhattan with New Jersey towns. In 1835 Hoboken was described as "a country retreat used much for children to walk in during the morning and in the afternoon the resort of multitudes of cocknies from New York. On a Sunday tens of thousands of visitors sometimes cross in the Hoboken ferry boats." By 1839 Red Bank and Long Branch, at greater distances from New York, had become more fashionable summer resorts. In the 1850s Jersey City and Hoboken were already the residences of a "very large portion of the merchants of New York [who] have deserted the old...part of town... now merely an aggregate of offices."

In New Jersey, however, railroads had the widest impact on the spread of settlement. Out-migrants from New Jersey's cities, as well as from New York, followed the railroads and established suburban communities. In 1832 the New Jersey Railroad Company was chartered to connect Jersey City, Newark, Elizabeth, and New Brunswick. In 1834 the Paterson and Hudson Railroad made its first run between Jersey City and Paterson. By 1840 all cities in the Region's New Jersey sector were linked to New York City by railroad and steam ferry.

By the early 1870s 420 miles of track operated by 13 different companies crisscrossed New Jersey within a radius of 40 miles from New York City. Each day 451 trains connected various New Jersey towns with terminals along the Hudson River. Numerous ferry lines then linked the terminals with Manhattan. In 1873 3,000 passengers were ferried daily between Jersey City and New York.

Newark was better connected by train with New York than was any other city. Daily 215 trains ran between the two, covering the nine miles in just thirty minutes. Other towns, more exclusively suburban, were almost as well served. Elizabeth, for example, had 123 daily train connections with New York City in 1873. Its growth in the preceding decade "having been caused nearly altogether by the influx of New York families—businessmen preferring to reside where they can have all the advantages of rapid and pleasant communication, pure air, low taxes and rents, and good society, to the disadvantages of high taxes and rents, and the disagreeable means of transit in the city of New York." Accordingly, Elizabeth's population more than quadrupled between 1850 and 1873.

Rutherford Park was described in 1873 as "one of the most progressive and popular suburbs of New York," in travel time "nearer Wall Street than 28th Street [in Manhattan is to Wall Street]." Many people no doubt responded to New Jersey's advantages of accessibility, clear air, and low taxes, for the population of New Jersey areas within 40 miles of Manhattan increased 40 percent between 1860 and 1870 while that of the City itself increased only 14 percent. One estimate, though somewhat exaggerated, suggested that "of the 400,000 souls living in this embryo city [northeastern New Jersey], at least 2/3 of them have come from the City of New York, proving...the wave of suburban emigration toward New Jersey...."

The industrial cities of New Jersey, moreover, spawned suburbs of their own. By the 1880s Belleville, Bloomfield, the Oranges, Montclair, and Morristown had developed as suburban refuges for New Jersey's as well as New York City's upper and middle classes. Already in 1873 one commentator had written:

In every direction, within an hour of New York we find the same signs of growth and active population; people of means and taste have taken absolute possession of the entire country, the old farm look has all but disappeared, houses have risen like magic, mere settlements have grown to be villages, villages to be towns, and towns to be cities.... The different stations on the lines of the railways have formed the nucleus of settlements. That with each year have grown and spread, until meeting, one continuous town has been formed. From Jersey City to Bergen Point, Elizabeth to Plainfield, Newark to Rahway, Jersey City to Englewood, Newark to South Orange, and

Rutherford Park to Paterson, have all become, as it were in the twinkling of an eye, one connected settlement, each adding enormously to its population every year. This is daily made manifest by the thousands and tens of thousands of people who every morning throng the chief railway lines leading to town [New York City] from their pleasant homes in New Jersey.

By 1900 about 3,000 miles of passenger railroad linked today's 31-county Region. The single most important focus of this passenger system was the same as was that of the rapid transit network—Manhattan. All the railroad lines which fanned out across the Region east of the Hudson River, and some of those which served New Jersey, terminated in Manhattan, either at Pennsylvania Station or Grand Central Station, both of which were built in the beginning of the 20th Century.

European immigration to the cores of the Region's cities and the movement of native residents to the cities' outskirts occurred simultaneously from 1820 to 1920. The Region's cities experienced an extraordinary growth in population and a rapid extension of their built-up areas in this period. Innovations in intraurban transportation, first in the use of horsedrawn buses and streetcars and later in the use of electrified streetcars, elevateds, and subways, promoted this residential development at increasing distances from the cities' centers. At the same time, the use of ferries and the construction of interurban transport systems, first of railroads and, around 1900, of interurban trolleys, often turned areas beyond the cities' boundaries into contiguous suburbs. This left undeveloped only those areas inaccessible to railroad stations. By the end of the period, in 1920, the Region's population had increased 2,500 percent, from about 375,000 to just over 9 million. Its built-up area had expanded from

about 10 square miles to almost 250 square miles.

The United States Census Office recognized the coalescence of a metropolitan region already in 1880. In a subsection of its 1880 publication, *The Social Statistics of Cites*, entitled "The Metropolis," the Office noted that:

> It seems proper, in treating of the vast population occupying the cities of New York, Brooklyn, Jersey City, Newark and Hoboken, to consider them not only as constituting five different municipalities, but as one great metropolitan community. This population has grown from one nucleus—the little trading post at the Battery—and its separation into different civil divisions is by physical and political lines, which have had little influence on the character of the people, their industries or their modes of life....

> There is no controlling reason why Flushing, New Rochelle, Yonkers and Paterson might not be included in the same community. Indeed, the villages and towns strung along the railways for 50 miles from New York are very largely made up of persons doing business in the city, or occupied in manufactures which there find their market. Wherever the line [defining the Region] may be drawn it must be an arbitary one, and it has been thought most proper to include only those larger towns which are most intimately allied with New York as their commercial center, and, as it happens which transport their raw material and their products from and to it largely by wagons.

> To adopt the opposite course, considering New York as New York, Brooklyn as Brooklyn, and Newark as Newark, would be misleading to one who might read the report of each particular city by itself. There is no reason to suppose that the western end of Long Island would have become the site of a great city had it depended on its own natural advantages alone; neither that Newark would have become a great manufacturing town had it not been for the distributing facilities in New York.

	1790	1820	1850	1880	1900	1910	1920	1930
New York	33.1	123.7	515.6	1164.7	1850.1	2331.6	2284.1	1867.3
Kings	4.5	11.2	138.9	599.5	1166.6	1634.4	2018.4	2560.4
Bronx[1]	1.8	2.8	8.0	52.0	200.5	431.0	732.0	1265.3
Queens	6.2	8.3	18.6	56.6	153.0	284.0	469.0	1079.1
Richmond	3.8	6.1	15.1	39.0	67.0	86.0	116.5	158.3
Westchester[2]	22.7	30.5	51.3	102.2	184.3	283.1	344.4	520.9
Rockland	3.3	8.8	17.0	27.7	38.3	46.9	45.5	59.6
Nassau[3]	9.9	13.3	18.2	34.0	55.4	84.0	126.1	303.1
Suffolk				53.9	77.6	96.1	110.2	161.1
Orange				88.2	103.9	116.0	119.8	130.4
Dutchess				79.2	81.7	87.7	91.7	105.5
Putnam				15.2	13.8	14.7	10.8	13.7
Hudson[4]	1.9	3.1	21.8	187.9	386.0	537.2	629.2	690.7
Essex[4]	9.6	15.5	56.2	189.9	359.1	512.9	652.1	833.5
Bergen[4]	{11.4}	{18.3}	14.7	36.8	78.4	138.0	210.7	365.0
Passaic[4]	{ }	{ }	22.6	68.9	155.2	215.9	259.2	302.1
Union[4]	6.4	12.0	17.7	55.6	99.4	140.1	200.1	305.2
Middlesex	13.1	17.8	28.6	52.3	79.8	114.4	162.3	212.2
Morris	16.2	21.4	30.2	50.9	65.2	74.7	82.7	110.4
Somerset	12.3	16.5	19.7	27.1	32.9	38.8	48.0	65.1
Monmouth	15.1	21.7	30.3	55.5	81.1	94.7	105.0	147.2
Fairfield							320.9	386.7
Total							9138.7	11642.8

1. Bronx County created from New York County in 1914.
2. Westchester County decreased in size in 1874 and 1895 when portions were added to New York County.
3. Nassau County carved out of Queens County in 1899.
4. Bergen and Essex Counties occupied the area today comprising Bergen, Essex, Passaic, Union and Hudson Counties. In the first half of the 19th Century Union County was carved out of Essex County; Hudson, out of Bergen; Passaic, out of parts of Bergen and Essex.

Figure 3-1. County Populations in the 22-County New York Metropolitan Region in Selected Census Years, 1790-1930. (Populations in thousands are in accordance with today's county boundaries.)

	1790	1800	1810	1820	1830	1840	1850	1860	1870	1880	1890	1900	1910	1920	1930
New York City	33.1	60.5	96.4	123.7	202.6	312.7	505.5	813.7	942.3	1164.7	1441.2				
Brooklyn[1]	1.6	2.4	4.4	7.2	15.4	36.2	96.8	279.1	419.9	599.5	838.5				
Greater New York City												3437.2	4766.9	5620.1	6930.4
Newark			5.0	6.5	11.0	17.3	38.9	71.9	105.1	136.5	181.8	246.1	347.5	414.5	442.3
Jersey City						3.1		29.2	82.5	120.7	163.0	206.4	267.8	298.1	316.7
Paterson						7.6		19.6	33.6	51.0	78.3	105.2	125.6	135.9	138.5
Kearny											—	10.9	18.7	26.7	40.7
Elizabeth						4.2		11.6	20.8	28.2	37.7	52.1	73.4	95.8	114.6
Bayonne											19.0	32.7	55.5	76.8	89.0
Hoboken											43.6	59.4	70.3	68.2	59.3
New Brunswick						5.9		11.3			18.6	20.0	23.4	32.8	34.6
Passaic											13.0	27.8	54.8	63.8	63.0
Orange											18.8	24.1	29.6	33.3	35.4
East Orange											13.3	21.5	34.4	60.7	68.0
Clifton											—	—	—	26.5	46.9
Irvington											—	5.3	11.9	25.5	56.7
Montclair											8.7	14.0	21.6	28.8	42.0
Plainfield											11.3	15.4	20.6	27.7	34.4
Perth Amboy											9.5	17.7	32.1	41.7	43.5
Bloomfield											7.7	9.7	15.1	22.0	38.1
Bridgeport								13.3	19.0	27.6	48.9	71.0	102.1	143.4	146.7
Yonkers									18.9	32.0	47.9	79.8	100.2	134.6
Mount Vernon												21.2	30.9	42.7	61.5
White Plains												7.9	15.9	21.0	35.8
New Rochelle												14.7	28.9	36.2	54.0
Newburgh												24.9	27.8	30.4	31.3

1. Kings County population 1860, 1870, 1880, and 1890.

Figure 3-2. Population of Selected Cities in the New York Metropolitan Region, 1790-1930 (In thousands).

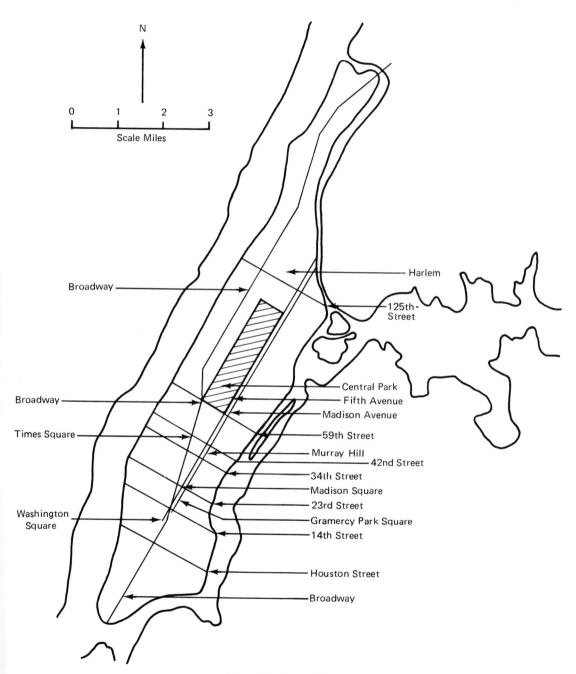

Figure 3-3. Principal Streets.

Chapter Four

1920-1975:
POPULATION GROWTH
AND SPREAD SETTLEMENT

Continuing growth of the Metropolitan Area from 1920 to the present necessitates that we review our very definition of the Region. The central cities and contiguous counties formed one generally recognized urban agglomeration already by the turn of the century, and more remote outer tiers of counties were drawn into the functioning Metropolitan economy and society.

The Prologue introduced the Tri-State Regional Planning Commission Area of twenty-one New York and New Jersey counties plus six planning districts in southwest Connecticut as one important definition of the Region (see page x). The Tri-State Commission came into existence only in 1965, however, long after the Region had in fact coalesced. But before the Tri-State Commission came into existence another planning group, the Regional Plan Association (introduced on page xi) had already in 1947 defined almost exactly this same region as the New York Metropolitan Region. The only difference between the 1947 Regional Plan Association Region and the later Tri-State Planning Commission Region was in Connecticut; the Association included only Fairfield County, rather than the six small planning regions later to be used by the Tri-State Commission.

For three reasons, therefore, will often speak of a *twenty-two county* Metropolitan Region after 1920. For one, it in fact functionally existed, as we shall see. Second, because all statistical data available before 1965 is county

data, Fairfield County having been a unit of statistical analysis long before the six small planning regions of southwest Connecticut were formed. Third, the Regional Plan Association conducted a number of excellent studies of this twenty-two county Region between 1947 and 1965. In 1965, when the Tri-State Commission came into existence and adopted almost exactly the definitions of the Region which the Regional Plan Association had been using for eighteen years, the Regional Plan Association expanded its definition of the Region to the thirty-one counties shown on Figure P-1.

Between 1920 and the present the population of our now twenty-two county Region doubled from nine million to eighteen million, and its built-up area expanded from about 250 to 2,500 square miles. It was, of course, the automobile which made this ten-fold expansion possible.

Core, Inner and Outer Rings

For best analysis of population trends since 1920, we will apportion the Region's counties into a Core, an Inner Ring, and an Outer Ring. Each category is based on a combination of criteria: the degree of urbanization in 1920, the availability of rapid transit facilities, the date of population stability, and the distance of counties from Manhattan.

The Region's Core counties include New York City's five boroughs plus Essex and Hudson counties in New Jersey. Each of these counties' populations was officially recognized as 90 to 100 percent urban already in 1920. All the Core counties are served by rapid transit facilities; no other counties in the Region are.

The populations in five of these seven counties stabilized in the period 1920-1950, or even declined. The Core, then, is the populous, highly urbanized heart of the Region.

The Inner Ring counties include Nassau, Westchester, Bergen, Passaic, and Union, surrounding the Core. By the late 19th Century some parts of these counties were urbanized, while other parts became suburbanized. These counties continued their suburban development up until 1970, and are today largely of mixed urban and suburban character. The remaining ten counties in the twenty-two county Region constitute the Outer Ring. They are on the fringes of advancing suburban development.

Population in the Region, 1920-1940

POPULATION IN THE CORE

For several decades before 1920 the Core and the Region's other counties had grown at about the same rate. The Core had maintained its 75 percent share of the Region's total population. With the Core's much larger population base, however, each decennial addition to its population in the decades prior to 1920 had been extremely large in actual numbers. Between 1910 and 1920, for example, more than a million people were added to the Core, and only half a million people to the rest of the Region. Between 1920 and 1940 the Core added 2 million more, three-fourths of them during the 1920s (Fig. 4-1).

The Core could not absorb such additions to its population without converting more of its living space to multiple-unit dwellings. The subdivision of single-family structures for multiple-family occupancy had begun in Lower Manhattan nearly a century before 1920. The replacement of such housing by multiple-unit dwellings, whether tenements or apartment houses, followed. By 1900 few single-family houses remained in Manhattan, and today only

one percent of Manhattan's population lives in one-unit structures. Even multiple-unit structures could no longer adequately house a population whose density per square mile passed 100,000 in 1910, and thus Manhattan's population peaked in 1910, and then declined by 600,000 during the next 60 years.

The other Core counties continued to add to their populations after 1910. At that time only Brooklyn and Hudson Counties were nearly fully built-up. To accommodate their growing populations after 1910, Brooklyn and Hudson Counties underwent housing conversion and replacement, though to a less spectacular degree than did Manhattan. In the 1920s Essex and Bronx Counties still had open space available for single-family units to house their growing populations, but already some sections of existing single-family houses in the Bronx were being replaced by six- to ten-story apartment buildings. The Grand Concourse, for example, a broad north-south boulevard, rivaled a number of Manhattan's avenues in the extent to which apartment blocks altered its appearance. By 1930 both Essex and Bronx counties had become nearly saturated, and thereafter their populations grew very little.

In 1920 only Queens and Staten Island among the Core counties remained significantly undeveloped. Unlike the other Core counties, neither then had mass transit access to Manhattan's job market. Subways linked Queens and Manhattan in about 1920. Thereafter Queens grew rapidly, although its large area, almost one-fourth of the Region's Core area, was not soon fully built-up. Sections of Queens which had the best access to Manhattan and which had developed even before 1920 changed character. Apartment blocks sprung up beside single-family houses in Forest Hills and other favored areas. At the same time new settlement expanded eastward to the Nassau County line.

Population growth in various parts of the Core between 1920 and 1940 was thus accommodated by converting single-family dwellings to multiple-family use, by replacing converted housing with multiple-dwelling units, and by developing available open space with either apartment buildings or single-family houses. The increase in dwellings units was especially pronounced in Queens and in the Bronx. The two boroughs were able to absorb 1.5 million people during the 1920s and 1930s, many of them former Manhattanites. The Region's Core counties as a whole grew by 1.5 million people between 1920 and 1930, and by .5 million between 1930 and 1940. In 1940 the Core's share of the Region's population had declined only slightly—to 71.5 percent—from its 75 percent share in 1920 (Fig. 4-2).

MASS TRANSIT IN THE CORE

Access to Manhattan is the principal explanation for the continuing increase in population in the Core outside Manhattan before 1940. Manhattan continued to offer the greatest share of the Region's jobs. It was also the principal focus of the Region's mass transport systems. Most people's choice of residential location was conditioned by these two factors together until some time after World War II.

We saw earlier that the principal function of mass transit has always been to move people from where they live to where they work and back again. In the 19th Century, places of work concentrated in the downtowns of CBD's of the Region's large cities. Residential areas, as we have seen, spread outward with each addition to the population. The design of the rapid transit system reflects the importance of the Core's CBD's and the impact of initial transport developments on the extent of residential development.

The arrangement of New York City's rapid transit network is quite simple (Fig. 4-3). Lines are closely spaced and intersect at Manhattan and Brooklyn. Manhattan is the primary node, still today the destination of about 80 percent of all the Region's mass transit users. Downtown Brooklyn remains a secondary node. The various Brooklyn lines converge there before again branching out to cross the East River into Manhattan. Although the Brooklyn CBD has diminished considerably in importance, the convergence of subway lines there reflects that it served a more important employment function when the subway system was first built. The lines radiate outward from these foci, with the spaces between spokes increasing away from them. Few lines connect the spokes. Not all directions away from Manhattan are equally well-served by these radial lines. The pattern reflects two things: the uneven population growth of the City, and the fact that the Manhattan CBD is not the geographical center of New York City.

The consolidated City network today reflects also the City's uneven spread of settlement in the past. The number of radial lines extending into the Bronx and Brooklyn is much greater than the number of lines to Queens. No lines reach out to Staten Island, five miles distant from Manhattan. The populations of the Bronx and of Brooklyn were much greater than were those of Queens or of Staten Island at the beginning of this century. Brooklyn, as a large independent city, built and extended its own pre-subway transit system as its population grew. The Bronx, as part of New York City, benefited from the construction of elevated lines connecting it to Manhattan, allowing people to move to the Bronx and yet be assured of getting to Manhattan quickly. Thus extensive networks and large populations had already developed in Brooklyn and the Bronx when the electrified rapid transit system started operations in the 1890s.

Both Staten Island and Queens remained unconnected to Manhattan by any form of mass transit *until* development of the subway. Since no major urban concentration had developed independently in these two areas, no internal extensive network had been required to meet internal needs. With few people to begin with and without links to Manhattan, the populations of Queens and Staten Island remained small, as we have seen. After World War I Queens was finally tied to Manhattan. Its population grew as a result, but the days of subway construction ended suddenly in 1940, and few lines today radiate eastward from Manhattan.

Since New York is politcally distinct from New Jersey, no effort was made to tie any of New Jersey's closely situated though undeveloped areas, such as Bergen County, to Manhattan. Jersey City and Newark, which grew rapidly in the 19th Century, developed their own transit systems. The separate Newark and Jersey City internal networks are relatively simple linear affairs serving small areas. In Newark one rapid transit line crosses the CBD and extends beyond it to residential areas. One extension connects with the Jersey City CBD, where it forks into two lines which then cross the Hudson River into Manhattan. These two links with Manhattan are provided by the Port Authority Trans-Hudson (PATH) tubes, a private railroad corporation until 1962. Thus, although the Region's rapid transit system focuses on the Manhattan node, its radials are concentrated in the northerly and southeasterly sectors.

GROWTH IN THE INNER RING

Before 1940 the Core registered the largest numerical increases in the Region's population, even though its rate of growth lagged behind that for the Region as a whole. Already in the 1920s and 1930s the Inner Ring's rate of growth exceeded that of the Core. In both decades Nassau County grew more rapidly than did any other county in the Region.

The Inner Ring contains numerous smaller industrial cities and railroad commuter suburbs. Many of these had been growing since before 1900. By the 1920s and 1930s towns such as Mount Vernon and Yonkers in Westchester County, and Englewood in Bergen County blossomed with apartment houses where one-family dwellings once predominated. Their residents were Manhattan-bound railroad commuters, as well as workers in local industries.

In some parts of the Inner Ring, Nassau County, for example, new single-family dwellings housed the growing population. Rising family incomes and the availability of a car allowed prosperous middle class families to choose more spacious lots in the Inner Ring over

denser settlement in the Core. Access to a railroad station by car enabled more and more such families to live farther away from the stations.

The intermittently built-up areas attached to railroad stations all along the Region's rail lines expanded as a result. In 1925 only two percent of the Region's densely developed residential land outside the Core was more than a mile from a railroad station, but this percentage increased steadily to 1940. Built-up areas coalesced into continuously settled areas all along the rail lines radiating outward beyond the Core. Even the interstices between the various spokes of the rail's radial network began to fill (Fig. 4-4).

In the 1920s and 1930s, therefore, both the extent and the pattern of Regional settlement changed. Mass transit facilities allowed the expansion of settlement in the Region's Core and promoted high-density land use. By 1940 the population in most Core counties had stabilized, and, except for Staten Island and western Essex County, few parcels of undeveloped land remained. The perimeter of continuous settlement around the Core's hub, Manhattan, was thus extended. The pattern of settlement changed as contiguous built-areas extended fingerlike along rail lines into the Region's Inner Ring.

Population in the Region Since 1940

Since 1940 the Region's population distribution and the extent and pattern of settlement have undergone a remarkable transformation. Between 1940 and 1970 the Core's share of the Region's population plummeted from 71.5 percent to 52.6 percent. Although the Core gained about 500,000 people during this period, both the rate of growth and the numerical increases in the Region's population were far higher in the Inner and Outer Rings than in the Core.

A variety of interdependent factors account for the differential growth rates between Core and periphery. First, new highway construction eased access to the Core from more places in the Region. Second, rising incomes enabled more people to become homeowners. Third, the desire for larger lots and more spacious accommodations could be satisfied only in the less built-up areas. Fourth, the changing ethnic composition of the Core's population frightened many Core city residents into abandoning the Core. Fifth, the Core offered a diminishing share of the Region's jobs, and settlement in nonCore areas became less tied to Core accessibility.

Between 1945 and 1950 the movement to the Inner Ring appeared to be simply a resumption of the trend begun in the 1920s, a trend which had been stemmed in the 1930s and early 1940s by the Depression and the war economy. The Inner Ring counties continued to grow more rapidly than did the Core or the Outer Ring, and Nassau County continued to be the Region's growth leader. Two factors, however, indicate that comparative population growth in the 1940s in the Region's three sectors differed markedly from that in the 1920s and 1930s. First, while the Core's population growth rate had nearly equaled that of the Region as a whole between 1920 and 1940, between 1940 and 1950 the Core's population grew at only one-half the rate of the Region as a whole. Second, *both* the Inner and the Outer Rings experienced growth rates about five times that of the Core. These factors were harbingers of Regional population trends in the 1950's and 1960s.

CHANGES SINCE 1950

Between 1950 and 1970 the Core's population declined; the Outer Ring's rate of growth accelerated and topped that of the Inner Ring. The Inner Ring's growth rate actually declined, and it is zero today. As a result of population redistribution within the Region in the 1950-1970 period, the Core's proportion of the total population fell from about two-thirds (67.7 percent) to just over one half (52.6 percent). The Inner Ring's share rose from 18.4 percent to 23.6 percent. The Outer Ring is now slightly more populous than the Inner Ring.

New York City had about 1 million more white out-migrants than white in-migrants bet-

ween 1950 and 1960 (Fig. 4-5). Brooklyn alone had nearly one half million more white out- than in-migrants. The total City population declined by only 100,000, however, because black, Puerto Rican, and foreign in-migration was larger than this out-migration, and because of the positive rates of natural increase.

The large white out-migration swelled the population of the Region's Inner and Outer Rings. Many of the white out-migrants from the Region's Core were themselves first or second-generation Americans, listed as foreign stock by the Census Bureau. Figure 5-8 shows that in 1970 the proportion of residents of foreign stock exceeded 30 percent in 10 of 15 Inner and Outer Ring counties. In all the Region's counties except Manhattan, Italians comprised the single largest foreign stock group.

In the decade 1960 to 1970 the Core's total population remained stable, although white out-migration and black, Puerto Rican and foreign in-migration changed the Core's population composition. During this decade growth in the Inner Ring slowed and barely matched the growth rate for the Region as a whole. The largest gains in population and the highest rates of increase were registered in the Outer Rings. Putnam County grew more rapidly than any other county in the Region, and Suffolk County gained the most people.

Since 1970 the Region's population has not grown at all. In-migration has been reduced, and birth rates have fallen. At the same time out-migration from the Region as a whole has increased. The population of both the Core and the Inner Ring have declined; that of the Outer Ring has increased only slightly. The proportionate share of the population in each sector thus remains about the same as in 1970.

ROLE OF THE HIGHWAYS

The first highways in the Region were built in the late 1920s and in the 1930s, both within and between densely built-up areas. By highways we mean parkways, expressways, turnpikes, skyways, and Interstate Highways; they are different from other roads in two ways. Access to highways is limited to widely spaced interchanges with other roads. The nation's first cloverleaf facilitating movement from one road to another was completed on Jersey City's Lincoln Highway in 1930. Second, higher travel speeds are allowed on roads designated highways.

By 1930 the Pulaski Skyway spanned the Jersey marshlands between Newark and Jersey City. In 1934 the Henry Hudson Parkway was completed along Manhattan's West Side and into the Bronx. Figure 4-6 shows that in 1945 New York City had nearly one-third of the highways in the greater 31-County Metropolitan Region as defined in 1965 by the Regional Plan Association.

These highways were designed with two purposes in mind: to supplement the rapid transit network by connecting outlying areas with Manhattan, and to circumvent the congestion building up in New York City's streets. The highway, then, was seen as a complementary alternative to rapid transit and to the street network. Before 1945 highway construction in the rest of the Region lagged. Only a few highways linked New York City and densely settled areas in New Jersey and Connecticut.

After 1945 both the rate of construction and the total highway mileage grew more rapidly in the Region's less-densely settled counties than in its built-up Core. By 1971, for example, only one-eighth of the Region's highway mileage was within New York City. Even though the number of miles of highway in the City had doubled between 1945 and 1971, it had expanded more than six-fold in the rest of the 31-county Region.

The shift of emphasis from construction in built-up areas to construction in less-developed parts of the Region answered demands from car owners that areas not served by any other transport network be served by new highways. Already in 1941 the highway planner Robert Moses had written, "It has long been a cherished ambition of mine to weave together the loose strands and frayed edges of the New York metropolitan arterial tapestry." In just five years, 1950-1955, the mileage of controlled-

access highways in the Region doubled to over 800. The Regional parkways, built earlier, were supplemented by newer expressways and turnpikes, such as the Long Island Expressway and the New Jersey Turnpike.

The complex pattern of streets in built areas was soon integrated with this new system of high-speed and restricted access highways which was superimposed on it. The combined highway and street network is a much finer network than that provided by mass transit. It grants accessibility to the interstices of the mass transit networks, thus diffusing accessibility. This has led to diffusion of settlement throughout the Region.

With greater accessibility almost everywhere within the Region, more and more people settled farther out from the Region's Core. Land was cheaper farther out, and a new house with a half acre of land around it was economically possible. The federal government helped by subsidizing home mortgages and by allowing deductions from taxed income for interest payments, as well as by subsidizing the highway construction. With new highways connecting people to the centers of employment, people chose to drive to work, rather than to live in cramped quarters in old residential areas and to commute by mass public transport.

As more and more people moved to the Inner Ring counties in the late 1940s and in the 1950s, and as the Outer Ring's population expanded prodigiously, the highways connecting these rings to the Core became increasingly congested. This had two results: it created a demand for even more highways, and it stimulated employers to move to where more of their actual or potential employees lived. Between 1955 and 1971 total highway mileage in the 31-county Region doubled, from over 800 to more than 1,600 miles.

THE HIGHWAY PATTERN

Most of the new highways have been constructed as part of the federal Interstate Highway System. This system was intended to connect metropolitan areas across the country

The George Washington Bridge, designed by Cass Gilbert, was opened in 1931. A lower level added in 1962 increased the Bridge's capacity by 75 percent. Linking the Palisades in Bergen County, New Jersey, with West 178th Street in Manhattan, the bridge was intended for motorists wishing to avoid Lower or Midtown Manhattan in reaching the Bronx or areas North and East of New York. The ready accessibility it provides to and from Manhattan and, of course, the spectacular view from the Palisades have encouraged high-rise housing development in Bergen County, which is now included in the New York SMSA and is sometimes called "New York's sixth borough." Crossing the Hudson from New Jersey, drivers may continue across Manhattan into the Bronx on Interstate 95 or swirl around these ramps onto the beautiful Henry Hudson Parkway along Manhattan's West side. (Photo courtesy of the Port Authority)

with one another. In the New York Region, however, it has forged links within the Region. Whereas most of the highways built before 1955 consisted of spokes radiating outward from the Region's densely settled Core, many of the Interstate System's highways link the spokes with one another. This is because many people who once worked in the Region's CBD's now both live and work in the suburbs. More highways

were needed to connect one suburban county with another.

As we can see in Figure 4-7, today's highway network consists of numerous roads radiating outward from New York City, the Region's center. These radials are linked by a series of concentric belts. The innermost belt, encircling Manhattan Island itself, is an example of one of the Region's first highways built to relieve con-

As we look South from the New Jersey shore of the Hudson River, the George Washington Bridge frames midtown and downtown Manhattan. The Empire State Building, with exterior lights on its top floors, seems a torch. (Photo courtesy of the Port Authority)

gestion on city streets. The next concentric belt, almost entirely within the Core, connects the counties surrounding Manhattan with one another. A driver following Interstate Highways 278 and 95, the New Jersey Turnpike and the Verrazano-Narrows Bridge, George Washington Bridge and one of the Long Island Sound bridges would cross most of the Region's radial highways. A third belt, composed of Interstate 287, now only partially completed, runs through parts of New Jersey's Inner and Outer Ring counties. It will connect with the completed portion in Westchester County via the New York State Thruway and the Tappan Zee Bridge across the Hudson River. If plans to build a bridge from Rye in Westchester County across Long Island Sound to Oyster Bay in Nassau County are carried out, this outer belt highway will be complete.

The Region's waterways are today major barriers to movement, although they once provided the Region's most important transport links. The Hudson River and its estuary bisect the Region. Waterways around Staten Island, Long Island Sound, the Harlem and East Rivers, and a number of smaller rivers subdivide the Region further. In the last one hundred years these water barriers have been spanned by numerous bridges and crossed by tunnels. The most notable of these provide crucial links in the Regional highway network and are shown in Figure 4-8.

Today more than 45,000 miles of road provide a network which penetrates nearly every square mile of the Region. The more than 1,600 miles of highway are the most important links in this network. Although limited access highways account for just over four percent of all mileage, they carry a disproportionate amount of traffic. One-third of all miles traveled by car in the Region are traveled on its highways.

The Spread of Settlement

These extensions of the highway network spread settlement, increasing the Region's built-up area to some 2,000 square miles, about 30 percent of the Region's total area. By granting accessibility to the interstices between the railroads' radials, highways have, moreover, enabled settlement to expand more uniformly away from the Core. The shape of the built-up area today thus resembles an ellipse more than a star.

Development has also eaten away at the amount of cultivated and pasture land in the Region. Today only about 1,000 square miles of the Region are still in farmland (Fig. 4-9). All but three of the Region's twenty-two counties have populations more than 75 percent urbanized, and only 18,000 people are classed as "rural-farm" by the Census Bureau. Dutchess County, the most important agricultural county

The graceful Throgs Neck Bridge, part of I 295, stretches from Queens in the foreground of this photograph to the Bronx in the North. It is generally thought of as separating the East River (here to the left) from Long Island Sound. The Bridge was completed in 1961. (Photo courtesy of the Triborough Bridge and Tunnel Authority)

Here we see the many complex approaches to the Lincoln Tunnel, with West 41st Street to the right. The Port Authority Bus Terminal is at the bottom of the picture. Manhattan's West Side here is still mixed in landuse, with tenements, warehouses, and loft buildings. The Hudson River piers visible here have been largely abandoned. (Photo courtesy of the Port Authority)

in the Region as measured by farm acreage, lost more than 40,000 acres of farmland just between 1964 and 1969. The Regional Plan Association estimates that in the larger 31-county Region 680 square miles of rural or vacant land were "urbanized" between 1960 and 1970. The decrease in farmland does not correspond exactly to the increase in developed land. Much land taken out of cultivation awaits development, and it meanwhile reverts to its natural vegetation. The large losses of farmland

in the Region are, however, indicative of rapid change along the frontier of residential development.

Some areas close to the original center of settlement on Manhattan remain undeveloped even today. Some 10,000 acres of the Hackensack Meadowlands in nearby Hudson, Essex, and Bergen counties form an empty carpet of salt meadow and marsh. Yet the Hackensack meadows are closer to Manhattan than are central Queens or Brooklyn. In New Jersey's northern Inner Ring Counties and in Westchester and Rockland, rough topography, such as the Watchung and Ramapo Mountains, has so far precluded development. Parklands and state forests have preempted other areas.

Coastal Connecticut and Long Island provide less formidable terrain for development. In these areas the absence of topographic barriers has promoted the extension of railroads and highways. Corridors of accessibility thus influenced the spread of settlement. Development east on Long Island and along coastal Connecticut is not only continuous, but it also extends farther than development does north and west at the same distance from Manhattan. The rapid population growth of Nassau and, more recently, Suffolk County reflects this topographic influence (Figs. 4-10 and 4-4).

POPULATION DENSITIES

The density of development, as measured by county population density statistics, declines outward from the Core's center, Manhattan. Population density differences result from several factors. First, higher densities in the

The Henry Hudson Bridge spans the Harlem River from the Bronx (in the foreground here) to the northern tip of Manhattan. The Hudson River is to the right. The Bridge is part of the Henry Hudson Parkway and was completed in 1936. The railroad tracks in the foreground are of the Penn Central's Hudson Division. Regular service connects Grand Central Station with suburbs along the east bank of the Hudson River up through Westchester into Putnam County. (Photo courtesy of the Triborough Bridge and Tunnel Authority)

Core suggest that it became residentially developed earlier than the periphery and that easier access to the center then resulted in higher densities. Second, higher densities have been maintained in the Core through historical inertia. More closely spaced housing, taller buildings, and smaller living space per dwelling unit continue to accommodate the Core's large population. Third, Core densities decline as land is redeveloped for commercial use or for lower-density housing, or as it is simply abandoned, as in Manhattan, Brooklyn, and Hudson Counties. Since 1910 Manhattan's density has fallen by one-third, from over 100,000 per square mile to 66,900 per square mile today. Fourth, population densities away from Manhattan, in the rest of the Core and then in the Inner and Outer Rings, decline with distance. Fifth, population densities in the Inner and Outer Rings have risen markedly with increased highway accessibility to Manhattan and the diffusion of employment opportunities into nonCore areas.

County-wide population density statistics nevertheless mask the degree to which individual areas in particular counties are actually developed. Some areas in counties with high densities are, as we have seen, still vacant. In all counties local residential zoning restrictions have affected land use and influenced the density of residential development and population.

The larger population density map of the Region today reveals the overall regularity of the density gradient in every direction from Manhattan (Fig. 4-11). Away from Manhattan's high density peak the slope of population is at first steep, punctuated occasionally by such smaller peaks as Newark and Paterson. Beyond the Core, especially, the density gradient flattens out even more. It fades almost imperceptibly into the low density terrain of the Region's Outer Ring.

The larger population increases in the Region's Inner and Outer Rings, especially in the last twenty years, have increased the Region's overall population density. Just between 1960 and 1970, for example, the Region's density increased from about 2,300 to more than 2,600 people per square mile. At the same time the differences between the peaks and valleys of the density map have diminished. The slope between Manhattan's high density and Putnam County's low density is less steep today than it was in 1960 or in previous decades in the 20th Century (Fig. 4-12).

	1920	+ or −	% Change	1930	+ or −	% Change	1940	+ or −	% Change	1950	+ or −	% Change	1960	+ or −	% Change	1970	+ or −	% Change	1973
The Core	6901.3	1553.3	22.5	8454.6	489.6	5.8	8944.2	503.1	5.6	9447.3	−131.1	−1.4	9316.2	117.9	1.3	9434.1	−182.8	−1.9	9251.3
Manhattan (New York)	2284.1	−416.8	−18.2	1867.3	22.6	1.2	1889.9	70.2	3.7	1960.1	−261.8	−13.4	1698.3	−159.1	−9.4	1539.2	−75.4	−4.9	1463.8
Brooklyn (Kings)	2018.4	542.0	26.9	2560.4	137.9	5.4	2698.3	39.9	1.5	2738.2	−110.9	−4.1	2627.3	−25.3	−1.0	2602.0	−94.9	−3.6	2507.1
Bronx	732.0	533.3	72.9	1265.3	129.4	10.2	1394.7	56.6	4.1	1451.3	−26.5	−1.8	1424.8	46.9	3.3	1471.7	−22.5	−1.5	1449.2
Queens	469.0	610.1	130.9	1079.1	218.5	20.2	1297.6	253.2	19.5	1550.8	258.8	16.7	1809.6	176.9	9.8	1986.5	−21.9	−1.1	1964.6
Richmond	116.5	41.8	35.9	158.3	16.1	10.2	174.4	17.2	9.9	191.6	30.4	15.9	222.0	73.4	33.1	295.4	16.6	5.6	312.0
Hudson	629.2	61.5	9.8	690.7	−38.7	−5.6	652.0	−4.6	−.7	647.4	−36.7	−5.7	610.7	−1.4	−.2	609.3	8.4	1.4	617.7
Essex	652.1	181.4	27.8	833.5	3.8	.5	837.3	68.6	8.2	905.9	17.6	1.9	923.5	6.5	.7	930.0	6.9	.7	936.9
Inner Ring	1140.5	655.8	57.5	1796.3	231.3	12.9	2027.6	543.3	26.9	2572.9	1227.4	47.7	3800.3	423.8	11.2	4224.1	−8.6	−.2	4215.5
Bergen	210.7	154.3	73.2	365.0	44.6	12.2	409.6	129.5	31.6	539.1	241.2	44.7	780.3	117.7	15.1	898.0	−.1	—	897.9
Nassau	126.1	177.0	140.4	303.1	103.6	34.2	406.7	266.1	65.4	672.8	627.4	93.3	1300.2	127.9	9.8	1428.1	−15.7	−1.1	1412.4
Passaic	259.2	42.9	16.6	302.1	7.3	2.4	309.4	27.7	9.0	337.1	69.5	20.6	406.6	54.2	13.3	460.8	7.0	1.5	467.8
Union	200.1	105.1	52.5	305.2	23.1	7.6	328.3	69.8	21.3	398.1	106.2	26.7	504.3	38.8	7.7	543.1	3.2	.6	546.3
Westchester	344.4	176.5	51.2	520.9	52.7	10.1	573.6	52.2	9.1	625.8	183.1	29.3	808.9	85.2	10.5	894.1	−3.0	−.3	891.1
Outer Ring	1096.9	295.0	26.9	1391.9	153.8	11.0	1545.7	387.0	25.0	1932.7	1089.7	56.4	3022.4	1251.1	41.4	4273.5	147.6	3.5	4421.1
Dutchess	91.7	13.8	15.0	105.5	15.0	14.2	120.5	16.3	13.5	136.8	39.2	28.7	176.0	46.3	26.3	222.3	7.4	3.3	229.7
Fairfield	320.9	65.8	20.5	386.7	31.7	8.2	418.4	85.9	20.5	504.3	149.3	29.6	653.6	139.2	21.3	792.8	−5.0	−.6	787.8
Middlesex	162.3	49.9	30.7	212.2	4.9	2.3	217.1	47.8	22.0	264.9	169.0	63.8	433.9	149.9	34.5	583.8	13.3	2.3	597.1
Monmouth	105.0	42.2	40.2	147.2	14.0	9.5	161.2	64.1	39.8	225.3	109.1	48.4	334.4	125.0	37.4	459.9	18.2	4.0	477.6
Morris	82.7	27.7	33.5	110.4	15.3	13.9	125.7	38.7	30.8	164.4	97.2	59.1	261.6	121.9	46.6	383.5	9.9	2.6	393.4
Orange	119.8	10.6	8.8	130.4	9.7	7.4	140.1	12.2	8.7	152.3	31.4	20.6	183.7	38.0	20.7	221.7	11.9	5.4	233.6
Putnam	10.8	2.9	26.9	13.7	2.9	21.2	16.6	3.7	22.3	20.3	11.4	56.2	31.7	25.0	78.9	56.7	6.8	12.0	63.5
Rockland	45.5	14.1	30.1	59.6	14.7	24.7	74.3	15.0	20.2	89.3	47.5	53.2	138.8	93.1	68.1	229.9	10.1	4.4	240.0
Somerset	48.0	17.1	35.6	65.1	9.3	14.3	74.4	24.6	33.1	99.0	44.9	45.4	143.9	54.5	37.9	198.4	2.8	1.4	201.2
Suffolk	110.2	50.9	46.2	161.1	36.3	22.5	197.4	78.7	39.9	276.1	390.7	141.5	666.8	458.2	68.7	1125.0	72.2	6.4	1197.2
Total	9138.7	2504.1	27.4	11642.8	874.7	7.5	12517.5	1435.4	11.5	13952.9	2185.1	15.7	16138.9	1792.8	11.1	17931.7	−43.8	−.2	17887.9

Figure 4-1. Total Population, Population Change, Plus Percent Change 1920-1973 in the Region by County and Core, Inner, and Outer Rings.

% of Total in	1920	1930	1940	1950	1960	1970	1973
Core	75.5	72.6	71.5	67.7	57.8	52.6	51.7
Inner Ring	12.5	15.4	16.2	18.4	23.5	23.6	23.6
Outer Ring	12.0	12.0	12.3	13.9	18.7	23.8	24.7
	100.0	100.0	100.0	100.0	100.0	100.0	100.0

Figure 4-2. Percent of Total 22-County Regional Population in Core, Inner Ring, and Outer Ring, 1920-1973.

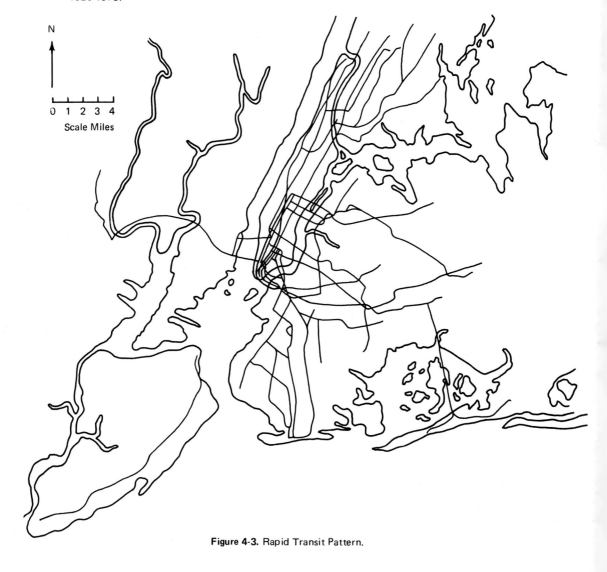

Figure 4-3. Rapid Transit Pattern.

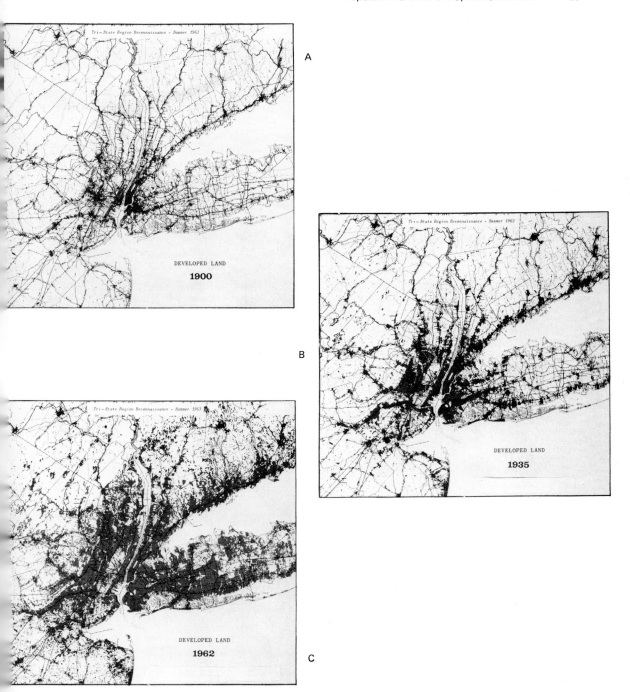

Figure 4-4. Tri-State Region Reconnaissance—Summer 1963.

	1950-1960			1960-1970		
	Total	White	Nonwhite	Total	White	Nonwhite
Core						
(New York City)	−828.3	−997.7	+169.4	−519.3	−955.0	+435.7
Manhattan (New York)	−364.4	−324.7	−39.7	−218.6	−197.5	−21.1
Bronx	−156.2	−194.6	+38.4	−88.3	−255.7	+167.4
Brooklyn (Kings)	−383.0	−476.1	+93.1	−280.0	−469.4	+189.4
Queens	+67.9	−6.7	+74.6	+19.2	−75.8	+95.0
Richmond	+7.4	+4.4	+3.0	+48.4	+43.3	+5.1
Hudson	−98.2	−107.5	+9.2	−45.5	−55.9	+10.4
Inner Ring						
Bergen	+152.8	+148.2	+4.1	+50.7	+41.9	+8.8
Nassau	+462.9	+444.3	+18.6	+14.4	−1.9	+16.3
Westchester	+108.2	+93.0	+15.2	+17.5	+1.2	+16.3
Outer Ring						
Rockland	+34.5	+32.8	+1.7	+71.7	+66.6	+5.1
Suffolk	+322.0	+304.8	+17.2	+328.5	+314.0	+14.5

Figure 4-5. Net Migration, 1950-1960 and 1960-1970, by Color in Selected Counties in the New York Metropolitan Region (in thousands).

	New York City	Rest of N.Y. Sector	N.J. Sector	Conn. Sector	Total
1927	1.6	1.0	1.0	−	3.6
1930	9.7	35.4	2.0	−	47.1
1935	25.7	111.2	10.5	−	147.4
1940	96.2	163.3	20.5	40.0	320.0
1945	111.9	171.5	20.5	45.0	348.9
1950	119.9	213.5	37.5	71.0	441.9
1955	149.8	377.0	217.6	74.0	818.4
1960	163.3	477.3	266.5	157.5	1064.6
1965	201.0	601.4	323.5	227.0	1352.9
1971	210.5	751.0	402.5	241.0	1605.0

Figure 4-6. Highway Mileage in the 31-County New York Metropolitan Region.

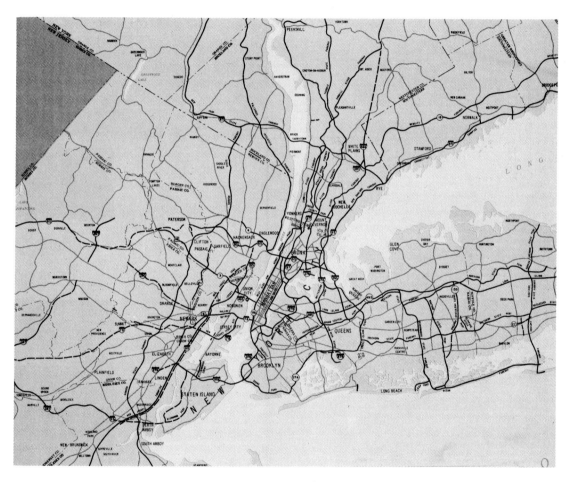

Figure 4-7. Regional Highways.

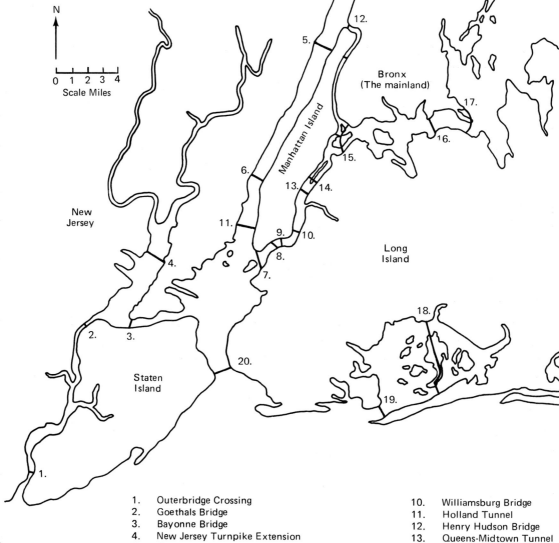

Figure 4-8. Major Highway Bridges and Tunnels.

1. Outerbridge Crossing
2. Goethals Bridge
3. Bayonne Bridge
4. New Jersey Turnpike Extension
5. George Washington Bridge. I 95 continues on across the tip of Manhattan into the Bronx. There are nine other highway bridges between Manhattan and the Bronx.
6. Lincoln Tunnel
7. Brooklyn-Battery Tunnel
8. Brooklyn Bridge
9. Manhattan Bridge
10. Williamsburg Bridge
11. Holland Tunnel
12. Henry Hudson Bridge
13. Queens-Midtown Tunnel
14. Queensborough Bridge
15. Triborough Bridge
16. Bronx-Whitestone Bridge
17. Throgs Neck Bridge
18. Cross Bay Bridge
19. Marine Parkway Bridge
20. Verrazano-Narrows Bridge

	Distance from Empire State Building to Approximate Center of Gravity of Population (in miles)	Area (in square miles)	Population 1970 (in thousands)	Population Density 1960 Per Square Mile (in thousands)	Population Density 1970 Per Square Mile (in thousands)	Farmland 1970 (in square miles)	Proportion of Land in Farms 1970 (in %)
Region		6909	17931.7	2.3	2.6	998.5	14.5
Core		477	9434.1	19.5	19.8	2.3	.5
Manhattan		23	1539.2	73.8	66.9	—	—
Hudson	4	47	609.3	13.0	12.9	.1	.1
Brooklyn	7	70	2602.0	37.5	37.2	—	—
Bronx	8	41	1471.7	34.8	35.9	—	—
Queens	8	108	1986.5	16.8	18.4	—	—
Essex	11	130	930.0	7.1	7.2	2.2	1.7
Richmond	11	58	295.4	3.8	5.1	—	—
Inner Ring		1261	4224.1	3.0	3.3	42.2	3.3
Bergen	12	234	898.0	3.3	3.8	10.1	4.3
Passaic	14	192	460.8	2.1	2.4	2.3	1.2
Westchester	19	443	894.1	1.8	2.0	23.9	5.4
Union	19	103	543.1	4.9	5.3	2.1	2.0
Nassau	20	289	1428.1	4.5	4.9	3.8	1.3
Outer Ring		5171	4273.5	.6	.8	954.0	18.4
Middlesex	25	312	583.8	1.4	1.9	50.9	16.3
Rockland	25	176	229.9	.8	1.3	6.3	3.6
Morris	25	468	383.5	.6	.8	45.4	9.7
Monmouth	31	476	459.4	.7	1.0	120.9	25.4
Somerset	33	307	198.4	.5	.6	78.9	25.7
Fairfield	40	626	792.8	1.0	1.3	35.7	5.7
Suffolk	42	929	1125.0	.7	1.2	95.7	10.3
Orange	48	832	221.7	.2	.3	245.7	29.5
Putnam	49	231	56.7	.1	.2	21.7	9.4
Dutchess	64	813	222.3	.2	.3	252.8	31.1

Figure 4-9. Concentric Development Out from the Manhattan Core.

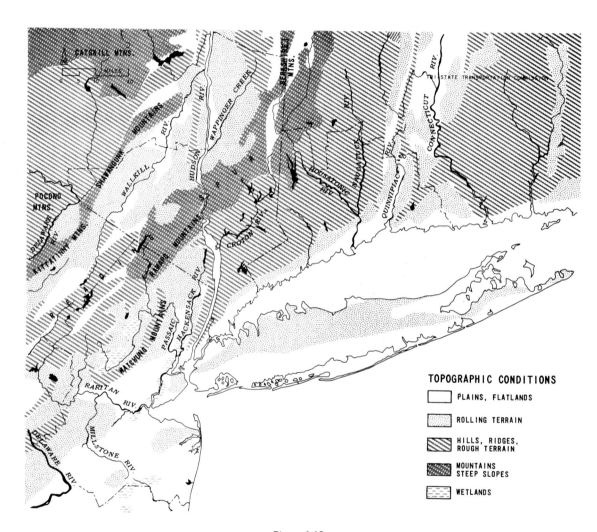

Figure 4-10.

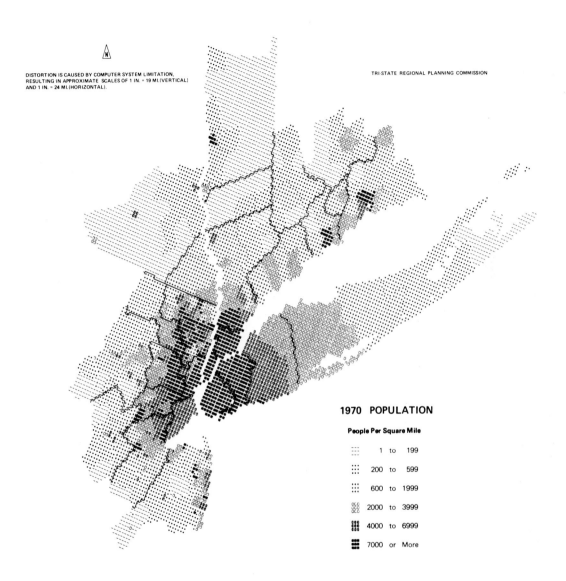

DISTORTION IS CAUSED BY COMPUTER SYSTEM LIMITATION,
RESULTING IN APPROXIMATE SCALES OF 1 IN. = 19 MI.(VERTICAL)
AND 1 IN. = 24 MI.(HORIZONTAL).

TRI-STATE REGIONAL PLANNING COMMISSION

1970 POPULATION

People Per Square Mile

	1 to	199
	200 to	599
	600 to	1999
	2000 to	3999
	4000 to	6999
	7000 or	More

Results from the 1970 census, displayed on this computer-produced map, show that the Region's people are concentrated in the central urban areas at densities requiring apartments, two-family houses and some single-family homes. Around the most densely settled area is a distinguishable "ring" of suburban communities.

Figure 4-11.

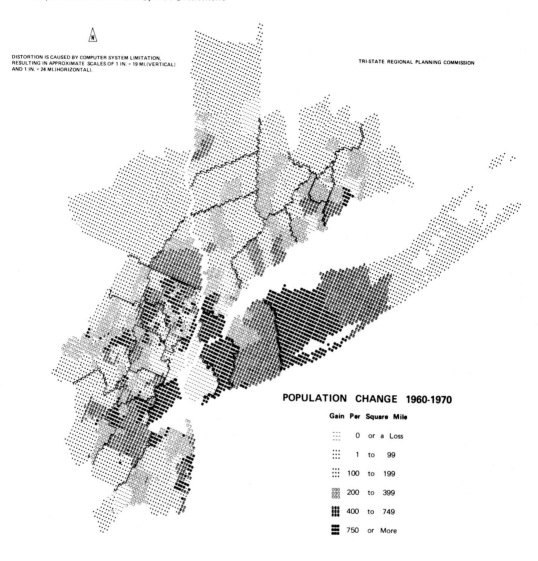

DISTORTION IS CAUSED BY COMPUTER SYSTEM LIMITATION,
RESULTING IN APPROXIMATE SCALES OF 1 IN. = 19 MI.(VERTICAL)
AND 1 IN. = 24 MI.(HORIZONTAL).

TRI-STATE REGIONAL PLANNING COMMISSION

POPULATION CHANGE 1960-1970

Gain Per Square Mile

:::	0 or a Loss
:::	1 to 99
:::	100 to 199
000	200 to 399
⌗⌗⌗	400 to 749
▬	750 or More

This map of the Tri-State Region was produced by a computer using U.S. census information. It illustrated how an overwhelming series of numbers can be organized into a visual statement—in this case a picture of growth occurring not in the cities, not in the far-out countryside, but at the suburban edges and newly accessible open sites. Places like western Suffolk County, Staten Island, Queens and Bronx can be seen in black as having experienced heavy growth from 1960 to 1970, while older central areas like Manhattan, Jersey City, Brooklyn, and Bridgeport have actually lost population.

Figure 4-12.

Chapter Five

1920-1975: NEW ETHNIC AND SOCIAL PATTERNS

In-migration has remained an important element in the Region's population growth since 1920. In this chapter we will examine continued immigration from Europe, and the more important newer migrant streams from Latin America and from other parts of the United States. Most recent arrivals have been drawn into the Region's Core, especially to New York City. As a result of simultaneous native out-migration from the Core to the Inner and Outer Rings, the Core and the Rings contrast markedly socially, and economically. We will look more closely at these differences later in this Chapter.

Continuing Immigration

The re-orientation of the immigrant source area since 1920 has had a conspicuous effect on the Region. The majority of in-migrants after about 1920 were Americans from the South and from Puerto Rico, although Europe and Latin America (including the West Indies but not Puerto Rico) have made substantial contributions. Between 1921 and 1974 the United States received about 13 million foreign immigrants, some 50 percent of the Europeans and 40 percent from the Western Hemisphere (Fig. 5-1).

FOREIGN IMMIGRATION

Eastern Hemisphere

European immigration has been relatively less important since 1920 than it was previously. Just over 6 million Europeans came to the United States during the last 50 years, the same number as came in each decade during the 40 years prior to 1920. The First World War curtailed European migration for a time. The National Origins Act, passed by the United States Congress in 1924, further restricted immigration by establishing national quotas based on the percentage of foreign-born persons of a specific nationality in the United States counted in the 1890 census. The 1924 law thereby gave preference to northwestern Europeans, who formed well over 90 percent of the foreign-born population in 1890, but whose migration since had already declined. The largest national quotas established in 1924 (German, English, etc.) were therefore rarely filled, reducing total European immigration even further.

During the 1930s the largest contingents of Europeans were political refugees from Naziism, the majority of them Jewish. In the decade after World War II nearly 2.6 million more European refugees arrived in the United States. Almost one-fourth of them settled in New York City. In 1949 the *Times* of London asserted that New York was "New Minsk, New Pinsk, or even New Naples [but] distinctly not New *York* or New *Amsterdam.*" In the 1950s, however, migration from Europe slowed as economic prosperity returned abroad and as political tensions abated. In 1965 113,000 European immigrants entered the United States; in 1972 some 90,000 came.

Even pagoda-shaped telephone booths mark New York City's Chinatown. Chinatown's core lies just South of Canal Street, adjoining the Civic Center, and is bounded on the East by Park Row and the Bowery. Chinese population has long expanded into adjoining areas of the Lower East Side, but nearly all of the leading Chinese institutions, as well as the restaurants and curio shops familiar to tourists, are found in China-town proper. Specialized shops for Chinese products and Chinatown's community organizations make it the main center for some 90,000 Chinese living in the Metropolitan Area. (Photo courtesy of the New York Convention and Visitors Bureau)

After 1965 immigration laws became less discriminatory, although the quota system continued. A quota of 120,000 was established for immigration from other countries in the Americas; for countries outside the Americas the limit was set at 170,000. Southern and Eastern Europeans and Asiatics benefited from larger quotas under the new law. As a result, between 1965 and 1972 the number of Italians entering the United States doubled, and the number of Greeks expanded five-fold. Filipino immigration increased 1,000 percent and Indian immigration 1,700 percent. Immigration from the United Kingdom and Germany on the other hand, was halved.

Many of these immigrants continued to settle in the New York Region, especially in the City. Older ethnic communities received a stimulus and grew for the first time in decades (Fig. 2-3). Italian neighborhoods were revitalized by a large influx of newcomers. Little Italy in Lower Manhattan today houses nearly 15,000 people, the majority Italians (Fig. 5-2). In 1974 New York City even announced plans to "preserve, restore, and invigorate" the neighborhood, largely as a concession to Italian-based political power in the City. Chinatown's population grew to some 70,000 in 1970, and densities increased. New communities of Sikh Indians established themselves in the Queens section of Richmond Hills.

Latin America

Immigration from Latin America (listed as "Other America" by the Bureau of the Census, and not including Puerto Rico), has, however, made the greatest impact on the Region. In 1970 New York City had 450,000 legal residents of Latin American origin. Another 150,000 lived in the rest of the Region. Latin American (including West Indian) migration to the United States, however, also involves large numbers of illegal aliens, most of them not counted in the Census. Estimates for illegal aliens in the United States range from 3 to 12 million. Immigration officials believe that as many as 1.5 million illegal aliens live in the New York Region, including 1 million in the City. Some 80 percent of 1.2 million of the Region's illegal aliens are thought to be Latin Americans. As a result, people of "other American" stock in the Region may number close to 2 million.

Special legislation enabled Cubans to immigrate in large numbers after 1961. The New York Region counted about 150,000 Cubans in 1970. About one-half lived in New York City, especially in the "El Escambray" section of Manhattan's Upper West Side between 125th and 145th Streets and farther north in Washington Heights and Inwood. Other more prosperous Cuban neighborhoods developed in the Astoria, Corona, and Flushing sections of Queens. Some cities in New Jersey have extraordinarily high concentrations of Cubans. In 1970 Elizabeth's population was 8 percent Cuban; Union City's, 28 percent; and West New York's, 34 percent.

Latin Americans other than Cubans include Dominicans from the Dominican Republic, Haitians, Colombians, and Peruvians. An exact count of their representation in the City or the Region is impossible because so many are illegal aliens. Legal Dominican residents number more than 50,000 in New York City, although illegal residents raise the total to well over 200,000. Estimates for the Colombian population in the City range from 80,000 to 160,000; for Ecuadorians, from 50,000 to 75,000; and for Peruvians, from 10,000 to 30,000. Dominicans are especially concentrated in Manhattan's Washington Heights; other more prosperous South Americans have established themselves in Queens, where part of the Jackson Heights-Woodside section is known as "Chapinerito," after a surburb of Bogotá, Columbia.

New York City's legal "other American" residents formed about 15 percent of its foreign stock (residents either born abroad or having a foreign-born parent) in 1970. Some 75 percent of the City's foreign stock of 3.3 million people were of European origin; their share of the City's foreign-stock population had tumbled from 90 percent in 1960. In 1970 Italy still led all other countries as the source area of the Region's foreign stock. Some 700,000 New York City residents were either born in Italy or to Italian parents in the United States.

UNITED STATES IN-MIGRATION

The greatest impact on the Region's population between 1920 and the present has been made by the immigration of native Americans. The twentieth century migration of blacks and Puerto Ricans into the New York Region has been a function of lack of economic opportunity in their home regions, of perceived economic opportunity in their home regions, of perceived economic opportunity in New York, and of the already-mentioned changes in national immigration laws. Large numbers of blacks from the South and of Puerto Ricans have not only helped increase the Region's overall population, but have further diversified it.

The Census Bureau's official 1970 count reported more than 2.5 million blacks and about 1 million Puerto Ricans in the 22-county Region. Together blacks and Puerto Ricans officially accounted for 20 percent of the Region's 18 million people in 1970. Net migration and natural increase since 1970, and an adjustment for the under-count of the black and Puerto Rican population in 1970, swells the black and Puerto Rican population to nearly 4.5 million by 1975, or about 25 percent of the Region's total population.

Black People in the Region

Population Increases. The history of black people in the New York Region dates to the founding of New Amsterdam in 1626. A number of black slaves were included among the first settlers. Importation of slaves to the Region directly from Africa began in 1655, and by 1723 some 1,360 blacks formed 24 percent of Manhattan's population. Thereafter Manhattan's black population increased only slowly, and the proportion of black people in the total population fell. In 1860, on the eve of the Civil War, Manhattan counted only 12,600 blacks, 1.5 percent of its total population. By 1920, however, black in-migration from the South and from the West Indies had gotten well under way. New York City's black population then numbered about 150,000, though it constituted only 2.7 percent of the City's population.

Several factors precipitated black migration to the Region's Core, especially to New York City, in the 1910s and 1920s. Unemployment in the South's cotton fields and the climate of racial antagonism pushed many black people northward, while at the same time jobs in war-related industries and in domestic service opened in the North. At the same time, European immigrants, who formerly filled such jobs, were arriving in fewer numbers. Blacks, accordingly, filled the need for cheap labor during the prosperous 1920s. By 1930 New York's black population had doubled to 327,700, and it formed 4.7 percent of the City's total population (Fig. 5-3).

The restriction of economic opportunity in the Region during the Depression of the 1930s reduced black immigration, and New York City's black population increased only 40 percent during the decade. In 1940 458,500 blacks, one-tenth of them West Indians, lived in the City, accounting for just over 6 percent of the City's population.

In the 1940s black migration from the South resumed, as labor shortages again developed in the Region during the Second World War. The flow of migrants persisted for well over a decade after 1945. Immigration from the British West Indies, however, declined after the imposition of a quota in 1952. By 1950 well over 800,000 blacks lived in New York City. Economic prosperity in the 1960s induced another spurt in migration. The relaxation of immigration laws in 1965 also prompted renewed black migration from the West Indian islands of Jamaica, Trinidad and Tobago, and Barbados. Between 1965 and 1970 some 80,000 West Indian settled in the City. Thus by 1970 New York City counted almost 1.7 million black people totaling just over 20 percent of the City's population and about two-thirds of the Region's total black population of over 2.5 million.

Concentration in New York City. The City's proportion of the Region's black population has remained fairly constant between 1920 and 1970, fluctuating between two-thirds and three-quarters of the total. As a proportion of the white population, however, the black population became more concentrated in the City during this half century. In 1920 61.5 percent of the Region's total population lived in New York City, while about 65 percent of the Region's total black population lived in the City. In 1970, however, the City's share of the Region's total population had been reduced to 44 percent, but the City had retained its high percentage (66 percent) of Regional black population. Obviously, whites were moving out of the City, and blacks were moving into the City but not into the suburbs (Fig. 5-4).

The continuing concentration of black people in New York City's five counties in 1970, and in the Core as a whole, reflects two factors: the large number increases in the black population within the Region's major cities, and the much more rapid growth in the Region's overall population outside the Core especially since 1930. The City's total population of about 7.9 million is today almost the same as it was in 1950. The population in counties beyond the City's five boroughs, meanwhile, has grown by 4 million just since 1950. Thus in 1970 New York City's black population was not only larger than that of any other city in the Region, but New York's black population also constituted a higher proportion (21 percent) of its total population than the proportion of any other big city (except Newark, 55 percent black) in the Region.

Black Communities Within the City. Within New York City Manhattan had until 1960 a larger black population than did any of the other boroughs. Also, the black share of Manhattan's total population was larger than was the black share of any other borough's total population. Black settlement in New York is comparable to earlier immigrant settlement in this regard, though it differs in other respects. Black people, for example, changed residential location not with improved economic conditions, as had been the case among earlier immigrants, but rather in accordance with the availability of any housing in any other area. Blacks were often replaced by more "desirable" tenants and were forced to move elsewhere. Black movement up Manhattan during the 19th Century, therefore, was not conditioned by blacks' economic prosperity, but, rather, by the appropriation of their housing in lower Manhattan.

Blacks, like earlier immigrants, had to accept the cheapest housing available in the City. Unlike earlier immigrants, however, they were frequently barred from areas of cheap housing by landlords' discrimination against "people of color." Unlike the Irish, Jews, or Italians, black people banded together not to enjoy a common linguistic, cultural, or religious tradition, but because discrimination left them no alternative. Blacks were tied together less by a common cultural heritage than by a common set of grievances.

The earliest concentration of freed blacks occurred in the Five Corners District in the 1820s and 1830s. Irish immigration into that area, however, soon forced blacks to move north into Hell's Kitchen and beyond into the West 60s. There a black district, San Juan Hill, developed around 1900. At about the same time black people made their initial inroads into Harlem. Between 1880 and 1900 speculators had built row after row of upper-middle income housing, both brownstones and apartments, in Harlem. More were built than could be sold. Landlords soon discovered that by renting their properties to blacks rather than waiting to sell them to whites they could realize higher profits. The increasing black population was desperately in need of housing and was willing to pay almost any price for it. Harlem offered an opportunity. In 1920 James Weldon Johnson, a well-known black writer, predicted that Harlem would become "the greatest Negro city in the world....And what a fine part of New York City [the Negro] has come into possession of!" Yet by 1927 a housing expert suggested that Harlem's buildings offered "the best laboratory for slum clearance...in the entire City." What had happened?

Between 1920 and 1930 Manhattan's black population doubled to 225,000 and about 75 per cent of it concentrated in Harlem. There the price of housing—Harlemites spent almost 50 percent of their earnings on rent—forced many families to crowd into houses and apartments designed for single families. Space was subdivided, and many people slept in shifts. Facilities deteriorated also because rural blacks at first did not easily adapt to urban living conditions, and because landlords refused to invest money for repairs. Black people were gouged because landlords recognized that blacks had to accept any available housing, regardless of its condition. These conditions led to inordinately high mortality and sickness rates. Infant mortality rates in Harlem were almost twice as high as for the City as a whole; death from tuberculosis exceeded the City's rate by almost 300 percent. In many respects Harlem thus resembled the Lower East Side ghetto at the turn of the Century.

In the late 1920s and through the 1930s Manhattan continued to hold about two-thirds of New York's black population. The Harlem ghetto expanded in all directions from its center in the West 120s. Southward the ghetto appropriated the older Jewish neighborhood as far as the northern edge of Central Park at 110th Street. Eastward Harlem encroached upon "Little Italy" in East Harlem. Westward movement was for a time limited by Morningside Heights and St. Nicholas Park. To the north the Harlem River served as a dividing line between black Harlem and the Bronx, still 98.3 percent white in 1940.

After 1940 the enormous black migration to New York City expanded the Harlem ghetto north of the Harlem River. Black movement followed subway lines which crossed Harlem into the South Bronx section of Morrisania. Between 1940 and 1950 the Bronx's black population grew 400 percent, to almost 100,000. The already sizable black ghetto in the Stuyvesant Heights section of Brooklyn expanded farther into Bedford, and Brooklyn's black population grew to more than 200,000 in 1950.

Between 1940 and 1950 the proportion of New York City black people in Manhattan declined from 65 to 37 percent. Significantly, the geographic trend among the black population was following that observed among the white population several decades earlier. Just as Manhattan was the first borough to experience white out-migration (as early as the 1910-1920 decade), Manhattan was the first borough to witness a black net out-migration. In the period 1950 to 1960 40,000 more blacks left Manhattan than came to settle. The growth in Manhattan's total black population in this decade was due solely to natural increase.

Since 1950, therefore, Manhattan's black population has remained relatively stable at about 400,000 people. Growth in the Bronx and Brooklyn has continued. The Bronx's black population increased 375 percent between 1950 and 1970, to more than 350,000. Today it extends both north and south of the original settlement in Morrisania. During the same period Brooklyn's black population grew over 200 percent, to more than 650,000 people. Black population is now concentrated not only in Bedford-Stuyvesant, but in contiguous sections to the East penetrated by subway lines, such as Brownsville and East New York. Today the populations of each of these three New York City boroughs, Manhattan, Brooklyn, and the Bronx, is about 25 percent black (Fig. 5-5).

Queens and Essex are the only other counties in the Region with large black populations. Since 1950 middle class black out-migration from the poorer ghettos of New York City to Queens has increased that borough's black population to more than a quarter million, about 13 percent of all Queens' residents. Growth has been especially concentrated in such areas as Jamaica and Springfield Gardens adjacent to Brooklyn and, again, along lines of subway access to Manhattan.

Essex County has the highest percentage black population of any county in the Region. After 1945 black migrants moved from the South to industrial employment opportunities, especially in Newark. Thus today black people

form 30 percent of Essex County's population and 55 percent of Newark's population (Fig. 5-6).

Puerto Ricans in the Region

Puerto Rican migration to the Region since 1920 has further diversified the Region's population. In 1970 the Census Bureau counted some 800,000 Puerto Ricans in New York City and just over 1 million in the Region as a whole. Puerto Rican leaders in New York City allege that the Census Bureau has undercounted the Puerto Rican population, and that it may be as large as 1.3 million. Many Puerto Ricans move back and forth between New York and the Island. Figures in the following pages, however, refer to the official 1970 count.

Puerto Rican immigration to the United States started at about the time Puerto Ricans were given United States citizenship by the 1917 Jones Act. In 1920 New York City counted 7,800 Puerto Ricans. By 1940 there were 61,000 persons of Puerto Rican birth in the City. Mass migration, however, did not occur until the 1940s.

Large-scale migration was prompted by a rapidly growing population in Puerto Rico. The predominantly rural economy could not absorb this growth, and many Puerto Ricans emigrated. New York, as the terminus of shipping lines, attracted the bulk of emigrants. After World War II the establishment of regular air service between San Juan and New York accelerated the flow. Between 1940 and 1950 New York City's Puerto Rican population expanded 400 percent, to 246,000.

New York City was the chief goal of Puerto Rican migrants. In 1950 83 percent of all Puerto Ricans on the mainland lived in New York City. Within the City the distribution of Puerto Ricans resemble that of earlier migrants. In 1950 some 56 percent of all Puerto Ricans in the City lived in Manhattan. The area of East Harlem known as "El Barrio" or "Spanish Harlem" was the focal point of settlement, although significant clusters of Puerto Ricans could be found on the West Side and the Lower East Side. In these districts Puerto Ricans replaced Europeans of the second generation, just as black people had a short time earlier moved into previously European ethnic neighborhoods.

In the 1950s Puerto Rican in-migrants to New York outnumbered those already settled in the City, and even exceeded black in-migration during the same period. In-migration and high birth rates among Puerto Ricans swelled their number in New York City to over 600,000, an increase of 150 percent over the number resident in the City in 1950. By 1960, however, Manhattan held over 37 percent of the City's Puerto Rican population. Many newcomers, as well as second generation Puerto Ricans, headed for Brooklyn and the Bronx. The Puerto Rican populations of these boroughs grew 450 and 300 percent, respectively. Whole neighborhoods in both boroughs became overwhelmingly Puerto Rican during the 1950s. Williamsburg, the former German and Jewish stronghold, in Brooklyn, is today at least half Puerto Rican; the South Bronx, 80 percent.

In the 1960s Puerto Rican immigration slowed. By the end of the decade and continuing to the present, more Puerto Ricans left the City than moved to it. Improved economic conditions in Puerto Rico and dissatisfaction with living conditions in New York account for this reverse migration to the island. High birth rates in the City (about 40/1,000, double the non-Puerto Rican white average), continued, and New York's Puerto Rican population numbered over 800,000 in 1970. This number included about 60 percent of all Puerto Ricans on the mainland and about 80 percent of those in the Region.

A rapid redistribution of the City's Puerto Rican population during the 1960s not only reduced Manhattan's share of the total further, but also resulted in an absolute decline in that borough. In 1970 Manhattan counted 40,000 fewer people of Puerto Rican birth and parentage than a decade earlier, while Brooklyn added some 90,000 and the Bronx 130,000. Manhattan's share of the City's Puerto Rican popula-

tion fell from 37 percent in 1960 to 23 percent in 1970. The Bronx's share increased from 30 percent to 39 percent during the same time, and that of Brooklyn grew from 29 percent to 33 percent. Together these three boroughs accounted for 95 percent of New York's Puerto Rican population in 1970, and almost 75 percent of the Puerto Rican population in the Region. Hudson County contains another 10 percent of the Region's total Puerto Rican population.

Rates of net migration (Fig. 4-5) examined in the previous chapter indicate the degree to which the Core's population, especially that of New York City, is being transformed. Between 1960 and 1970 about 1 million whites left the City, while at least 600,000 blacks and Hispanic-speaking peoples were added. Unofficial statistics released in 1974 indicate that the pace of change between 1970 and 1973 picked up. In just three years more than 400,000 whites left the City, and nearly 250,000 blacks and Hispanic peoples arrived. It is estimated that in 1973 non-Hispanic whites constituted 56.8 percent of the City's population, blacks and Orientals 25.3 percent, and Hispanics 16.1 percent (1.8 percent unattributed).

Core-Ring Contrasts

The large in-migration of blacks and Hispanics to the Region's Core has created enormous contrasts between the Core and the rest of the Region. Blacks and Hispanics today account for well over one-third the Core's population, but for less than 8 percent in the rest of the Region. The contrasts between the Core and the Rings are more than just ethnic, however. Lack of resources and education, discrimination, language barriers, and a myriad of other handicaps suffered by the in-migrants to the Core further differentiates the Core from the Inner and Outer Ring counties. The Core's population is today poorer, less educated, and older than that of the surrounding counties. More of the Core's housing stock is older as well, and most people live in multiple-unit dwellings, many of which are dilapidated.

In the early 1920s Sutton Place, along the East River in the upper 50s, was a district of run-down brownstones. Soon, however, the site was discovered and colonized by the 5th Avenue rich, who converted it into one of Manhattan's most attractive residential streets. The home on the northeast corner of Sutton Place and East 57th Street, shown here in 1936, was that of Mrs. William K. Vanderbilt, and next door lived Miss Anne Morgan. The street is still one of the handsomest in the City. (Museum of the City of New York)

INCOME LEVELS

An examination of Figure 5-7 reveals the striking decline in the relative level of per capita income in the Region's Core since 1939. In 1939 average incomes in the Core were seven percent higher than in the Region as a whole. In 1970 they were six percent lower. The Inner Ring, by contrast, has emerged as the Region's wealthiest sector, with Westchester County's 30 percent higher per capita incomes leading the way.

Manhattan's high per capita income standing is deceptive. It masks the disparity between the rich and the poor in that borough. Figure 5-8 shows the Region's counties' median family incomes. Median income is the amount which divides the distribution into two equal groups, one having incomes above the median and the other having income below the median. By that measure Manhattan emerges as the third-poorest county in the Region, half of its families earning less than 9,000 dollars annually by 1969. Only Brooklyn and the Bronx have relatively more poorer families. Other statistics indicate that relatively more families in Manhattan (37.8 percent) than even Brooklyn (37.4 percent) had incomes of less than 7,000 dollars in 1969. Manhattan's unusually high *average* per capita income results from the enormous incomes earned by some of the 12.4 percent of its families with incomes exceeding 25,000 dollars. Considerable numbers of Manhattanites also have very high incomes from investments (Fig. 5-9).

The Core is today poorer than the rest of the Region and becoming still poorer. The 1960 median income of Core families was 89 percent of the median income for the Region as a whole. By 1969 this proportion had dropped to 85 percent and in 1974 to 81 percent. The disparity in incomes among the black, Puerto Rican, and non-Hispanic white population is also revealing. In 1970 one out of three Puerto Rican families had incomes of less than 4,000 dollars; the proportion for blacks was one family in four; for whites, one in nine.

In a survey of 31 large American cities in 1974, New York City ranked 19th in its real annual per capita income figures. The cities' real annual incomes reflect the incomes' purchasing power and are computed by taking the median per capita income and adjusting it to reflect cost-of-living differences. Further analysis in 19 cities indicated that New York's real income had risen only 1.6 percent between 1960 and 1970, placing New York next to last, just ahead of St. Louis, in the rank-ordering of cities according to increasing real incomes.

POVERTY

Poverty, as measured by the number of welfare recipients, is endemic in New York City. The City has 26 federally recognized poverty zones, which are eligible for certain categories of federal aid (Fig. 5-10). These zones include 40 percent of the City's total population. In the ten poorest of these, more than 30 percent of all residents received some form of welfare payments in 1971. Between 1965 and 1971 poverty spread beyond such designated poverty zones into adjacent neighborhoods, and the number of welfare recipients climbed from some 478,000 to more than 1.25 million.

Poverty in the City today is most pervasive in the Bronx and in Brooklyn. In the Bronx poverty is spreading rapidly from the South Bronx, Hunts Point, and Morrisania northward into Tremont and beyond. These sections saw a three- to ten-fold increase in their welfare populations between 1965 and 1971. In some subsections of these districts, more than 50 percent of the people receive welfare. In Brooklyn, poverty has spread east and west from Bedford-Stuyvesant and Brownsville into East New York, Bushwick, Williamsburg, and Fort Greene. In the rest of the Core in 1971 Newark had proportionately more welfare recipients than did New York!

A comparison of Figures 5-5 and 5-10 confirms that in New York City poverty is largely identified with the City's black and Puerto Rican populations. The City's Human Resources Administration estimated in 1971 that nearly 48 percent of the City's one million Puerto Ricans were receiving some form of welfare assistance, and that 32 percent of the City's 1.7 million black residents were also on welfare rolls.

In the Inner Ring, by contrast, per capita as well as median family income figures are rising more rapidly than those for the Region as a whole. In 1969 median family incomes of over 13,100 dollars in three of the five Inner Ring Counties and in four of ten Outer Ring Counties placed these seven counties among the 25 richest in the country.

EDUCATION

Education, when measured by the proportion of the population 25 years and older with at least four years of college, correlates highly with income (Fig. 5-11). In the Region as a whole, 12.5 per cent of its 25-year old and older population has had four or more years of college. In the Core the proportion falls to 10.2 percent, and in the Inner Ring it rises to 16.2 percent. In Hudson, the Bronx, and Brooklyn counties, only 5.6 to 6.6 percent of the population has completed a college education. In fact the hope that future generations in the Bronx will be able to equal that borough's already low educational achievement rate is dim. Only 6 percent of the South Bronx's school-age population in 1974 read at or above grade-level!

The extraordinarily high proportion of college-educated residents in Manhattan, a proportion exceeded only by Westchester County (the richest in the Region as well as the best-educated), again masks the disparity between its well-to-do, well-educated, largely white population, and its poor, less-educated black and Hispanic population.

AGE STRUCTURE

Not only is the Core's population poorer and less well-educated than is that of the Rings, but it is also older. White out-migration has been of younger families with children. Older whites have remained behind. In 1930 by only 3.8 percent of New York City's population was over 65 years old; by 1950 this proportion had risen to 7.7 percent; and by 1970, to 12 percent. This has raised the median age of the Core's population (Fig. 5-12). A second set of statistics confirms this pattern: an unusually high proportion of New York City residents live alone. In fact in 1974, 25 percent of the City's households were made up of single people; in Manhattan 42 percent of households were occupied by singles. One-third of all people living alone were 65 years old or older in 1974. According to Figure 5-8 31.7 percent of the Region's population is under 18 years old. In the Core the proportion of the youthful population drops to 28.9 percent, and in Manhattan to 21.6 percent.

Away from the Core's center, the proportion of younger people rises. The above Regional average shares in Essex County and the Bronx are explained by the impact of a high proportion

of young black and Hispanic families with many children in these counties' age structures. In the Inner Ring, the proportion of people under 18 barely exceeds the Region's average. The families in the Inner Ring counties are often second-generation suburbanites whose children are now themselves marrying and moving out farther. Many such mobile young people, starting families of their own, have moved on to the Outer Ring. In a number of Outer Ring counties nearly forty percent of the population is under 18.

HOUSING

Core Housing Stock

Figure 5-8 reveals that the Core's housing stock is much older than is that of the rest of the Region. The 1970 data indicate that in the five first-settled Core counties, 74.6 to 84.7 percent of all housing was built before 1950. A large share of The Core's housing dates from the 19th Century. Much of it has not been maintained, and it has deteriorated beyond repair. Obsolete housing is increasing faster in New York City than it can be replaced by new housing units. In 1973 23,000 new housing units were erected in the City, and at that rate it would take 125 years to replace existing housing stock, more than 70 percent of which is already at least 25 years old.

In the poorest areas of the City where the housing is oldest and least well-maintained, abandonment of buildings by landlords and tenants alike has created a landscape reminiscent of devastated European cities after World War II. In 1974 the South Bronx (including Morrisania and Hunt's Point and with a total population of about 400,000) contained 114 acres of rubble-strewn vacant lots. An estimated 5,000 buildings had been abandoned but were still standing. Of 80,000 South Bronx buildings, three-fourths were considered "dilapidated." Some 20 percent had no running water, and 50 percent were sporadically without heat. Robert Moses commented already years ago that "...this Bronx slum and others in Brooklyn and

Manhattan are unrepairable. They are beyond rebuilding, tinkering, and restoring. They must be leveled to the ground." A Puerto Rican South Bronx community leader maintained in 1974 that "we're a real immigrant ghetto. ...,"

The South Bronx slum is reminiscent of earlier immigrant ghettos in many ways. A doctor serving the area commented in 1973 that "the South Bronx is a necropolis—a city of death." Its infant mortality rate of 23.3/1,000 was nearly 50 percent higher than that of the City as a whole. Tuberculosis cases averaged 52.5 for ever 1,000 residents, compared with a city average of 22.6 and a national average of 21. Some 25 percent of reported cases of malnutrition in the City occurred in the South Bronx. Other areas in the City—East Harlem, Brownsville, Bedford-Stuyvesant, for example—and in Newark are comparable decayed and death-ridden in the mid 1970s.

Urban Renewal

Private and public urban renewal projects in the City have not met the City's needs. The West Side Urban Renewal Project covers twenty Manhattan blocks from 87th to 97th Streets along Central Park West, Columbus, and Amsterdam Avenues. It is one of the nation's largest recent projects for low- and middle-income families. *The New York Times* observed in 1974 that since the project's inception in 1962 it "has transformed Columbus Avenue in the 90s from a deteriorated stretch of low-rise blight into one of the city's most striking highrise environments, echoing the concepts of Le Corbusier, the late master builder, who envisioned the ideal city as a series of tall towers surrounded by open spaces." Only 4,720 units of the West Side Project were completed by 1974, however. Many other less well-known low- and middle-income housing projects are dispersed throughout the City. These are generally concentrated in the worst housing areas.

The largest and most spectacular new housing developments in the City generally serve middle-and upper-income needs. Co-op City,

built between 1968 and 1970 in the northern Bronx, houses some 60,000 middle-income people, many of them relocated from areas in the South Bronx. Starret City in southern Brooklyn is New York's largest housing development of the 1970s. Its 46 buildings, some as high as 20 stories, occupy a sprawling tract of landfill and marshes along Jamaica Bay west of Kennedy Airport. Starret City houses some 25,000 people, and it was constructed through the Mitchell-Lama Program Housing Program established in 1955. The Mitchell-Lama Program channels state and city financial aid and provides low mortgages and real estate tax abatements to private builders willing to invest in new middle-income housing. By 1974 some 56,000 Mitchell-Lama units had been built in the City.

A number of other publicly supported projects are under way in 1975. They include the well-publicized Battery Park City and the "new town in town" on Roosevelt Island. Battery Park City is going up on one square mile of landfill in the Hudson River off lower Manhattan. Some 16,000 units housing 50,000 people will be contained in four-story townhouses as well as 34-story towers. On Roosevelt Island in the East River between mid-Manhattan and Queens some 5,000 units of one of the handsomest of recent large-scale developments are reaching completion in 1975. Like other projects, however, Roosevelt Island will serve middle- and upper-income residents more than it will satisfy the needs of the City's poor minorities.

Suburban Housing

Housing in the Inner and Outer Rings is not only much newer than in the Core, but it is also in better condition. Such housing, however, is available only to fewer and fewer of the Region's residents. In 1974 the median cost of one-family homes in the Region exceeded 40,000 dollars, a price which only 85 percent of the Region's families could afford (Fig. 5-13).

Cost is not the only deterrent to out-migration by the Core's poorest residents; land use politices have also excluded the migration of low- and moderate-income people to the suburbs. Communities in the Region, as throughout the nation, have local zoning laws banning apartments which the middle class might be able to afford. In Suffolk County, for example, 88.7 percent of all dwelling units are in one-unit structures. Zoning laws also often require that single-family houses be built on large lots with costly materials or methods.

In 1975 the New Jersey Supreme Court found such laws to be racially as well as economically exclusionary, however, and the Court ruled that zoning laws must serve the "general welfare" not only of the locality but of the surrounding region as well. This New Jersey ruling may have an impact on zoning laws in other localities in the Metropolitan Area. Cases challenging existing exclusionary zoning laws are already before the courts in Middlesex, Bergen, Somerset, Morris, Nassau, Suffolk, Westchester, and Fairfield counties. In New Jersey legislation is being prepared to establish regional housing goals for communities.

Patterns of Legal Immigration to the United States from 1821 to 1974

Year	Total Immigration	Northern and Western Europe	Southern and Eastern Europe	Western Hemisphere	All Other Countries
1821-1830	143,439	66.7%	2.2%	8.1%	23.0%
1831-1840	599,125	81.8	1.0	5.6	11.6
1841-1850	1,713,251	93.0	0.3	3.6	3.1
1851-1860	2,598,214	93.6	0.8	2.9	2.7
1861-1870	2,314,824	87.8	1.4	7.2	3.6
1871-1880	2,812,191	73.6	7.2	14.3	4.9
1881-1890	5,246,613	72.0	18.3	8.1	1.6
1891-1900	3,687,564	44.6	51.9	1.0	2.5
1901-1910	8,795,386	21.7	70.8	4.1	3.4
1911-1920	5,735,811	17.4	58.9	19.9	3.8
1921-1930	4,107,209	31.3	29.0	36.9	2.8
1931-1940	528,431	37.6	28.3	30.2	3.9
1941-1950	1,035,039	47.2	12.9	34.4	5.5
1951-1960	2,515,479	36.8	16.0	39.6	7.6
1961-1965	1,450,312	23.8	12.9	54.8	8.5
1966-1974	3,421,452	└─ 28.0 ─┘		47.0	25.0

Note: Between 1790 and 1820, it is estimated 250,000 immigrants entered the U.S.

Source: Immigration and Naturalization Service

Figure 5-1.

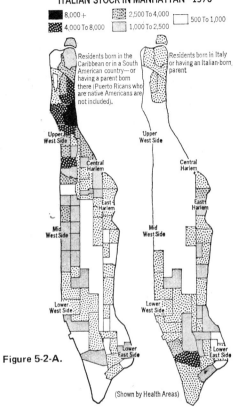

CARIBBEAN, SOUTH AMERICAN AND ITALIAN STOCK IN MANHATTAN – 1970

8,000+   2,500 To 4,000   500 To 1,000
4,000 To 8,000   1,000 To 2,500

Residents born in the Caribbean or in a South American country—or having a parent born there (Puerto Ricans who are native Americans are not included).

Residents born in Italy or having an Italian-born parent.

(Shown by Health Areas)

Figure 5-2-A.

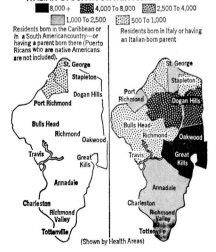

CARIBBEAN, SOUTH AMERICAN AND ITALIAN STOCK IN STATEN ISLAND – 1970

8,000+   4,000 To 8,900   2,500 To 4,000
1,000 To 2,500   500 To 1,000

Residents born in the Caribbean or in a South American country—or having a parent born there (Puerto Ricans who are native Americans are not included).

Residents born in Italy or having an Italian-born parent

(Shown by Health Areas)

Figure 5-2-B.

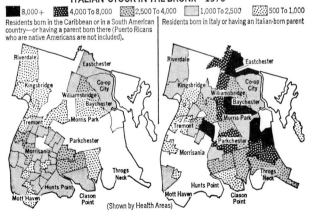

CARIBBEAN, SOUTH AMERICAN AND ITALIAN STOCK IN THE BRONX – 1970

8,000+   4,000 To 8,000   2,500 To 4,000   1,000 To 2,500   500 To 1,000

Residents born in the Caribbean or in a South American country—or having a parent born there (Puerto Ricans who are native Americans are not included).

Residents born in Italy or having an Italian-born parent

(Shown by Health Areas)

Figure 5-2-C.

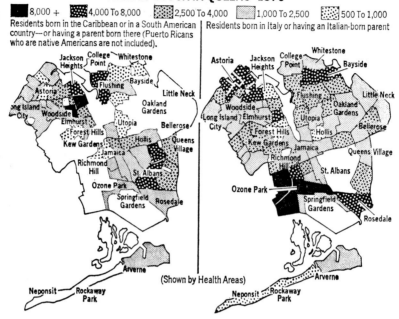

CARIBBEAN, SOUTH AMERICAN AND ITALIAN STOCK IN QUEENS-1970

■ 8,000 + ▦ 4,000 To 8,000 ▧ 2,500 To 4,000 □ 1,000 To 2,500 ⬚ 500 To 1,000

Residents born in the Caribbean or in a South American country—or having a parent born there (Puerto Ricans who are native Americans are not included).

Residents born in Italy or having an Italian-born parent

(Shown by Health Areas)

Figure 5-2-D.

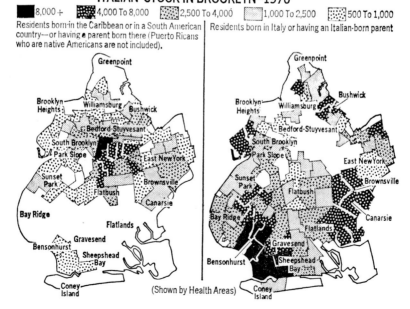

CARIBBEAN, SOUTH AMERICAN AND ITALIAN STOCK IN BROOKLYN-1970

■ 8,000 + ▦ 4,000 To 8,000 ▧ 2,500 To 4,000 □ 1,000 To 2,500 ⬚ 500 To 1,000

Residents born in the Caribbean or in a South American country—or having a parent born there (Puerto Ricans who are native Americans are not included).

Residents born in Italy or having an Italian-born parent

(Shown by Health Areas)

Figure 5-2-E.

	1900		1910		1920		1930		1940		1950		1960		1970	
	Total	%	Total	%	Total	%	Total	%	Total	%	Total	%	Total	%	Total	%
New York City	60.7	1.8	91.8	1.9	152.4	2.7	327.7	4.7	458.5	6.2	845.5	10.7	1088.0	14.0	1668.1	21.1
Manhattan	36.2	2.0	60.5	2.6	109.1	4.8	224.7	12.0	298.4	15.8	384.5	19.6	397.1	23.4	380.4	24.7
Brooklyn	18.4	1.6	22.7	1.4	31.9	1.6	68.9	2.7	107.3	4.0	208.5	7.6	371.4	14.1	656.2	25.2
Bronx	2.4	1.2	4.1	1.0	4.8	.7	12.9	1.0	23.5	1.7	97.8	6.7	163.9	11.5	357.7	24.3
Queens	2.6	1.7	3.2	1.1	5.1	1.1	18.6	1.7	25.9	2.0	51.5	3.3	145.9	8.1	258.0	13.0
Richmond	1.1	1.6	1.2	1.4	1.5	1.3	2.6	1.6	3.4	1.9	5.4	2.8	9.7	4.4	15.8	5.3

Figure 5-3. Total Black Population and Black Population as a Percent of the Total Population in New York City by Borough, 1900-1970. (Totals in thousands.)

Total Black Population, Black Population as a Percent of the Total Population, and Percent increase of the Black Population by Sector in the New York Metropolitan Region (22-County), 1960-1970.

	1960	**1960**	**1960-1970**	**1970**	**1970**
	Black Population in Thousands	Black Population as % of Total Population	Black Population Increase %	Black Population in Thousands	Black Population as % of Total Population
Core	1312.2	14.1	53.0	2008.3	21.2
Inner Ring	182.2	4.8	57.2	286.4	6.7
Outer Ring	154.3	5.1	48.9	231.1	5.4
Region	1648.7	10.2	53.2	2525.8	14.1

The Sector Share of the Total Black Population in 1960 and 1970. (in %)

		1960		**1970**	
Core		79.6		79.5	
Inner Ring		11.0		11.3	
Outer Ring		9.4		9.2	
Total		100.0		100.0	

Figure 5-4. Regional Distribution of Black Population.

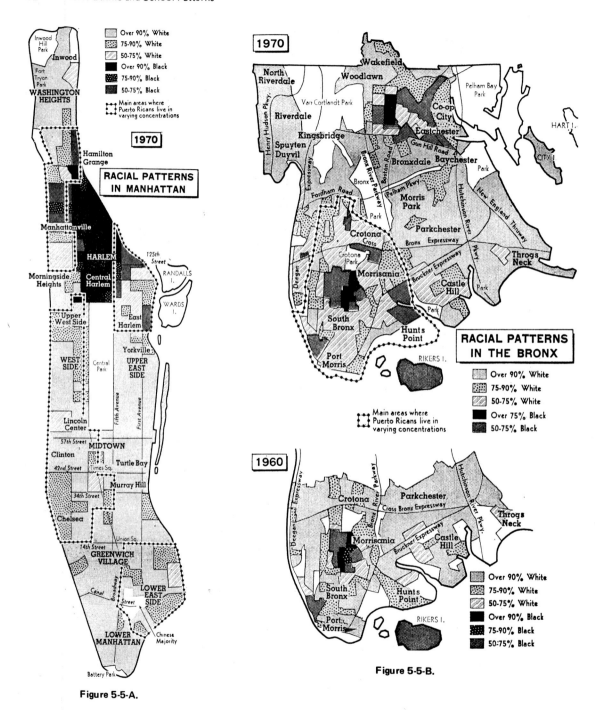

Over 90% White
75-90% White
50-75% White
Over 90% Black
75-90% Black
50-75% Black
Main areas where Puerto Ricans live in varying concentrations

1970

RACIAL PATTERNS IN MANHATTAN

Figure 5-5-A.

1970

RACIAL PATTERNS IN THE BRONX

Over 90% White
75-90% White
50-75% White
Over 75% Black
50-75% Black

Main areas where Puerto Ricans live in varying concentrations

1960

Over 90% White
75-90% White
50-75% White
Over 90% Black
75-90% Black
50-75% Black

Figure 5-5-B.

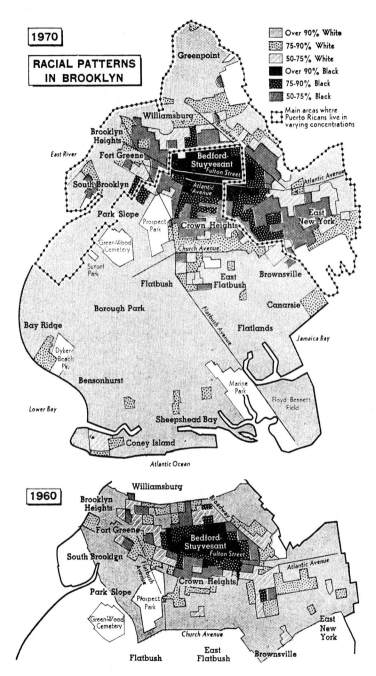

Figure 5-5-C.

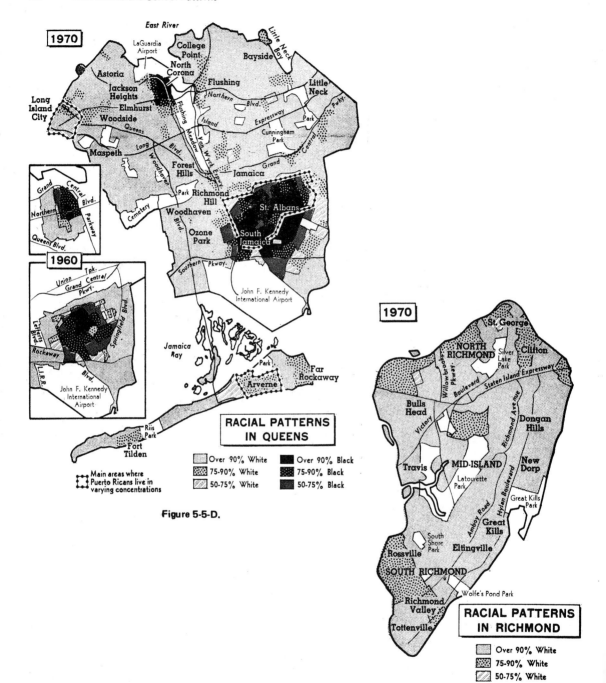

Figure 5-5-D.

RACIAL PATTERNS
IN QUEENS

	Over 90% White		Over 90% Black
	75-90% White		75-90% Black
	50-75% White		50-75% Black

Main areas where
Puerto Ricans live in
varying concentrations

RACIAL PATTERNS
IN RICHMOND

	Over 90% White
	75-90% White
	50-75% White

Figure 5-5-E.

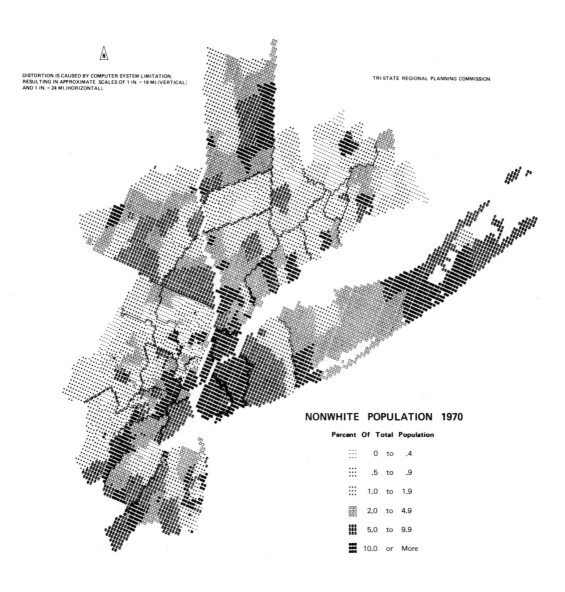

DISTORTION IS CAUSED BY COMPUTER SYSTEM LIMITATION,
RESULTING IN APPROXIMATE SCALES OF 1 IN. = 19 MI.(VERTICAL)
AND 1 IN. = 24 MI.(HORIZONTAL).

TRI-STATE REGIONAL PLANNING COMMISSION

NONWHITE POPULATION 1970

Percent Of Total Population

	0 to	.4
	.5 to	.9
	1.0 to	1.9
	2.0 to	4.9
	5.0 to	9.9
	10.0 or	More

Each square mile in the metropolitan region contains its own unique share of blacks, orientals and other nonwhites. Blacks constitute more than 90 percent of the nonwhite component of the population.

Figure 5-6.

Sector and County / Year	1939	1947	1956	1970
Core	107	106	98	94
Manhattan	163	149	114	134
Hudson	88	88	84	82
Brooklyn	101	91	89	78
Bronx	84	93	89	75
Queens	79	93	106	103
Essex	102	121	104	96
Richmond	80	83	87	90
Inner Ring	83	89	115	116
Bergen	85	79	109	116
Passaic	72	102	86	89
Westchester	93	103	124	130
Union	85	85	109	108
Nassau	74	78	125	119
Outer Ring	81	84	86	96
Middlesex	69	68	83	90
Rockland	75	65	70	96
Morris	81	68	92	106
Monmouth	86	74	82	93
Somerset	73	58	89	105
Fairfield	90	119	114	119
Suffolk	76	73	72	86
Orange	88	88	69	78
Dutchess/Putnam	75	83	62	86

Figure 5-7. Relative Levels of Per Capita Personal Income in the 22-County New York Metropolitan Region, by County and Core, Inner and Outer Rings, 1939, 1947, 1956, and 1970. (As % of average income for entire region.)

	Median Family Income 1969 (in thousands of dollars)	Population 25 Years and Older with 4 Years College or more 1970 (in %)	Median Age of Population 1970 (in years)	Population Under 18 Years of Age 1970 (in %)	Housing Built before 1950 as % of All Housing 1970 (in %)	Housing–One-unit Structure as % of All Housing 1970	Foreign Stock Population 1970 as % of Total Population
Region	11.3	12.5		31.7			37.1
Core	9.6	10.2		28.9			40.7
Manhattan (New York)	9.0	20.7	35.5	21.6	76.1	1.1	38.6
Hudson	10.7	5.6	33.0	29.3	84.7	13.0	42.1
Brooklyn (Kings)	8.9	6.6	30.7	31.5	80.7	8.8	41.4
Bronx	8.3	6.2	30.1	31.8	76.6	6.1	35.8
Queens	11.5	10.2	35.5	26.3	64.7	26.1	50.5
Essex	10.7	12.2	31.1	32.4	74.6	31.5	30.0
Richmond	11.9	9.1	28.4	34.7	54.5	50.3	35.1
Inner Ring	13.6	16.2		32.8			37.4
Bergen	13.6	15.6	33.0	31.9	54.6	61.7	39.2
Passaic	10.9	8.4	31.3	32.2	65.5	42.1	37.0
Westchester	13.8	21.0	33.1	31.6	60.8	45.1	38.4
Union	12.6	14.0	33.6	31.3	60.0	57.1	36.3
Nassau	14.6	17.0	30.9	34.9	45.4	80.3	36.2
Outer Ring	12.4	14.0		36.7			29.0
Middlesex	12.0	11.2	27.5	35.8	39.4	66.2	31.5
Rockland	13.8	18.4	27.0	39.5	33.6	70.5	33.9
Morris	13.4	19.9	28.3	36.6	41.9	76.4	27.0
Monmouth	11.6	14.3	28.4	36.1	45.9	74.4	24.2
Somerset	13.4	19.0	29.3	36.3	44.2	73.7	30.1
Fairfield	13.1	17.6	30.9	33.9	54.5	61.7	33.6
Suffolk	12.1	12.0	26.4	39.7	27.5	88.7	28.1
Orange	10.1	10.0	28.7	34.7	60.4	65.5	22.8
Putnam	12.0	12.8	27.5	39.6	44.6	85.9	30.1
Dutchess	11.7	14.0	29.2	34.1	50.0	65.0	23.2

Figure 5-8.

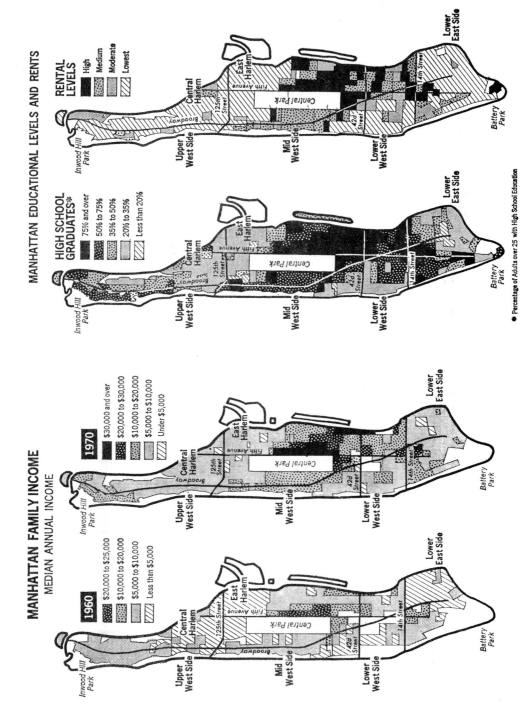

MANHATTAN FAMILY INCOME
MEDIAN ANNUAL INCOME

1970
- $30,000 and over
- $20,000 to $30,000
- $10,000 to $20,000
- $5,000 to $10,000
- Under $5,000

1960
- $20,000 to $25,000
- $10,000 to $20,000
- $5,000 to $10,000
- Less than $5,000

MANHATTAN EDUCATIONAL LEVELS AND RENTS

RENTAL LEVELS
- High
- Medium
- Moderate
- Lowest

HIGH SCHOOL GRADUATES*
- 75% and over
- 50% to 75%
- 35% to 50%
- 20% to 35%
- Less than 20%

*Percentage of Adults over 25 with High School Education

Figure 5-9.

98

PEOPLE RECEIVING WELFARE IN MANHATTAN

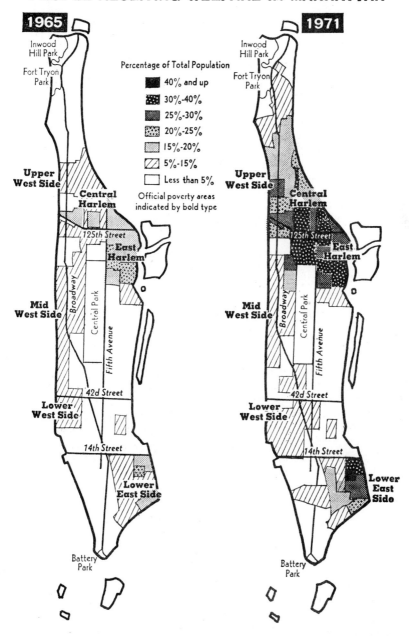

1965

Inwood
Hill Park

Fort Tryon
Park

Upper
West Side

Central
Harlem

125th Street

East
Harlem

Mid
West Side

Broadway

Central Park

Fifth Avenue

Lower
West Side

42d Street

14th Street

Lower
East Side

Battery
Park

1971

Inwood
Hill Park

Fort Tryon
Park

Upper
West Side

Central
Harlem

125th Street

East
Harlem

Mid
West Side

Broadway

Central Park

Fifth Avenue

Lower
West Side

42d Street

14th Street

Lower
East
Side

Battery
Park

Percentage of Total Population

- 40% and up
- 30%-40%
- 25%-30%
- 20%-25%
- 15%-20%
- 5%-15%
- Less than 5%

Official poverty areas
indicated by bold type

Figure 5-10-A.

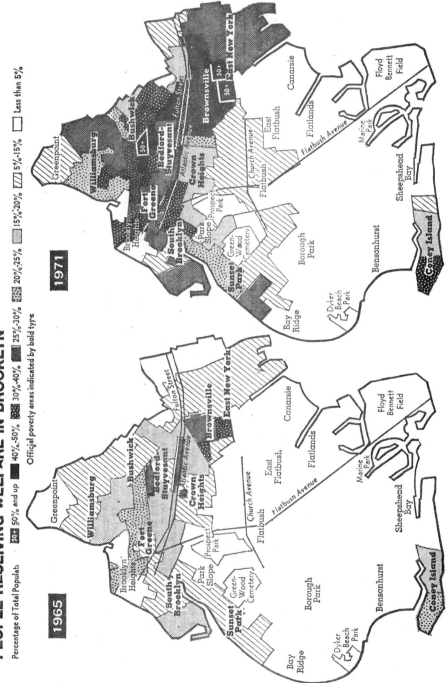

PEOPLE RECEIVING WELFARE IN BROOKLYN

Percentage of Total Populat

50+ 50% and up
40%-50%
30%-40%
25%-30%
20%-25%
15%-20%
5%-15%
Less than 5%

Official poverty areas indicated by bold type

Figure 5-10-B.

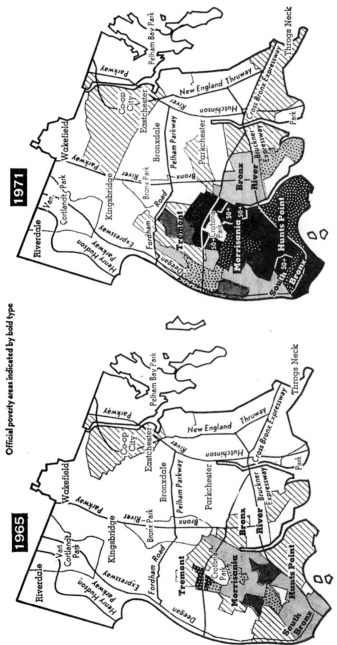

Figure 5-10-C.

PEOPLE RECEIVING WELFARE
IN RICHMOND

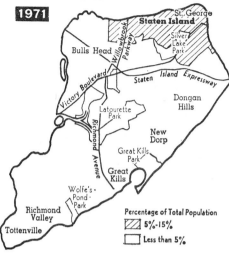

Figure 5-10-D.

PEOPLE RECEIVING WELFARE IN QUEENS

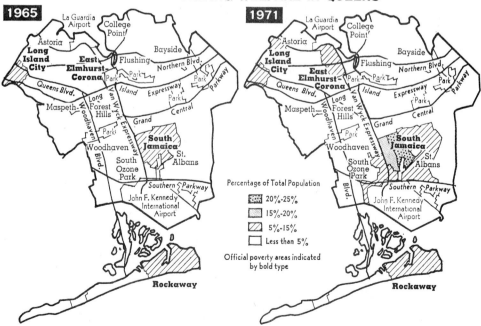

Figure 5-10-E.

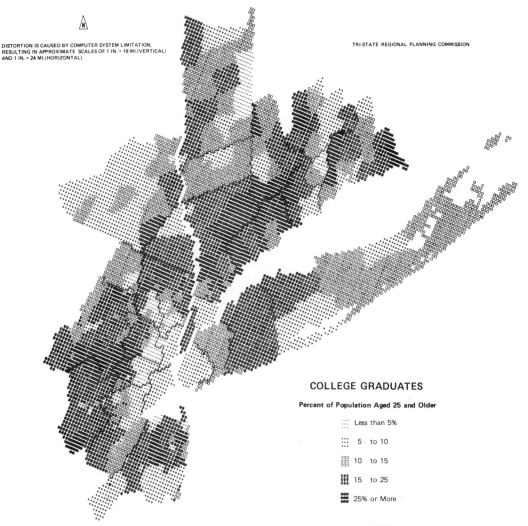

TRI-STATE REGIONAL PLANNING COMMISSION

DISTORTION IS CAUSED BY COMPUTER SYSTEM LIMITATION, RESULTING IN APPROXIMATE SCALES OF 1 IN. = 19 MI.(VERTICAL) AND 1 IN. = 24 MI.(HORIZONTAL).

COLLEGE GRADUATES

Percent of Population Aged 25 and Older

- Less than 5%
- 5 to 10
- 10 to 15
- 15 to 25
- 25% or More

In 1970, when the U.S. Census was conducted, the Tri-State Region had an advantage in college graduates as a share of the general population 25 and older compared with the share of these people in the national population. Some 10.7 percent of the nation's citizenry 25 and up were college graduates; 12.7 percent of the Region's over 25's had graduated from college.

The number of regional college grads living in each community counted by the Census was divided by the total population over 25; this computation gave the share of college graduates living in every town, city or borough. These varying percentages were next broken down into five percentile ranges: 5—10 percent, for example, is one range. A symbol was used to designate each range, and the appropriate symbol was coded into all the square-mile cells in the community.

Figure 5-11.

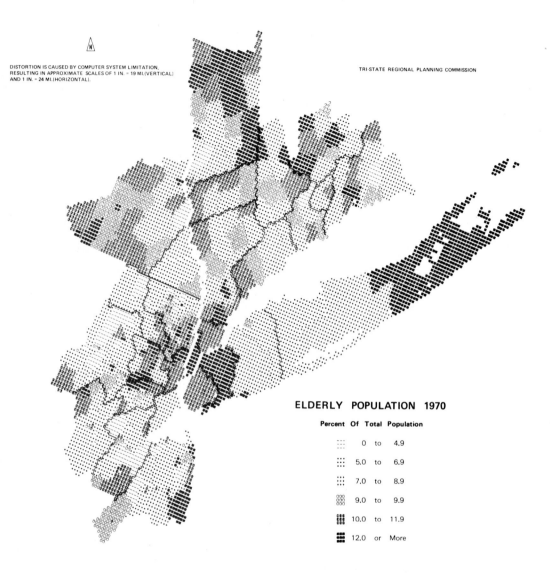

DISTORTION IS CAUSED BY COMPUTER SYSTEM LIMITATION,
RESULTING IN APPROXIMATE SCALES OF 1 IN. = 19 MI.(VERTICAL)
AND 1 IN. = 24 MI.(HORIZONTAL).

TRI-STATE REGIONAL PLANNING COMMISSION

ELDERLY POPULATION 1970

Percent Of Total Population

	0	to	4.9
	5.0	to	6.9
	7.0	to	8.9
	9.0	to	9.9
	10.0	to	11.9
	12.0	or	More

People who are at least 65 years old constitute 10.4 percent of the Regional population, according to the U. S. census. Here, localities in the Region have been placed by computer calculation into six arbitrary groups according to the percent of elderly population per square mile that they contain. The red lines indicate the boundaries of the 21 counties of New York and New Jersey and six planning regions in southwest Connecticut that are parts of the New York Region.

Figure 5-12.

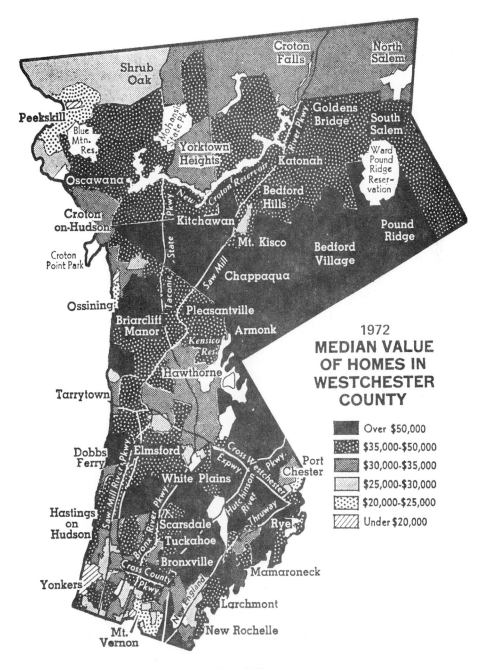

1972
**MEDIAN VALUE
OF HOMES IN
WESTCHESTER
COUNTY**

███	Over $50,000
▓▓▓	$35,000-$50,000
▒▒▒	$30,000-$35,000
░░░	$25,000-$30,000
∷∷∷	$20,000-$25,000
▨▨▨	Under $20,000

Figure 5-13.

Chapter Six

TRANSPORTATION WITHIN THE REGION

Through this book we have used the extent of urban and contiguous suburban settlement to define the Metropolitan Region. This presents, however, only a static picture. It is the movement and commutation and interconnection of people and of activities within and across the Region which define its dynamic integration. People move from their homes to their jobs to shopping centers and to various recreational and leisure activities. The network of movements among all of these locales binds the Region into a functioning entity. A family may live in one community, work in another twenty miles in one direction, shop ten miles in the opposite direction, and go to school or to the movies in a third legal entity in still another direction! These intraregional movements are made by car, by subway, by train, or by bus, and all of these facilities of transportation support the Region's internal connectivity. Each of these modes of transportation uses a network which binds all or parts of the Region.

The Development of the Networks

The rapid transit network and the railway network tell us a great deal about the Region prior to the 1920s. By examining the configurations of these networks we can determine which areas offered employment and which areas developed large population concentrations. These systems together provided the only important links within the Region before the automobile. Areas lacking rapid transit or railroad service remained undeveloped.

Since the 1920s the Region has changed dramatically. A new form of transportation has appeared, and the older railroad network has been altered as a result. The car and the truck and the highway system have changed patterns of growth and movement in the Region. Simple patterns have become complex. Previously unintegrated areas have been tied to the Region; land once farmed is now thickly settled or industrialized. Other places have seen their economic or residential prominence decline. The functions of developed areas are not always what they once were: some older residential areas are now open lots, and once-busy CBD's have deteriorated. These changes can be traced to widespread car-ownership and to the construction of the new highway system. The car and the highway have added flexibility to the transportation system, which has in turn created a greater variety in the use of the Region's land.

Before about 1920 the horse-drawn carriage was the only private means of transportation. But only the rich could afford to buy horses, to feed them, and to pay a driver to take care of them. The roads available to horse-drawn vehicles were terrible. Most people had to rely upon public transportation.

This changed when the automobile began to be produced cheaply in large numbers. With that, the demand for surfaced roads and wider highways increased. Once these were built, more and more people came to prefer private transportation to get from one place to another. This diffused all activities, decreasing use of the rapid transit and railroad lines because they are fixed and relatively less and less convenient! Thus a need/use cycle has been established to the detriment of the transit and rail systems. The result of highway, bridge, and tunnel construction in the last fifty years has been a change in the internal structure of the Region. The patterns of population distribution and of population growth have shifted, and the foci of employment have dispersed. The highway system, first thought to be a complement to the existing transport network, became instead a rival and replacement.

Use of the commuter railroad in the Region has declined more than use of rapid transit because the railroad is in more direct competition with the highway in providing Regional service. Highways connected all those places earlier served by the railroad, and they also opened to new residential settlement many areas into which the railroad had not reached. Since highways provided a flexibility which the fixed-line and scheduled railroads could not, many commuters switched their mode of travel from trains to cars. As rail use declined, the rail lines lost money, and many lines of track were simply abandoned. This abandonment is illustrated by the reduction in the number of miles of commuter railroad track in the 31-county Region: from 3,000 in 1900 to 2,000 in 1950 to 1,086 in 1971. For every mile decrease in railroad mileage there has been a comparable increase in superhighway mileage. The automobile was largely responsible for the death of the commuter railroad.

Mass transit methods evolved from the omnibus era to the subway age because the populations of New York, of Jersey City and of Newark, the Region's most populous cities, grew so quickly. Cities whose populations did not grow or spread out so rapidly never made the technological transition from the trolley car to the elevated train or the subway, and so when the automobile appeared, these smaller and less

congested places gave up all thoughts of ever needing a public rapid transit system. As a result, only those few places which built rapid transit facilities first are today served by public systems. No new lines of rapid transit have been built since 1940, but the network is just about as extensive today as it was when first opened. Today there are 268 route miles of track in the Region's rapid transit systems: 237 miles of elevated and subway lines in Manhattan, Brooklyn, Queens, and the Bronx; 14 miles of electrified surface track on Staten Island; 13 miles of subway and surface track owned by the Port Authority in Hudson County and linking Jersey City with Manhattan and Newark; and 4 miles of subway and surface track in the city of Newark. Had highways not been built with such enthusiasm during the last thirty-five years, however, it is probable that this present rapid transit network would have been improved and extended.

Circulation Within the Region

METHODS OF TRAVEL

Let us now look at how each of the transportation networks we have described is used today. In the thirty-one county Region about forty million trips are made each day by some means of transportation other than walking. This daily population movement, its direction, and the networks used underscore the unity of the Region by emphasizing the degree of interaction within it. In order to understand this interaction, we have to answer how and why some twenty million people make forty million daily trips.

About eighty percent of all trips are made by automobile. The proportion of car trips increases every year. Nevertheless, twenty percent of all trips are still made on mass transit facilities, half of these by bus and the other half by rapid transit and trains. While the number of trips by rapid transit and train equals only ten percent of total trips made, these trips account for twenty percent of all movement when measured by distance traveled. Subways and trains are especially important to commuters who must generally cover long distances than other travelers.

Almost half of all journeys-to-work are made by mass transit, either because mass transit is just as convenient as driving, or because the car is needed at home for household errands. Employment in the Region is still highly concentrated in areas well-served by mass transit facilities. Going to work by mass transit is often easier than driving on congested highways during rush hours and parking in the limited and expensive space available near areas of high employment concentration. Even if it were more convenient to drive to work than to ride rapid transit, many suburbanites would have to leave their cars at home because shops and schools in suburbia are frequently accessible to those who stay home only by car.

Shopping centers sprouted at suburban highway interchanges to serve the spread-out auto-dependent suburban population. The Roosevelt Field Mall in Garden City, Long Island (Nassau County), shown here, opened in 1956. With a gross leasable area of over two million square feet, it is the size of many a small city's downtown. Macy's, Gimbel's, and Alexander's, three major Manhattan department stores, all have stores at Roosevelt Field.

In the background low-rise industrial structures line the railroad tracks, and in the residential right background, the size of the trees indicates that this is a close-in, relatively mature suburb. (Photo courtesy of Roosevelt Field Mall)

As a result, most nonwork-related trips, which account for about 60 percent of all trips, are made by car. Most of them are short distance movements beginning and ending in the same county. Nonwork-related trips in those counties of the Region which have no rapid transit service are made almost solely by car. In the Core counties, which have rapid transit, a higher proportion is made by subway and bus.

Travel to Shop and School

About 85 percent of shopping or school trips are restricted to intra-county movements, although, as we will see, this varies across the Region. Stores, schools, and recreational facilities have dispersed faster than job concentrations, and almost as rapidly as has the Region's population. Gimbel's, Macy's, and other department stores which once had an outlet only in Manhattan, now have branch stores in shopping centers located at the foci of automobile traffic patterns. New schools were built wherever the school-age population was numerous enough to support a new facility. As a result, all the Region's counties can provide most of the services their residents require.

In the Region's Core counties 78.6 percent of all shopping trips have their origin and destination in the same county. This proportion increases in outer counties. In the Inner Ring counties, those counties contiguous with the Core counties and into which population first grew beyond the Core counties, 88.7 percent of shopping trips are confined to the county in which the shopper lives. In the fringe counties of the Region, its Outer Ring, this proportion rises to 93 percent. School and recreational travel is even more exclusively intra-county movement.

What explains the proportional differences of intra-county travel within the Region? One reason is that the Core counties are smaller than the Outer Ring counties. A shopper could travel twenty miles or more in Suffolk County, for example, and still remain within the County, but he could not travel so far in the Core counties without crossing county boundaries. Second, the

rapid transit network of the Core counties encourages inter-county travel, especially to and from Manhattan, where a wider variety of stores is attractive.

Travel to Work

The travel pattern and the mode of travel for journeys to work is different. The automobile becomes relatively *less* important, and inter-county movement *more* important. Only 54 percent of all trips to work are made by car, and only sixty percent of all work-trips have their destinations within the county where they originate. Nevertheless, the travel differences among the Core, Inner Ring, and Outer Ring counties which we found when examining travel to shops and schools hold true for travel to work as well. People in the Outer and Inner Ring counties are much more likely to drive to work. About eighty percent of the population in these Rings drives to work, whereas in the Core counties only thirty percent of workers do.

There are proportionately fewer car trips to work than to shop because even though employment is more dispersed than it once was, it is still a great deal more concentrated than are other widely used facilities such as shops and schools. This explains why a higher proportion of travel to work crosses county boundaries. It also suggests why public transportation, which has always served to link areas where people live to where they work, continues to play an important role in journeys to work. Many jobs, as we will see in Chapter Eight, are still clustered in relatively few places. And since most people try to get to these places at the same time, it makes a great deal more sense to use public transportation than to get caught up in rush-hour traffic jams.

Travel to work by car is much more frequent farther out from the Core counties. In the Inner and Outer Ring counties, there is no rapid transit network, and even bus service is unavailable in the less-densely settled parts of these counties. Railroads stations are readily accessible on foot to only ten percent of the developed land outside New York City. As one might expect, car ownership per household generally increases away from the Region's Core (Fig. 6-1). As population densities decline and mass transit facilities vanish, car ownership rises.

Cars are a necessity—not a luxury—in most parts of the Inner and Outer Rings. Car ownership throughout the Region depends less on a family's income than on the availability of mass transit. Nassau County, for example, does not have the highest percentage of households with cars even though it has the highest median family income (Fig. 6-2). This suggests that even though more people in Nassau could afford cars, cars are less necessary there. In fact 25 percent of all travel in Nassau is still by railroad or bus. Because some form of mass transit is available in high-income Nassau, the rate of car ownership is lower than it is in lower income counties with less mass transit service.

JOURNEY-TO-WORK PATTERNS

The Tri-State Region's travel-to-work pattern is the single most important index of how functionally interrelated the Region is. Forty percent of all trips to and from work cross county boundaries. To a high degree the Region is in fact a single operating unit.

The Region's commuting pattern is quite simple, no matter how complex Figure 6-3 may appear to be. This table merits close inspection. Most people live and work in the same county. Those whose travels take them from county to another almost always move to a Core county or toward a Core county. Those who work neither in their home county nor in one closer to the Core are most likely to work in a county within the same Ring. There is very little movement away from the Region's Core counties.

Workers from the Core county of Hudson, for example, are most likely to work in another Core county, e.g. Manhattan or Essex. Twenty-three percent do so. They are less likely to work in an Inner Ring county, no matter how close. Only nine percent do this. Workers living in Hudson County are least likely to travel to the Outer

Ring. Only an insignificant number, which does not even show up on the table, travels that far outward from the Region's Core.

As another example we might look at the Inner Ring county of Bergen. Most Bergen County workers, 60 percent, remain in Bergen to work. Some 27 percent commute to one or another Core county; about 8 percent to another county in the Inner Ring, and about 1 percent to an Outer Ring county.

What exerts this strong centripetal force on the Region's commuting patterns? Why does such a high percentage of workers stay in or move toward the Core counties? There are, quite simply, more jobs and better jobs in a few of the most centrally located counties. This becomes apparent in Figure 6-4.

With more than 25 percent of all jobs in the Region, Manhattan, and especially its CBD, is the most significant net importer of workers. Manhattan has many more available jobs than workers, and must import workers to fill its jobs. The only other counties in the Region which finds themselves in this job-surplus position are Essex, Union, and Dutchess. All other counties are net exporters of workers.

This does not mean, however, that all the workers resident in each county stay in their home county to work. Figures of *net* county import and export of workers are quite different from individual workers' case histories. Queens illustrates this very well. There are 482,000 jobs available in Queens, and 850,000 workers living there. Some 368,000 must work elsewhere. Not all of the 482,000 available jobs are actually filled by Queens residents. Figure 6-3 shows that only 36 percent of the employed population in Queens works in Queens. Only 305,000 of the 482,000 available jobs are filled by Queens residents. The remaining 177,000 jobs are held by commuters—by and large residents of Brooklyn, Nassau and Suffolk Counties. A total of 545,000 workers who live in Queens work elsewhere, 374,000 of them in Manhattan.

The general pattern should now be quite clear. The vast majority of inter-county commuters work in the Core or at least in a county closer to the Core than the one in which they live. Residents of Suffolk who commute out of their home county to work, for example, are most likely to work in Nassau County, which is closer to New York City than is Suffolk. They are next most likely to work in New York City. Within the City, Manhattan is the strongest magnet for all inter-county commuters.

The Manhattan Magnet

Manhattan actually attracts one-half of *all* inter-county commuters. Figure 6-3 shows that Manhattan exerts the greatest pull on workers in ten of twenty counties and combined planning regions of the Tri-State Region. Even among workers living in the other ten counties, Manhattan is the second or third most important destination. This emphasizes again that the Region's work travel pattern is still highly focused on the Region's first and most important core.

In general the importance of Manhattan as a commuter's destination declines with distance. In the nearby counties of the Bronx and Queens, as we have seen, more people commute to Manhattan than work in the county in which they live. Manhattan is a strong magnet for workers from the City's other boroughs as well, though its attraction is not so strong in the other Core counties, Essex and Hudson. It diminishes further in the Inner Ring counties and reaches a low in the Outer Ring. Only one percent of Dutchess County's workers commute to Manhattan.

Distance, time, and cost of travel are obviously important factors in explaining this. But what may be more important is understanding why people commute to Manhattan at all. Manhattan, and especially its CBD, continues to have a disproportionately large share of the Region's jobs. Many of the best and high-paying jobs in the Region are to be found in Manhattan. People with high-paying jobs can afford the time and money cost of commuting greater distances. Reverse commuting, or movement away from the Core, is almost insignificant in the overall

pattern. Perhaps four percent of the Region's working population commutes from its particular Ring outward. Some 96 percent of Manhattanites and 91 percent of Queens residents, for example, work in New York City. That there is any reverse commuting at all, however, evidences a trend in the Region: the ever-greater dispersion of jobs as the Region continues to decentralize. New jobs are being added in the Inner and Outer Ring counties while the number of jobs in the Core counties has in most instances declined both absolutely and relatively. Job opportunities in the nonCore counties increase, and the trend to move out, or at least to commute out, increases concomitantly.

The Manhattan CBD remains, nevertheless, the Region's travel hub. In 1971 about 3.2 million people entered the CBD daily. Of these, 1.7 million came to work, and 1.5 million came to shop to enjoy its cultural and recreation facilities, or simply to look around.

Most people reached the CBD by subway (Fig. 6-5). Although both the total number of subway riders and the proportion of people commuting by subway declined between 1963 and 1971, rapid transit is still the single most important form of travel to the Manhattan CBD. In this way hub-bound travel differs significantly from travel to shop or to work in the rest of the Region, where, as we pointed out earlier, the car is a necessity, and all other forms of transportation are comparatively unimportant.

Even travel to the Manhattan CBD has changed in recent years. Fewer people come to the CBD each year now than previously, and more of those who do come arrive by car. Hub-bound auto travel creates problems not only in Manhattan, but for the Region as a whole. Next we will look at the Region's transportation problems more closely.

PROBLEMS TODAY

Preference for the Automobile

For most people in the Region, there are several advantages in owning a car. First, the car is the fastest means of travel for short trips within the Region. For longer trips only the railroad is quicker. Second, the car is generally the most convenient means of getting from one place to another, especially in the Inner and Outer Rings. It offers privacy and a freedom of movement independent of timetables. Third, the car lets people enjoy a semi-rural life-style in the suburbs, without depriving them of urban opportunities; and fourth, the cost of maintaining a car has risen less steeply than has the cost of public transportation. For all these reasons, combined with increasing public affluence, car ownership in the Region increased by 37 percent between 1960 and 1970, while the Region's population grew only 11 percent. There are fewer carless families and more multi-car households in the Region today than ever before.

The Car Versus Mass Transit

The car's popularity has, however, hurt public transportation. Only one-fourth of all trips made in the Region on any day are made on public transportation. Subway ridership has declined from 2.2 billion in 1947 to 1.1 billion in 1974. The car is being used not only where there are no alternative forms of transportation, but also in the Region's Core counties, where subways, railroads, and buses are widely available.

These facts suggest not only that people like cars, but that they dislike mass transit. Subway riders object to the system's noise, dirt, danger, and overcrowding. They object to the long waits between trains and to the uncomfortable conditions of waiting platforms, and they feel that mass transit service is overpriced. The subway fare has risen 700 percent in less than thirty years.

The increased popularity of the car and the declining use of public transportation pose numerous problems for the Region, and these problems' solutions depend upon how people in the Region want to live in the future. The decisions which shape the way we live today were made many years ago, and the decisions we make today will shape how we live in the future.

Many people are today unhappy with the effects of decisions about transportation made in the last fifty years. They are especially unhappy to see similar decisions being made now for the future. Although more people use cars every year, drivers can see the negative impact that the car has made on the Region and its people as a whole. Highways and parking lots are wasting a great deal of land. Sunlight decreases year after year because of the pall that cars' engines cast over the sky. Cars require enormous amounts of rapidly diminishing natural resources, such as petroleum and steel. The Region's older cities are dying; cars are strangling them. Cars also disable the carless poor and elderly who must rely on public transportation but cannot because it is not there. And it is not there because most people prefer that their money be spent on highways rather than mass transit facilities.

Planning for the Future

Cars' relative advantages of flexibility and comfort for the large numbers of people who drive them must be weighed against their relative disadvantages for the Region as a whole. If the Region's future social, economic, and aesthetic well-being are more important than is the comfort of today's drivers, then measures must be taken to inhibit car use and to stimulate public transport development. To achieve these goals a coordinated Regional effort would have to be made along several lines. Money would have to be diverted from highway to transit construction. Tolls for cars would have to be raised and fares for mass transit lowered. Land-use zoning would have to promote higher residential densities in order to encourage mass transit extensions. Public transit facilities would have to be renovated to make them more attractive.

Discouraging Car Use

There are indications that the Region is coming to grips with some of these issues. There is widespread consensus in the Region today that the highway building of the 1950s and 1960s must be stopped. A typical editorial in *The New York Times* inveighed against another highway for Long Island which has "had enough of concrete ribbons squeezed out of a giant tube....If the past three decades of sprawl have taught anything, it is that new highways do not relieve congestion. They invite more of it...." Plans to connect Westchester with Nassau County across Long Island Sound by way of a Rye-Oyster Bay Bridge have evaporated in the face of heated local opposition. Proposals for Lower Manhattan and Mid-Manhattan Expressways to cut across Manhattan have been shelved. In both instances the expressways' advocates felt that these routes would relieve congestion on narrow cross-town streets. Opponents countered that more cars and trucks would in fact be lured to the area, since the new routes would link New Jersey and Long Island more directly than do the peripheral routes across the Bronx or Staten Island.

Currently controversy rages over the redevelopment of the elevated fifty-year-old West Side Highway, south of 72nd Street to the Battery along the Hudson River. One recent City-endorsed proposal calls for a billion dollar "Westway" financed under the federal government's Interstate Highway program. Most of the proposed six-lane road would run fully enclosed through landfill replacing ships' piers in the Hudson River. Advocates are making a concession to mass transit proponents by agreeing to reserve a highway lane for express bus service during rush hour. This plan's opponents, however, argue that most of the billion dollars would be better spent on subway construction, and that a less extravagant Westway scheme would be preferable.

The best way to halt increasing usage of private cars may be to stop building highways. Some people feel that congestion is its own cure. Simply by letting the highways become saturated, by allowing the Long Island Expressway, for example, become "the world's longest parking lot," drivers may become so discouraged that they will turn to mass transit. So far this cure has not worked.

As pointed out earlier, the number of people coming to the Manhattan CBD has declined, but the number of people arriving by car, as well as the number of cars, have increased. Between 1963 and 1971 the vehicle entry into the CBD increased 16 percent. Not only do more cars enter the CBD now than formerly, but the proportion arriving during rush hours between 7 and 10 in the morning has increased from 22.7 to 25.2 percent. Expressways, which were thought to have reached the saturation point thirty-five years ago, such as the usable part of the West Side Highway, are now increasingly congested. Furthermore, more cars today are using the Manhattan Street system to get to the CBD.

Therefore a halt in highway construction probably is not the most effective way to discourage people from using those highways which already exist. Not building highways in order to force drivers to find another way to get to work may actually have the undesired effect of encouraging employers to relocate to where their employees live. This is in fact one of the reasons cited by employers for moving out of the Region's Core counties.

Other policies to discourage car use may yield similarly disappointing results, but might be tried, nevertheless. Placing new tolls on all river crossings into Manhattan and raising tolls substantially where they already exist might discourage drivers. In 1975 the Port Authority announced a number of revisions in its toll rates on crossings between New Jersey and Manhattan and Staten Island. Tolls increased from one dollar to one and a half dollars for cars without passengers, and decreased to 50 cents for motorists forming car pools of three persons or more in one automobile. This is the first revision in the toll structure since 1927. The Port Authority commented:

> It is no longer in the public interest to offer special inducements to motorists who choose to drive to work. On the contrary, there is general agreement on all levels of government that commuters should be encouraged to make maximum use of public transportation or to form car pools.

If the Port Authority's toll charges had risen

as rapidly as New York City mass transit fares rose during the same period, however, they would now be seven dollars. Studies indicate that unless tolls are raised substantially, they will affect highway users hardly at all. When the Triborough Bridge and Tunnel Authority doubled tolls in 1973 on its bridges and tunnels, and increased the Verrazano-Narrows Bridge toll from 50 to 75 cents, it experienced a traffic loss in the first year of just under 8 percent. Higher gasoline prices and automobile taxes might also discourage car use and stabilize levels of ownership. These cost increases might come as national policies, or as the results of international economic trends.

Proposals to redistribute current traffic in space and time have also been suggested. Creating pedestrian malls from existing CBD streets would limit auto accessibility and also be a boon for the walker. In Manhattan several such malls have been tried experimentally. It has been suggested that cars even be banned entirely from Manhattan island. Staggering work hours and a system of congestion pricing might help to regulate traffic flow. Congestion pricing consists of encouraging highway use during nonrush hours by lowering tolls and discouraging it during rush hours by raising tolls.

Encouraging Mass Transit

Programs designed to discourage car use might be coupled with programs to encourage use of mass transportation. Otherwise we may very well inadvertently continue the trend of driving employers to the Inner and Outer Rings to join their employees. Mass transit accessibility to the Core counties would have to be maintained and improved not only to offset a decline in car use, but eventually to pull more people back to the Core.

Passage of the National Mass Transportation Assistance Act of 1974 is one indication of a revived interest in public transportation. Some 11.8 billion dollars is to be distributed nationally on the basis of total population and population density. Between now and 1980 the New York

Region will obtain 20 percent of this fund. A recently passed New York State transportation bond issue to improve railroad service gives added hope to public transport supporters.

Although these and other state and local funds are meant to improve and extend the mass transit system, soaring costs of operating the system as it is may very well delay most capital projects. Money set aside for construction may be used to defray current operating expenses and limit further fare increases. New York City and the Metropolitan Transit Authority (MTA), which operates most rapid transit and rail facilities in the New York sector of the Region, have already made decisions to delay subway construction in order to hold down fares.

New Projects

The completion target dates for four projects which would provide more effective transit service between Manhattan and the undeveloped Queens portion of the system have been advanced until the early 1980s. Included in the delay are the connections linking the already completed new East River Tunnel with existing Manhattan and Queens lines, a superexpress line along Long Island Railroad tracks, and connections and extensions into Southeast Queens. Also delayed are projects to extend two lines into the northernmost reaches of the Bronx and the highly publicized and controversial Second Avenue line in northern Manhattan. Construction of the Second Avenue line is already well under way at four widely separated points (Fig. 6-6).

Other projects will not be completed for at least another twenty years. The southern section of the Second Avenue subway, the "cup handle" route in Manhattan's lower East Side, and various extensions of lines in Brooklyn and Queens are not scheduled to open until the 1990s. If the past is any guides to the future, however, delays until the next century should be expected. The Second Avenue line was planned seventy years ago. Half a billion dollars for its construction was set aside fifty years later.

Subsequently the Third Avenue Elevated line was torn down in anticipation of its replacement by the Second Avenue line, and so Manhattan is now without rapid transit service along either Third or Second Avenues.

Two other major construction programs which have been postponed would have provided links from the Region's Core to two of its three airports at the edge of the Inner Ring. Both a high-speed rail link between Mid-Manhattan and Kennedy Airport and an extension of rapid transit service from Newark to Newark Airport and on into the Plainfield area of Union-Somerset-Middlesex counties have been jeopardized. The two routes were to have been built by the Port Authority of New York and New Jersey, but because either state may veto any Port Authority plans, the approval of both states to build both lines will be needed before construction can begin on either line.

Construction costs are the major deterrent to all these projects. That some of these projects have been started indicates that the problem is not one of recognizing the need for more mass transportation facilities. That the necessary sums of money are unavailable does suggest, however, that a total commitment to mass transit is still lacking. In other metropolitan parts of the world the commitment is greater, and construction is moving forward rapidly. The Brazilian government, for example, has allocated 7 billion dollars to a five-year program to speed construction of mass transit networks in Rio de Janeiro and Sao Paulo. In Tokyo 10 miles of new subway are added annually. Within a decade Tokyo will have 350 miles of subway, the world's largest network. Sixteen miles of Montreal's recently opened system were completed in four years. In Germany no fewer than a dozen cities will have mass transit facilities by the 1980s.

In New York, by contrast, the last subways were built 35 years ago, and current construction is at a virtual standstill. The emphasis today is to maintain present fares, renovate decrepit stations, and replace old subway cars. Each incrase in fares has led to a decline in sub-

way riders. To stabilize patronage the MTA has decided on massive fare subsidies, but these subsidies must come out of construction funds. A number of stations have been redesigned. Murals, better lighting, and more seating capacity have been added. The entrances to some stations have been made more inviting by widening stairwells and installing translucent roof covering. Some new, air-conditioned cars have been introduced, but since an average of only 200 cars is replaced annually, it will take another 36 years to replace all of the present rolling stock.

Much money has gone for merely cosmetic changes. Real revitalization and innovation awaits a larger commitment from the state and federal governments. Individual governments in the Region simply do not have the money to reverse the decline of the Region's mass transit facilities. Even programs designed to reduce costs are initially expensive. Automation of trains and unmanned stations would decrease payrolls, but would be enormously expensive to institute. Other plans to save money and to make the fare system more equitable might actually cause further loss in subway ridership. Charging more for longer distance travel or travel during rush hours may be fair, but its impact in the long run may be to reduce passengers.

Rail and Bus Service

More headway has been made in other forms of mass transportation, in rail service and buses. The Region's rail network is now almost totally electrified. Inefficient operating companies in the New York sector have been replaced by the MTA. New cars are rapidly replacing old ones. Rundown stations have been renovated. Though the New Jersey sector of the Region lags in rail improvements, the Region as a whole has benefited. Figure 6-5 shows that rail ridership has dropped, but not so much as subway ridership.

Bus service has improved even more than rail service. Most bus rides cover very short distances, and on a regional scale buses have played a minor role in the transportation system. Today, however, more and more buses use the Region's limited access highways. Express bus lanes have been set aside on a number of them, and bus patronage has increased as a result. More people arrived in the Manhattan CBD by bus in 1971 than eight years earlier. More reserved lanes and more express buses on the Region's streets may very well be the best way to attract drivers away from their cars. Buses are more flexible than rail and subway lines, and both schedules and routes could be made even more convenient than they are now.

A number of places in the Region have experimented with dial-a-ride systems. People who need transportation call a bus to pick them up and deliver them to a central location. From there they can easily switch to more regular transit service. Even without such innovations, buses' flexibility remains a popular feature. Buses' least attractive feature, their slowness, can be changed by adding more buses, each with fewer stops. Such service is already widely available within New York City.

A comprehensive program extending, renovating, and innovating mass transit facilities, combined with plans making car use less convenient would hold out the promise of reversing the trend of present transport use patterns and providing more efficient transportation for everyone throughout the Region.

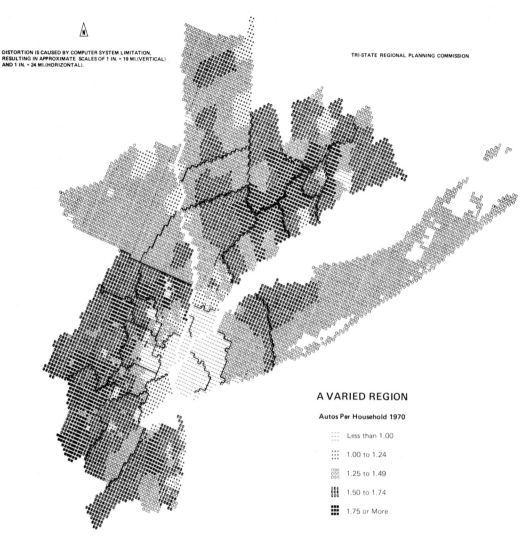

TRI-STATE REGIONAL PLANNING COMMISSION

DISTORTION IS CAUSED BY COMPUTER SYSTEM LIMITATION, RESULTING IN APPROXIMATE SCALES OF 1 IN. = 19 MI.(VERTICAL) AND 1 IN. = 24 MI.(HORIZONTAL).

A VARIED REGION

Autos Per Household 1970

Less than 1.00

1.00 to 1.24

1.25 to 1.49

1.50 to 1.74

1.75 or More

Despite the uniqueness of the Tri-State Region as an urban-suburban concentration whose citizens use plenty of mass transportation, U.S. census facts demonstrate the important position of the private car in most parts of this area.

Nearly 95 percent of the 8400 square miles in the Region average one or more autos per household, as shown in this map, printed by computer using census data. This is typical of the nation.

The localities whose square miles average less than one car per household are relatively scarce, accounting for fewer than 500 square miles out of the 8400. However, these square miles hold almost half of the Region's people.

Figure 6-1.

Core	Average # of Cars Per Household	% of House- holds With- out Cars	% of House- holds with More than Two Cars	Population Density Per Square Mile	Median Family Income (dollars)
Manhattan	.23	21.5	1.6	67,808	8,982
Bronx	.43	37.6	4.7	35,721	8,306
Kings	.47	41.5	5.3	34,013	8,858
Hudson	.73	59.1	12.0	12,936	9,696
Queens	.78	63.6	13.0	18,393	11,554
Essex	.98	68.4	25.7	7,181	10,684
Richmond	1.07	80.1	23.9	5,138	11,892
Inner Ring					
Passaic	1.23	79.1	36.4	2,389	10,931
Westchester	1.25	82.6	36.0	2,020	13,782
Union	1.35	85.8	41.4	5,288	12,591
Bergen	1.44	89.7	45.3	3,838	13,595
Nassau	1.50	91.7	49.3	4,952	14,631
Outer Ring					
Orange	1.21	83.7	32.9	266	10,129
Dutchess	1.33	87.8	39.0	273	11,661
Connecticut[1]	1.40	86.3	45.3	1,127	12,052
Monmouth	1.41	88.6	44.3	965	11,663
Middlesex	1.44	90.0	45.2	1,869	11,981
Suffolk	1.49	93.1	48.1	1,211	12,083
Rockland	1.51	90.8	50.4	1,304	13,752
Putnam	1.59	93.8	50.5	245	11,994
Morris	1.59	94	55.3	819	13,419
Somerset	1.61	93	56.9	647	13,432

1.   This includes the six planning regions of the Tri-State Region.

Figure 6-2. Automobile Availability, Median Family Income, and Population Density in the Region (1970).

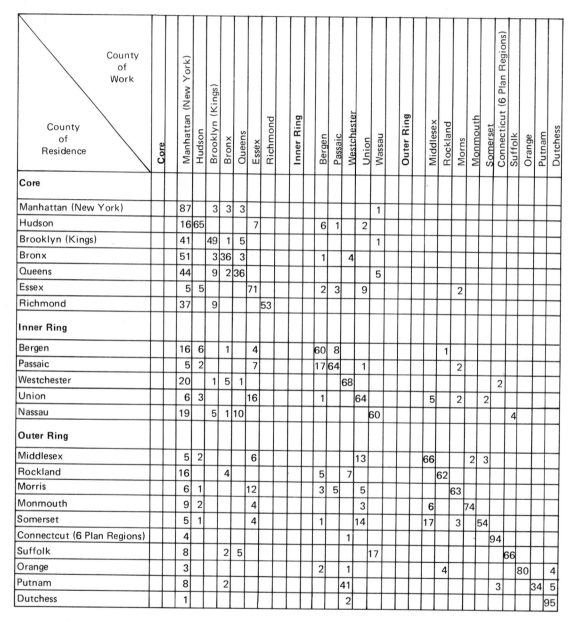

County of Residence \ County of Work	Core	Manhattan (New York)	Hudson	Brooklyn (Kings)	Bronx	Queens	Essex	Richmond	Inner Ring	Bergen	Passaic	Westchester	Union	Nassau	Outer Ring	Middlesex	Rockland	Morris	Monmouth	Somerset	Connecticut (6 Plan Regions)	Suffolk	Orange	Putnam	Dutchess
Core																									
Manhattan (New York)		87		3	3	3								1											
Hudson		16	65			7				6	1		2												
Brooklyn (Kings)		41		49	1	5								1											
Bronx		51		3	36	3				1			4												
Queens		44		9	2	36								5											
Essex		5	5				71			2	3		9							2					
Richmond		37		9				53																	
Inner Ring																									
Bergen		16	6		1		4			60	8							1							
Passaic		5	2			7				17	64		1					2							
Westchester		20		1	5	1						68									2				
Union		6	3		16					1			64			5		2		2					
Nassau		19		5	1	10								60									4		
Outer Ring																									
Middlesex		5	2			6							13			66			2	3					
Rockland		16			4					5	7						62								
Morris		6	1			12				3	5		5					63							
Monmouth		9	2			4							3			6			74						
Somerset		5	1			4				1			14			17		3		54					
Connectcut (6 Plan Regions)		4										1									94				
Suffolk		8			2	5								17								66			
Orange		3								2	1						4						80		4
Putnam		8			2							41									3			34	5
Dutchess		1										2													95

Figure 6-3. Percent of Workers Employed in County of Residence and Other Counties in Tri-State Region, 1970. (Percent omitted when commutation to another county is less than 1% of work force in county of residence.)

	Bronx	Kings	New York	Queens	Richmond	Dutchess	Nassau
Resident Workers	506	927	679	850	108	75	551
No. of Jobs in County	269	627	2068	482	60	76	459
Export or Import (−)	237	300	−1389	368	48	−1	92

	Orange	Putnam	Rockland	Suffolk	Westchester
	79	18	81	377	359
	69	10	62	284	315
	10	8	19	93	44

	Bergen	Essex	Hudson	Middlesex	Monmouth
	370	364	247	223	155
	312	304	235	193	120
	58	−30	12	30	35

	Morris	Passaic	Somerset	Union	Conn.[1]
	153	188	76	232	609
	120	181	56	246	588
	33	7	20	−6	21

1. Connecticut planning regions in the Tri-State Region.

Figure 6-4. Import or Export of Workers by County, 1970.

Mode	1963 People (in thousands)	1963 Percent	1971 People (in thousands)	1971 Percent
Auto/taxi	752	22.9	842	26.6
Bus	252	7.6	256	8.1
Truck	94	2.8	72	2.3
Subway	1977	60	1789	56.5
Railroad	177	5.4	172	5.4
Ferry	38	1.2	36	1.1
Total	3290		3167	

Figure 6-5A. Mode of Daily Entry into the Manhattan CBD in Thousands of People and as a Percent of All Entering.

HOW AND WHERE PEOPLE ENTER THE HUB
ON A TYPICAL DAY

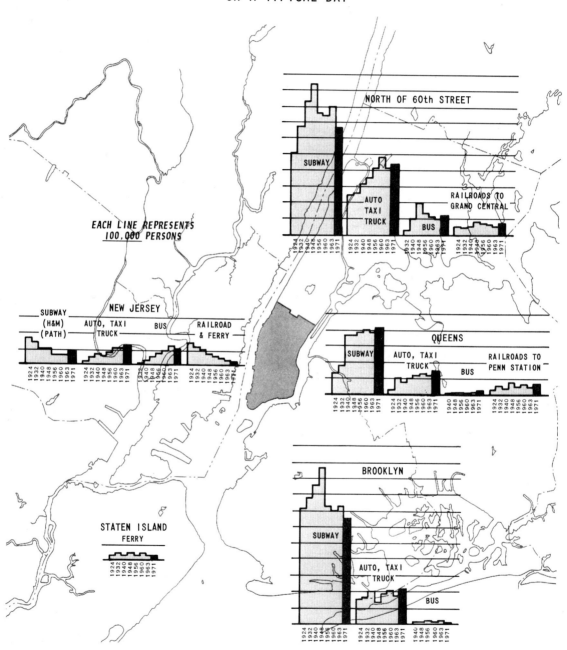

Figure 6-5-B.

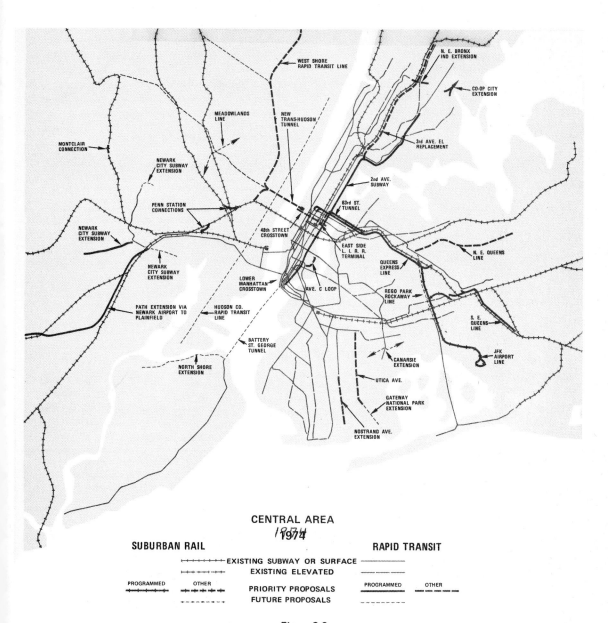

CENTRAL AREA

1974

SUBURBAN RAIL

|←+++++→| EXISTING SUBWAY OR SURFACE ————

|←+++→| EXISTING ELEVATED ————

PROGRAMMED   OTHER

PRIORITY PROPOSALS

FUTURE PROPOSALS

RAPID TRANSIT

PROGRAMMED   OTHER

Figure 6-6.

Chapter Seven

THE REGION'S ECONOMY: THE PREDOMINANCE OF MANUFACTURING

It is customary to think of Metropolitan New York as a financial center, a hub of foreign trade, a capital of corporate headquarters, a center of medical research, a commercial center, a market for culture and fashion, a scientific and research center, and a home base for mass communications. In each of these fields the Region is indeed a world center. The Region's leadership in these fields, however, is less important to its economic existence than is the Region's leadership in manufacturing, which provides about 24 percent of all jobs in the Region. Service industries make up the Region's second major economic sector, providing about 22 percent of all jobs in the Region; retail trade is third, providing some 15 percent; and government fourth, providing about 12 percent (Fig. 7-1).

Manufacturing in the Region

Metropolitan New York is the nation's premier manufacturing center. It is first whether measured in employment, number, and variety of industrial plants, or value of production.

DIVERSITY

The most striking characteristic of the Region's manufacturing base is its diversity—diversity of product, of process, and of location. Of the 418 categories in the United States

Census Bureau's industrial lexicon, 394 are found in the Metropolitan SCA. The presence of such a broad range of manufacturers is a valuable asset to any single manufacturer, for it assures him of close sources of supply for components and materials. Thus he can assemble his product economically, and he does not need to maintain expensive inventories or special, seldom-used equipment. To the manufacturer who sells to other industries, the Region's diversity assures a substantial immediate market for even the most specialized goods.

The New York Region is much less dependent upon any one industrial activity than are other leading industrial regions. The ten largest industrial categories in terms of employment account for only 25 percent of the area's manufacturing employment and about 20 percent of industrial plants. These ten leading industries, in rank order of employment, are women's dresses, radio and TV transmitting equipment, women's suits and coats, periodicals, aircraft, newspapers, plastics products, pharmaceuticals, electronic components, and commercial printing. In metropolitan Pittsburgh, by contrast, steel mills account for over 30 percent of industrial employment. In Detroit motor vehicles account for almost 20 percent, and in both Los Angeles and Saint Louis aircraft manufacture accounts for over 10 percent.

Following the ten leaders in the New York Region is a group of twenty-three types of industries, each of which employs more than ten thousand workers. These industries include the production of motor vehicles, games and toys, aircraft parts, lighting fixtures, machinery, metal stampings, nonferrous wire, leather handbags, and toiletries.

The next group of sixty-four activities, each of which employs between five and ten thousand workers, includes the manufacture of advertising displays, costume jewelry, dolls, photographic equipment, semi-conductors, special industry machines, printing machinery, dies and tools, sheet metalwork, cans, rubber products, paints, and plastic materials. This group also contains the production of organic chemicals, cyclic intermediates, bookbindings, corrugated boxes, automotive cloth trimmings, and confectionery products.

Finally, another 161 industrial activities in the Region each employ between one and five thousand workers, and another 136 industries count Area-wide employment of under one thousand workers each.

MANUFACTURING EMPLOYMENT

The 1972 *Census of Manufactures* reports that 1,623,300 people hold manufacturing jobs in the metropolitan area. This labor force excludes the 193,700 employed in separate Central Administrative Offices of manufacturing firms.

New York's role as the nation's corporate headquarters has led many to believe that the Region's manufacturing employment is composed mainly of Central Administrative Office jobs. In fact, the proportion of production workers is just about the national average, and actually exceeds the proportion in Los Angeles, Milwaukee, Boston, Philadelphia, Cleveland, and many other industrial metropolitan areas.

Since the end of World War II, total manufacturing employment in the Region has grown by the relatively small amount of 7 percent. This small growth has been due to a fundamental restructuring of the Region's manufacturing complex. In general, employment has risen in the technology-oriented,

high-wage industries, and fallen in the low-wage industries.

Most notable has been expansion in the durable goods sector, where employment rose 31.5 percent from 1949 to 1969. Durable goods production now absorbs almost 45 percent of Regional employment, in contrast to 36 percent in 1949. The high growth components have been electrical equipment, machinery, instruments, metal fabrication, and transportation equipment.

Employment in the nondurable sector, by contrast, declined 7 percent, due principally to the attrition of the apparel industry, which declined by over 27 percent. Excluding apparel, employment in the nondurable sector actually rose by 6.3 percent. Significant expansion occurred in chemicals, rubber and plastics, paper products and printing.

Garment manufacturing in the Region, about half of which is concentrated in Manhattan, has suffered the out-migration of manufacturers of standardized clothing items—uniforms, work clothes, underwear, hosiery—and of production of cheaper dresses and outerwear lines. Those segments of the industry more attuned to fashion trends and higher product values—better dresses, coats, sportswear, accessories—have grown in the Region. They maintain vital links to Manhattan's design, advertising, and merchandising complex.

Excluding apparel, the rise in total durable and nondurable employment has been 18.5 percent. Thus apparel's decline has masked vigorous growth in the rest of the Region's industrial structure. The Region's ability to withstand such a deep and fundamental restructuring of its industrial base reflects the basic health of the Region's economy.

PLANTS

The diversity of Regional manufacturing is further evidenced by the number of plants in the Region. In 1972 there were 41,693 manufacturing plants and over 1,000 Central Administrative Offices (Fig. 7-2). This number of plants is about 15 percent of the total in the United States. The great number of small plants in the Region—27,335 employ less than 20 people—actually does not represent a significantly different proportion of the total than that in other major industrial centers. Small-scale manufacturing is concentrated in Manhattan, where 38 percent of the area's small plants can be found.

No single plant accounts for more than two percent of the Metropolitan Area's manufacturing employment.

VALUE OF PRODUCTION

The Metropolitan Area's industrial output, as measured by the value of shipments from its manufacturing plants, was fifty-six billion dollars in 1972. Of this, 28 billion dollars represents the cost of material inputs, and 28 billion dollars was the value added within the Region.

The value of production is fairly evenly distributed among industrial categories. The largest category, apparel, accounts for less than 16 percent of shipments and for 13 percent of value added. This had declined greatly from the late 1940s, when apparel accounted for almost 22 percent of total value added and for more than a quarter of shipments. After apparel, the leading industries are chemicals, printing, and food production, each with about 11 percent of total shipments.

Industries Which Favor a Metropolitan New York Location

Before examining the pattern of industrial locations within the Region, we must differentiate those industries which serve local needs from those activities which serve wider national or even international markets. No region can survive economically by providing goods and services to itself; it must export goods and services to wider markets in order to pay for the food, energy, raw materials, and other items it must import. What types of manufacturing industries concentrate in the New York Region, and why?

Many Regional industries will need to be large just to serve the Region's huge population, but while we saw that no specific handful of industries dominate Regional employment, there are a few industries in which the Region does have a very high share of the nation's total employment.

In general, those industries exhibit a few common characteristics. For one, many of these industries manufacture consumer goods which move directly to national markets without additional fabrication. Also, most of these goods are of high value relative to their bulk or weight. Thirdly, most of these products are unstandardized, that is, they vary frequently. The reasons why the Region attracts industries with these characteristics will become apparent as we analyze the Regions's locational advantages for manufacturing.

LOCATIONAL ADVANTAGES

A manufacturer's decision of where to build a factory is based on a large number of both economic and noneconomic considerations. The pressure of competition generally makes economic factors most important, but if there is little competition in an industry, or if the differences in the economic advantages among different locations are small, noneconomic factors may be decisive. In some cases manufacturers can avoid direct price competition by product differentiation; that is, they make their product somehow different from its competition, in fact or at least in the public mind through distinctive advertising or packaging.

For an area as large and diversified as Metropolitan New York, some of the large group of locational factors that might be important in other contexts can be counted as unimportant in analyzing the advantages and disadvantages of the Region as a whole. The availability of low cost space of a specific size is one major locational factor, but in most industries a manufacturer can find a desired site somewhere in the New York Region as readily as elsewhere in the country. Also, the quality and availability of water in the Region is at least as adequate as in other areas. Taxes are another general locational factor which can be ignored in comparing the Region as a whole with the rest of the country.

Four other factors are more important in explaining what industries locate in the Region, or why they stay in the Region: inertia, transport costs, labor supply and costs, and external economies. Of these four factors considered by an industrialist in locating a factory, the New York Region is actually quite weak in the first two, but offers advantages in the second two considerations.

In examining these four locational determinants and the industries which are sensitive to them, we must remind ourselves again always to differentiate carefully between those economic activities in which the New York Region leads the nation, and those which are actually most important in providing employment within the Region. The New York Stock Exchange, for example, is the most important in the world, but it does not employ so many workers as does the Region's glass industry, which is relatively unimportant on a national scale.

Inertia

The location of many industries can be understood only by reference to history, because the factors which originally placed them in the Region may no longer be present. Today they either gain no economies at all from their location, or else they may gain only economies specific to the firm. That is, any specific company may have sunk investment in plant or equipment, or in the training of a skilled labor force. Several industries in the New York Region composed of unusually large plants, such as electrical equipment, aircraft, and chemicals, grew up in the Region in order to be near their financiers or founders, but these locational factors are often no longer relevant. In their cur-

rent location these industries gain few advantages in either production or marketing which they could not gain elsewhere, and some of them would even probably locate elsewhere if they were starting out afresh today. The chemical industries along the Arthur Kill in New Jersey, for instance, face serious problems of waste disposal and air pollution abatement at their present location, but they are committed to that location by investment in plant and trained labor force.

Transport Costs

For a second group of industries, the most important factor in their decision of where to locate is the cost or problems of moving raw materials to the plant or of getting their products to the market. The New York Metropolitan Region generally is not attractive for transport-sensitive industries which serve national markets. In the past these industries did favor New York, but as the nation's center of population shifted West, as Asia and Canada came to be as important in American foreign trade as Europe, and as the New York Region's lack of raw materials contrasted sharply with the Midwest, many of these industries, especially the heavy industries, moved away.

The few transport-sensitive industries serving national markets which remain in Metropolitan New York can be accounted for either by the port or by economies of scale long ago achieved in large plants. These industries include copper refining, confectionery products, manufacture from imported chemicals, the manufacture of brooms and brushes, and the processing of vegetable oils.

Those transport-sensitive industries which are underrepresented in the Region are, however, finding less and less disadvantage in being in the New York Region, even though it is at the edge of the nation and far from the center of national markets or the main domestic sources of raw materials. Many American industries have been dispersing throughout the country in the past thirty years because of the depletion of

America's highest grade raw materials, the substitution of imported raw materials, and the decline of transport and raw material costs as a percentage of delivered-item cost in most industries. Thus New York is slowly *losing* its preponderance in some transport-sensitive industries, but at the same time the Region has been *gaining* some industries which have previously been under-represented in the Region. Metal working, refrigeration equipment, valves and fittings, and auto assembly have all generally grown in the New York Region as they have dispersed out from previous concentration in the Midwest.

Labor

When examining the Region's labor supply, we must distinguish between industries which rely on skilled labor and industries which rely on unskilled labor. The Region does contain many plants for which the availability of unskilled labor is a locational determinant, but few industries actually locate in the Region for its unskilled labor. On a national scale, plants for which low-skilled labor is the primary locational determinant locate in the South or in rural areas. Continuing immigration to New York of people from abroad and, more recently, of Puerto Ricans and southern blacks, has long provided a low-wage unskilled labor pool, but today skilled labor supplies are actually a much more important factor in attracting industries to the Region.

Industries requiring substantial pools of skilled labor are generally concentrated in the nation's metropolitan areas. Of these areas, New York has held an important role both by virtue of historical reasons—a skilled labor supply being largely self-reproductive whatever the original reason for development—and for reasons of economies of scale.

The extraordinary size and diversity of the Region's skilled labor pool is a locational attraction which can even outweigh the fact that wages in the Region are generally high. The differences in wages paid skilled laborers from one region to another, however, are less important to an industrialist than are differences in wages paid unskilled labor from one region to another. There are three reasons for this. For one, employers in areas short of skilled labor can usually speed up on-the-job training of local semiskilled workers, rather than try to attract skilled workers from other areas by paying extra high wages to skilled workers. Also, plants which employ skilled labor are often branches of large corporations which pay uniform wages across the country. Thirdly, many of these industries are of a sort which can avoid direct price competition by brand name advertising and other product differentiating techniques. Thus they can pay a little more in wages and charge a little more for their product. For these reasons the *supply* of skilled labor can be more important than actual *wages*. The Region's wages for skilled labor are, in fact, particularly *above* national levels in precisely those industries concentrated in the Region (e.g., apparel) and *below* national levels in those skilled labor industries underrepresented in the Region (e.g., metal working).

Labor Supply. The Port Authority of New York and New Jersey defines seven labor market areas within the Metropolitan Region. These conform to the labor markets defined by the United States Bureau of Labor Statistics, with one exception. The Port Authority combines Monmouth County in New Jersey with the Perth Amboy Labor Area, because Monmouth County is in fact tied to the Perth Amboy Area's two counties, Middlesex and Somerset, by a substantial interchange of labor. Such interchange is of course true for all of the Labor Areas in the Metropolitan Area. Since Labor Areas are based on the residence of labor, each exports workers to industry in adjacent Labor Areas and even beyond. We will use Port Authority statistics in examining the Regional labor force because, as part of the Authority's efforts to attract new industry to the Region, the Authority monitors statistics not so well observed by other governmental agencies.

The Resident Labor Force. The 1970 adult

civilian labor force resident in the Port Authority's 18 county Metropolitan Region was 6.9 million people—4.3 million men and 2.6 million women (Fig 7-3). This includes all people twenty years and older either employed or looking for work. An additional 641,000 teenagers, aged fourteen to nineteen, were either employed or looking for work. The Regional labor force is augmented further by commuters from outside the Metropolitan Area in New Jersey, New York, Connecticut, and even Pennsylvania.

The New York sector, with a resident labor force of 4.9 million, or 70 percent of the Area total, contains the Region's two largest labor markets: New York City and Nassau-Suffolk. The 2 million people in the New Jersey sector's resident labor force are more evenly distributed among its four labor markets, although the largest, comprised of Essex, Morris, and Union Counties, includes the cities of Newark and Elizabeth, two well-established industrial and business centers.

How the Labor Force is Employed. In 1970 there were 7.5 million jobs in the Region. This figure exceeds the number in the labor force because of dual job holding and in-commutation.

Manufacturing is the largest industry category, with 1.8 million jobs, or 24 percent of the Regional total (Fig. 7-1). As Regional manufacturing industries have become increasingly technologically-oriented, this labor force has moved toward the professional and technical fields.

The figure shows that manufacturing jobs are the most important sector of total employment in the New Jersey part of the Metropolitan Area, where they account for about one-third of total jobs. The importance of manufacturing in the state of New Jersey as a whole is a weakness in that state's economy. In the New York part, by contrast, manufacturing jobs are only one-fifth of the total.

Service industry jobs constitute the second largest group in the Region as a whole. These include business and professional services, legal, medical and health services, and amusement and recreational activities. The service group's 1.7 million jobs are about 22 percent of the Regional total. Again the figure clearly differentiates the New York and New Jersey parts of the Metropolitan Area. The service industry group is the leading employer in the New York part, although manufacturing jobs are a close second.

The only other industry category that employs over one million people is retail trade, whose 1.1 million jobs account for 15 percent of the Area's total. More than one-half of all Metropolitan retail jobs are in New York City, a figure in keeping with the City's share of total Regional population.

Skills of the Region's Labor Force. Regional employment can be analyzed not only by categories of industrial employers, but also by categories of skills of employees. Members of each occupational group may, of course, be employed in each industry category, as each industry category may employ workers from each occupational group (Fig. 7-4). The largest occupational group in the Metropolitan Area consists of clerical workers, with 1.6 million employed. Occupations in this group include secretaries, stenographers, typists, office machine operators, accounting clerks, bank tellers, cashiers, telephone operators, insurance adjusters, stock clerks, shipping and receiving clerks.

Electronic data processing plays a growing role in routine clerical operations, but the demand for clerical personnel has not declined appreciably. This is in part because of the continuing development of the Metropolis' headquarters function, and partly due to the proliferation of clerical operations in all businesses.

The service workers and laborers are the Region's second largest employed group, numbering 1.3 million. Typical service and labor occupations include waiters and waitresses, household workers, janitors, cooks, policemen, hospital attendants, bakers, beauticians, and airline stewardesses. One must be especially careful not to confuse the occupational category of service workers with the industry category of service industries. Many service workers are employed in the personal and business service industries, but manufacturing industries employ 56,000 workers in this occupational category.

The occupational category of operatives includes over 1.2 million area residents, more than 700,000 of whom work in manufacturing industries. Operatives usually operate a machine or motor vehicle, assemble components or pack materials, and they are generally considered semi-skilled.

The number of professional and technical workers in the Region, just under 1.2 million, accounts for 15.5 percent of the total labor force. This impressive number is equal to the entire work force of Metropolitan Washington, D.C. This large pool of specialized skills is attractive to manufacturers, although only 189,000 of these workers are directly employed by manufacturing industries.

The fifth largest occupational category, the craftsmen, consists of mechanics and journeymen, the most skilled of the manual work force. About 38 percent of these 936,000 workers are in manufacturing industries.

Some 771,000 people in the Region are classified as managers, officials, and proprietors, 132,000 of whom are in manufacturing industries. This occupational classification goes considerably beyond what is normally regarded as executive talent and embraces all functions requiring leadership and managerial or supervisory skills. This occupational group usually accounts for 10 or 11 percent of employment in the Region as in the nation as a whole, although there are internal shifts within the category. Managers of branch stores replace owner-operators of retail shops, for instance, but the number of managers in manufacturing, finance, and insurance has increased.

There are 583,400 Regional workers classified as sales workers, two-thirds of whom work in wholesaling or retailing establishments.

All of these figures detailing the labor force, its skills and employment, emphasize the predominance of manufacturing industries in the economy of the Region as a whole.

External Economies

A number of industries manufacture products for which demand is variable and unpredictable, due to seasonality, fashion, or changing technology. The rapidly changing requirements of manufacture prevent manufacturers of these products from achieving internal economies of scale. The variability necessitates frequent and rapid retooling, which prevents standardized mass production. Specialized equipment rapidly becomes obsolete, and the internal division of labor cannot go very far when the product is changed frequently. Thus plants among these industries are usually small, using little horsepower per worker.

Most firms have only one plant, because the manufacturer cannot take advantage of the economies of a multiplant firm—the sharing of overhead costs by a number of plants. The variability of the product precludes sharing advertising costs or the purchase of raw materials in bulk. Decisions are unique to each plant, and supervisory personnel cannot be spread among plants.

Because these firms cannot invest heavily in specialized machinery or in inventories of raw materials, capitalization is minimal. Little capital is needed to start a business, and so new competition can enter the market easily.

These firms cannot keep on hand all of the materials or personnel which they might need only occasionally, and thus their overriding locational need is the ability to tap a pool of facilities—of space, of skills, of supplies, and of freight services—to be able to tap this pool at a moment's notice, and to be able to share these facilities. These pools of facilities upon which any individual manufacturer can draw whenever he needs them are known as *external economies,* and they are a substitute for a company's achieving internal economies of scale.

Small manufacturers, and manufacturers of unstandardized products, agglomerate and multiply wherever external economies can be found. By agglomerating, they achieve economies which are internal to the large plant or the multiplant firm. Industries dependent upon external economies generally include fashionable apparel, embroidery and trimmings, small leather goods, toys and dolls, periodicals and books, and electrical components.

Because of the unique number and diversity of manufacturers and services in Metropolitan New York, the external economies found in the Region are commeasurably attractive. In the 19th century industries dependent upon external economies grew up in New York, largely because of the City's great size. Once established, they attracted additional industries to the cluster, and such clusters continuously spawn new industries.

Space. Rentable space is one important external economy, and there is more rentable space for industry in the New York Region than in any other metropolitan area in the country. If each new industrialist had to design and build his own facility, his capital requirements to get started would be much higher, and it would take some time. In the New York Region a manufacturer can almost invariably find suitable space for his production, in an area zoned for industry, with a rail siding or near a highway, or appropriate to whatever his needs might be. He can share a large building with one or more other companies if he needs only a small space. By renting, of course, he also retains his flexibility to move or expand.

Services. Not only space, but also services can be shared by small firms. Commercial laboratories provide technical and research services on a contract basis; designers of all types can be hired. Manufacturers of unstandardized products can thus obtain these services and many others when they need them without committing themselves to a fixed cost over a long term. Availability when the manufacturer needs a service or item decreases the need for in-plant overhead, and thus the manufacturer is free of tying up capital in a facility he needs only part of the time. The specialized suppliers and the owners of the specialized services, on the other hand, are able to make their profit because the

needs of a large group of customers are more reasonably stable than those of an individual producer.

Labor. The pool of skilled laborers in the Region provides a third external economy. Workers can be hired as needed. As already noted, workers' availability can sometimes be more important than their wage level.

Freight Forwarders. A fourth external economy offered by the New York Region is the pool of freight forwarders. Their function is to combine small shipments of several manufacturers to make up full carloads or truckloads. This is important for small producers, or for producers whose product may be of high value, but of low bulk.

Buyers. New York City's role as the national marketplace for products of unstandardized industries is still another important external economy. Stores all over the country send their buyers to New York, or contract with resident buyers, to inspect rapidly changing products. Producers of goods want to be represented in New York, where they can reduce their advertising and other selling costs by sharing the time of visiting buyers.

Thus the Region's producers can draw on a great variety of facilities that either are not available elsewhere, or are available in New York at low cost, because the suppliers have such a large market in the cluster of producers. The short production cycle and the unpredictable variability of the unstandardized product—whether a high fashion dress, a toy, or the editorial in a magazine—emphasize the need for speed. The producer must be able to obtain his material, equipment, and the advice of specialists on a moment's notice, and he cannot store material or buy without inspection.

The key to the importance of external economies for these manufacturers is their products' lack of standardization. The specifications for standardized products, by contrast, can be planned in advance with relative assurance, and large numbers of identical items are produced. Standardized products for local markets are produced locally (newspapers, bread, etc.), but standardized products made for national markets generally seek the cheapest labor, transport, and other costs.

If a product becomes standardized, the producer can internalize economies of manufacture—build his own plant wherever land is cheapest, produce wherever unskilled low-wage labor can be utilized in routine operations, and hire his own full-time support staff (lawyer, electrician, etc.). Thus it is a general principle that standardized production for national markets migrates out of New York, even though the company or industry may have gotten its start in the Region. Products which have migrated out include simple dresses, uniforms, press-work, binding, mailing, radio and television sets, vacuum tubes, and other standardized components. Some of these manufacturing processes have by now, of course, migrated out of the United States altogether and established themselves in foreign cheap labor markets. Some industries keep the unstandardized operations in New York and move the standardized operations out. The garment industry illustrates this in the contrast between fashionable dresses and uniforms. Similarly, magazine editorial offices might stay in New York, while the printing and shipping is done elsewhere.

Weaknesses

Industries which rely on external economies have two built-in weaknesses, and these weaknesses can affect the entire economy of a Region dependent upon such industries. For one, a growth in demand for any unstandardized manufactured product may lead to greater employment, but it will not necessarily result in more output per worker, that is, to increased productivity. This is because the manufacturer hires more workers *rather than* invest more capital in specialized production equipment, which he fears would soon become obsolete.

Secondly, industries which have a low level of capitalization, and are thus easy for new competition to enter, always squeeze down both profit margins and wages per unit of output. Because productivity does not keep pace with increases in employment, per capita income is held down.

This has been a problem with which the New York Region has struggled for years: Regional per capita income has not risen so fast as the growth in the number of jobs would lead one to hope. This is a reflection of the importance of external-economy industries in the Regional economy.

THE BUSINESS SPIRIT

It is difficult to convey the "mood" of a group of industries, but the characteristics of business in the external economies industries so well define what many consider the spirit of New York, that they must be surveyed. The existence of external economies enables anyone to start a business with just a small investment and a short-term commitment. What the businessman needs in large supply are a good idea and nerve. These industries are gambles and, for the spirited entrepreneur, almost gambols as well. One toy, one publication, one dress, one electrical component, or one fashion accessory which "catches on" can make its manufacturer very rich. Great deals of money can be made fast. Money can be lost, too, but since these industries are capitalized at a minimal level, the amount which can be lost is peanuts compared to what can be made. Profits as a percentage of sales may be small, and these manufacturers always complain about business. Profits as a percentage of invested capital, however, can be enormous. Each product marketed is a throw of the dice. The garment industry, an industry which ranks first in New York and in which New York ranks first in the nation, is just such an industry.

New York's role as a leading center of external-economies-dependent industries combines particularly with its role as the world's leading financial center (discussed below) so that to some observers the chase after the dollar is a fixation of New Yorkers. Anthony Trollope noted this over one hundred years ago:

> Every man worships the dollar, and is down before his shrine from morning to night.... Other men, the world over, worship regularly at the shrine... but the New Yorker is always on his knees.

Interest in the dollar, however, often is not rapacity so much as adventurousness. Trollope recognized this too:

> . . . the New Yorker (is not) a hugger-mugger with his money. He does not hide up his dollars in old stockings and keep rolls of gold in hidden pots. . . . He builds houses, he speculates largely, he spreads himself in trade to the extent of his wings, and not seldom somewhat further. . . . His regret at losing his money is by no means commen-

surate with his desire to make it. In this then is a living spirit which to me divests the dollar worshiping idolatry of something of its ugliness. The hand when closed on the gold is instantly reopened.

Anyone who does not understand the "sport" of capitalism, that making money can be fun—even more fun than having it—can never understand much of the New York business world.

	All Jobs	Mfg.	Ag. & Mining	Const.	Transportation Communication Public Utilities	Wholesale Trade	Retail Trade	Finance Insurance Real Estate	Services	Govt.
Total Metropolitan Area	7528.5	1815.5	33.7	361.8	502.8	517.3	1133.9	621.5	1651.7	890.3
New York Sector	5433.1	1129.2	10.4	255.5	371.5	391.9	818.9	523.8	1265.8	666.1
New York City	4236.4	871.3	3.4	180.0	319.8	340.1	578.4	472.1	971.8	499.5
Nassau-Suffolk	777.3	163.1	4.9	50.1	31.1	32.6	165.5	33.0	182.2	114.8
Westchester-Rockland	419.4	94.8	2.1	25.4	20.6	19.2	75.0	18.7	111.8	51.8
New Jersey Sector	2095.4	686.3	23.3	106.3	131.3	125.4	315.0	97.7	385.9	224.2
Bergen-Passaic	526.9	181.6	2.6	32.4	24.6	36.9	86.6	19.7	95.1	47.4
Essex-Morris-Union	859.4	259.4	7.2	41.1	52.6	53.0	127.3	58.0	173.4	87.4
Hudson	286.0	118.1	0.1	7.7	34.6	17.5	33.0	10.0	36.8	28.2
Middlesex-Somerset-Monmouth	423.1	127.2	13.4	25.1	19.5	18.0	68.1	10.0	80.6	61.2

Figure 7-1. Major Industry and Place of Work of Port-Authority 18-County Metropolitan Area Employment 1970, (in thousands).

	Mfg. Estab.	With 20 or More Employees	1972 Total Employees (in thousands)	Production Workers (in thousands)	Value Added (million $)	Capital Expend. (million $)	1967 Total Employees (in thousands)	Value Added (million $)
SCA	41693	14358	1623.3	1027.5	28383.2	1233.0	1818.5	23767.7
NY-NJ SMSA	28419	9466	951.3	590.7	15145.9	584.6	1147.4	13803.5
New York	14929	4360	431.5	225.6	6404.5	201.0	482.3	5666.8
Bronx	1397	532	41.2	32.2	573.0	27.9	52.7	570.7
Richmond	144	55	6.0	4.6	166.4	12.5	7.7	136.7
Queens	2773	1076	113.6	85.3	1899.9	83.2	132.3	1680.7
Kings	5072	1993	165.6	132.6	2534.4	94.2	220.3	2190.7
Rockland	242	95	14.2	9.5	517.2	19.6	14.0	371.9
Westchester	1368	469	68.4	33.5	1080.3	47.4	73.3	956.3
Putnam	37	12	.7	.5	12.4	.7	1.2	13.7
Bergen	2457	874	110.1	66.9	1957.8	98.1	107.2	1469.4
Nassau-Suffolk SMSA	4193	1220	150.2	97.7	2527.5	111.3	164.8	2229.7
Nassau	2524	680	93.5	55.7	1622.6	64.5	116.0	1639.8
Suffolk	1669	540	56.7	42.0	904.9	46.8	48.8	589.9
Newark SMSA	4600	1748	271.2	160.7	5608.7	269.9	263.7	4071.1
Essex	2157	769	104.0	65.4	1913.8	83.2	123.6	1762.9
Morris	658	242	42.4	20.5	833.6	40.3	38.4	546.0
Somerset	276	115	25.8	13.8	627.3	31.6	28.6	329.1
Union	1509	622	99.0	61.0	2234.0	114.8	101.7	1762.2
Jersey City SMSA (Hudson County, N.J.)	1909	742	94.9	71.2	1899.2	91.8	107.2	1584.9
Paterson-Clifton-Passaic SMSA (Passaic Co., N.J.)	1591	669	75.6	54.8	1180.8	58.7	82.8	1037.2
New Brunswick-Perth Amboy-Sayreville SMSA (Middlesex Co., N.J.)	982	514	80.1	52.4	2021.5	116.7	81.6	1472.5

D-Data withheld because bulk of contribution was from one corporation.

Figure 7-2. Census of Manufacturing Data for the 18-County SCA.

	Age 20 and over	Supplemental Age 14-19
Metropolitan Area	6,921	641
New York Sector	4,879	438
New York City	3,482	286
Nassau-Suffolk	948	108
Westchester-Rockland	449	44
New Jersey Sector	2,042	203
Bergen-Passaic	559	54
Hudson	261	23
Essex-Morris-Union	747	73
Middlesex-Somerset-Monmouth	475	53

Figure 7-3. Age and Residence of the Port Authority 18-County Metropolitan Area Labor Force in 1970 (in thousands).

Clerical Workers	1613.3
Service Workers and Laborers	1259.4
Operatives	1201.9
Professional and Technical Workers	1166.0
Craftsmen	935.6
Managers and Administration	770.8
Sales Workers	583.4

Figure 7-4. Inventory of Occupational Categories in 18-County Port Authority Region in 1970 (in thousands).

Chapter Eight

INDUSTRIAL LOCATIONS WITHIN THE REGION

Reasons for Site Selection

Several fairly obvious locational pressures have shaped the pattern of industrial settlement in the Region. Many operate the same within the Region as they do in considering the Region as part of the nation. Manufacturing industries want cheap and easy transportation, space, a labor force, access to outside services, and a low tax rate. We must now review how each of these factors operates in the Metropolitan Area before defining specific Metropolitan industrial belts. One consistent theme to be noted is that most of these factors today favor the dispersal of industry from the Region's central cities. Everywhere the suburbs gain population and jobs, while the cities are drained of opportunity.

TRANSPORTATION

The successive development of different modes of transportation has probably been the single most important factor in industrial location decisions. Each new transport mode or facility redistributes locational advantages. One hundred years ago the convenience of water transport, both deep-water and barge, favored industrial sites on Manhattan Island, along the shores of the East River and Newtown Creek in Brooklyn, the Morris Canal in Newark, Yonkers on the Hudson River, and Bridgeport on Long Island Sound. Industries which depend upon water-borne American or imported raw materials still cling to waterfront sites. Examples include the coffee, chocolate, and sugar processing industries along the Hudson River in New Jersey and in Brooklyn; the petroleum refining and petrochemical complex along the Arthur Kill; and the copper smelting, refining and fashioning industries also along the Arthur Kill.

Next the railroad lines appeared to serve existing nuclei of settlement and industrial activity. At the same time, however, the railroads encourage the spread of industry into other towns along the tracks. Another important effect of the railroads was to grant New Jersey a great advantage over New York parts of the Region. Most of the lines stopped at the Hudson River, and thus Long Island suffered higher transport costs and delays. Between 1899 and 1919 the New Jersey parts of today's Metropolitan Area industrialized so rapidly that New Jersey's share of total Metropolitan Area manufacturing employment grew from 20 percent to 33 percent.

Truck transportation became important after about 1920, and it offered new freedom in industrial site selection. The highways opened up suburban land previously inaccessible for industrial development, while at the same time vehicles began to choke the central cities. The multitude of trucks and, more important, of private cars, caused intolerable congestion on city streets. Industries located or relocated in the suburbs, where they could receive their raw materials and ship out their products by truck.

Also, the labor force came to the plants by private car; low-density dispersion of both housing and industry made mass transit infeasible. Industrial activity in the old city centers soon grew more slowly than in the suburbs, and it finally began to decline. Even those industries which serve local consumer markets, must have low transport costs, and must carefully time their deliveries (e.g., newspapers, bakers, breweries, bottlers) have dispersed out from the central cities, following the population and seeking the most convenient Regional distribution points.

The more widespread accessibility offered by trucks diluted New Jersey's railroad advantage, and generally reduced any site's locational advantages.

Air transport has added a new dimension. All existing industrial districts have good access to the Region's three major airports, but the Region also has 33 smaller general aviation airports of significant value to industry. Only the lowest bulk and highest value raw materials or finished products usually move by air, but business managers, consultants, and product designers frequently must fly to check with suppliers or customers. The Region's most important general aviation airports include Caldwell Airport in Essex County, Linden Airport in Union, Teterboro Airport in Bergen, McArthur and Republic Airports in Suffolk, White Plains Airport in Westchester, and Flushing Airport in Queens. Extensive improvements are planned at this latter, which is adjacent to the College Point Industrial Park, and at Suffolk Airport in conjunction with an industrial park there.

SPACE REQUIREMENTS

Manufacturing industries' search for space has been another factor pulling them out of the Region's older city centers. Many of the industrial structures in the cities are worn out or have been made obsolete by new manufacturing processes.

In the past forty or fifty years many industries have developed continuous material flow systems with automatic processing controls. For such production methods, the size and shape of the building must be determined by the process, and the site must not restrain the shape of the structure. The production process is designed, and then the building is tailor-made to be wrapped around the process. Such manufacturing plants are usually single-story, and they require considerable plot space per worker. Where the value of land in a central city is high, or where the land is divided into small parcels and difficult to assemble into a larger site, industry is discouraged. The suburbs have, of course, been quick to plan spacious industrial parks with preferred highway or rail access, thereby hoping to hold down residential property taxes.

Industrial expansion in the central cities is also often discouraged by zoning requirements or other urban regulations. The history of the group of industries known as "nuisance industries," including slaughtering, rendering, soap making, tanneries, paints and varnish, chemicals, petroleum and copper refining, illustrates this. As late as the 1920s many of these industries were still concentrated along the East River and along Newtown Creek between Brooklyn and Queens. They were forced farther and farther away from the central business district by zoning, fire regulations, and waste disposal problems.

Already by the early 20th century Westchester County and Northern Long Island had attracted upper class residential settlement, thus closing those areas to the nuisance industries. Estuarine areas in New Jersey were developed by heavy industry, and still today these industries can be found in Newark Bay, along the lower Raritan River, and along Arthur Kill.

REGIONAL WAGE DIFFERENCES

Differences in wage rates within the Region are not an important industrial locational determinant. Only a few intra-Regional differences may be noted. Those manufacturing plants employing unskilled labor at low rates, and willing to accept the consequent high employee turnover and absenteeism, remain in the core cities.

The aircraft industry, concentrated in parts of Nassau, Suffolk, and Bergen counties, and the petroleum refining and chemical industries in Hudson, Middlesex, Union, and Richmond Counties are notably high wage industries. They do pull up general wage levels a bit where they are concentrated.

Examination of Regional workers' residences reveals that the Region's higher-paying occupations are dominated by suburbanites. The three categories of professional and technical workers, of managers, and of craftsmen include 34 percent of New York City working residents, 37 percent of all United States workers, and 41 percent of workers in the New York Region who live outside the City.

EXTERNAL ECONOMIES

From what has already been said about external economies, it can be assumed that maximum advantage of external economies can be gained from the most central location. In terms of the Region, the most central location is Manhattan, and small establishments both among industries and within any industry favor a Manhattan site, or one close in to it. Of the 14,929 manufacturing plants in Manhattan in 1972, some 10,569 of them employed fewer than twenty people, and these plants totaled 38 percent of all plants so small in the entire Region. The external economies available in Manhattan grant significant advantages in opening or operating an industrial plant there. Small establishments may not survive, but new ones are always springing up.

Even within Manhattan external economies dictate a high degree of concentration of certain industries or activities. The garment district occupies less than twenty city blocks between 34th and 41st Streets, 6th and 8th Avenues, and the fur industry the blocks just to the South. Special retailing and wholesaling districts can also be identified: diamonds on 47th Street between 5th and 6th Avenues; art along Madison Avenue, centering at 75th Street and along East 57th Street; flowers at 28th Street and 6th Avenue; draperies and floor coverings along 5th Avenue from 23rd to 34th Street; and church supplies and vestments along Barclay Street and Park Place, west of Broadway; to name just a few. These specialized shopping districts attract out of town buyers, and add to the City's fascination.

TAXES

Industries are always mindful of both the level and the form of taxes levied upon them. They generally prefer property taxes, because the industries then have numerous allies in fighting a rise in taxes. Many businessmen feel that corporate income taxes, on the other hand, often reflect an anti-business attitude.

The major taxes on general business in New Jersey are a corporate business tax (on both net income and net worth), a sales and use tax, and real and tangible business personal property taxes. New Jersey relies heavily upon business taxes and local property taxes for all government financing; it levies no personal income tax. In New York the principal taxes on business are those levied on net income, sales and real property. New York does not tax personal property, and only New York City imposes a local tax on corporate income. Machinery, equipment, utilities and materials used in production are exempt from the state tax. Manufacturing supplies are also exempt from local sales taxes outside New York City, but machinery and equipment as well as supplies are subject to the local tax in the City.

Real property taxes vary from community to community. Within the Metropolitan Area in 1970 the rate per $1,000 of full value varied from $33.93 in Queens to $60.63 in Long Beach, in Nassau County.

Thus the general pattern of taxation, greatly simplified, shows that combined taxes are highest in New York City and in the Region's other older central cities, and that taxes are higher in New York State than in New Jersey.

Regional Industrial Belts

Figure 7-2 presents a county-by-county analysis of the 1972 *Census of Manufacturers* of the 18-county SCA. From these data and from other sub-county analyses of Regional manufac-

This unit at the Du Pont Company's plant near Parlin, New Jersey (Middlesex County), is for the continuous production of "Cronar" polyester photographic film base. The plant, unique in the photographic film manufacturing field, has a five story open air structure for the chemical mixing and formulation of base making. It is clearly capital-intensive, and typifies the petroleum and chemical industries along the Raritan River. (Photo courtesy of E.I. Du Pont de Nemours and Co.)

turing, we can generalize that about two-thirds of manufacturing in the New York-Northeast New Jersey SCA is concentrated in two broad industrialized belts. One is in New Jersey, and the other is entirely within New York City. (Fig. 8-1).

INDUSTRY IN NEW JERSEY

Two-thirds of industrial employment in Northern New Jersey is found within a belt stretching from Southern Bergen and Passaic counties as far south as Perth Amboy in Middlesex County. This belt, thirty-four miles long and fourteen miles wide, may be subdivided into the Newark-Perth Amboy District, the Bergen-Passaic District, and the Hudson County District. The more than 8,000 plants in these three districts employ about 500,000 people.

Newark-Perth Amboy District

This district lies at the convergence of all major land transportation routes in Northeast New Jersey. The district has excellent maritime facilities in Port Elizabeth, Port Newark, and along the Arthur Kill. Newark Airport is also in the center of the district. The excellence of all of these transport facilities underlies the district's industrial prominence. The district's leading city, Newark, has been a business and manufacturing center since colonial days, and is still a headquarters of major insurance companies, financial institutions, and corporations.

Chemicals and electrical equipment and supplies are the leading industries in the district. Petroleum refining concentrated along the Arthur Kill is not a leading employer, but it provides basic materials to the district's important producers of organic chemicals, drugs, pharmaceuticals, paints and coatings. Nonferrous metal (especially copper) smelting, refining, rolling, drawing and casting is an important employer, and provides raw materials to the electrical equipment and supplies industries. The capital intensity of the industries in this district is shown in the continuing high capital expenditure in Union and Middlesex Counties, which returns as high value added per production worker.

Bergen-Passaic District

The southern portions of these two counties are most heavily industrialized; the northern and western portions, especially of Passaic County, are more rugged, and less-settled generally. Paterson, in Passaic County, was the nation's first organized industrial district. Alexander Hamilton initiated industrial settlement to tap the waterpower potential at the falls of the Passaic River.

Textiles and textile finishing industries once dominated in this District, but today the manufacture of electrical equipment, rubber and plastics products, paper and allied products, and chemicals are all important.

Hudson County District

Hudson County contains some 2,000 establishments employing almost 100,000 workers. With important port facilities, railroad termini, and as a focus of major highways, the County has experienced every stage of industrial development and progressive redevelopment. In Bayonne, for example, much of the heavy manufacturing is being replaced by lighter processing and fabricating activities. Heavily developed as the County already is, it still includes over 5,000 acres in the Hackensack Meadowland just now being developed for industrial and distribution activity.

Electrical equipment and supplies is the leading industry, the major items being communications equipment and electronic components. Apparel is the second largest industry. Food processing is also important, much of it based upon imported raw materials. Maxwell House Coffee, for instance, is roasted in Hoboken. The County's important chemical industry produces soaps, detergents, toiletries and industrial chemicals.

Suburban New Jersey

Outside these three districts, industrial settlement in the New Jersey portion of the Metropolitan Region is diffused. Important subclusters exist, such as the concentration of production of industrial chemicals, plastics and synthetics, and drugs in the Raritan Valley, but overall development is essentially suburban; the approximately 3,900 plants employ about 250,000 people.

INDUSTRY IN NEW YORK

On the New York side of the Region some 60 percent of industrial employment lies within a belt stretching fourteen miles north-south and about seven miles east-west. This belt is entirely within New York City, and subdivides into a Bronx District, a Manhattan District, and a Western Brooklyn-Western Queens District. The 25,000 plants in this belt employ about 660,000 workers.

Manhattan

About 25 percent of Manhattan employment is in manufacturing, which includes 431,500 manufacturing employees plus some 86,000 employees of Central Administrative Offices of industrial concerns. There are more industrial jobs in Manhattan than in any other county in the nation.

Actual production, however, has been moving out of the county since World War II, to be replaced by office activities. Much of the borough's industrial space, in multistory lofts, has given way to new office buildings or to apartment buildings, and industry has relocated in other boroughs or in the suburbs. The industry that has remained is closely tied to the Manhattan transaction economy. Figure 7-2 shows only about one-half of manufacturing industry employees to be production employees, a share comparable only to the shares in more suburban Westchester, Morris, and Somerset Counties.

The value of space in Manhattan dictates the

Here a technician checks the probes used in testing integrated circuits at RCA Solid State Division, Somerville, New Jersey (Somerset County). The circular mount permits a computer-controlled test machine to make many simultaneous tests on an integrated circuit: a tiny electronic device that helps operate TV sets, radios, home appliances, automobiles, medical instrumentation, and many industrial systems. Many high-technology laboratories or manufacturing plants have spread out across the more suburban counties of the New York Metropolitan Region. (Photo courtesy of RCA)

use of multistory buildings for manufacturing. In a typical loft building several industrial tenants are commingled with wholesale and retail and service establishments. About 80 percent of the borough's industrial space is in such buildings. Most occupants rent or lease space, and share a great variety of other external economies.

Manhattan's external economies attract small young firms: 70 percent of its industrial plants employ fewer than 20 persons. Thus Manhattan can be said to spawn new industries through diverse stages of initial growth.

Two industries account for 72 percent of Manhattan's manufacturing employment: apparel with 43 percent and printing and publishing with 29 percent.

The apparel industry includes the design, marketing and distribution of the industry's output as well as its manufacture. While the production of fashion apparel remains in Manhattan, the lower priced lines have moved elsewhere in the Region and beyond. Women's apparel is the preponderant element in the garment industry, but men's wear, millinery, infant's wear, apparel accessories, textile specialties, and footwear are also produced.

Of the 117,200 people employed in the printing and publishing industry, less than one-half are actually production workers in printing. The majority of workers are in editorial work and distribution phases of the industry. Art work, collation, editing, design and layout of published materials are the bases of the Manhattan industry. Manhattan prints only a fraction of the material it prepares for the press. Actual printing is significant only in commercial printing, business forms, bookbinding, services to the printing trade and publishing newspapers.

Other manufacturing industries in Manhattan cover a broad range of goods. In the production of many specialty items usually associated with a large urban area, such as instruments, jewelry, toys, sports equipment, art goods, and notions, the manufacturing is closely related to Manhattan's marketing complex.

In the future the transaction orientation of manufacturing in Manhattan will probably continue to grow, with increasing specialization and diminution of the work force in actual physical production.

Western Brooklyn—Western Queens District

This important industrial district consists of Astoria, Long Island City, Maspeth, Greenpoint, Williamsburg, the Brooklyn Navy Yard,

In this photograph we can see Brooklyn's waterfront activity around Upper New York Bay and the East River. Gowanus Bay is in the right foreground, with the Bush Terminal Piers to the right. The Gowanus Canal cuts into Brooklyn. Port Authority grain elevator piers line the left side of Gowanus Bay. The scythe-shaped breakwater defines Erie Basin; the breakwater (completed 1864) was built by ships dumping the rock they had carried as ballast from overseas ports. The Atlantic Basin farther around Brooklyn opens to the Buttermilk Channel between Brooklyn and Governors Island. The entire section of Brooklyn between Gowanus Bay and the Atlantic Basin is known as Red Hook, in the center of which can be seen the immense low-rent Hook Housing Project of the 1930s. The Brooklyn-Queens Expressway cuts off Red Hook from the rest of Brooklyn, and drivers on this Expressway can either head North or enter the Brooklyn-Battery Tunnel to Manhattan. The squat white building on the northern tip of Governors Island is an air shaft for that tunnel. The IND subway also tunnels toward downtown Brooklyn and then to Manhattan shortly after bridging the Gowanus Canal.

The three bridges across the East River linking Brooklyn and Manhattan are, in order going upriver, the Brooklyn Bridge (1883), the Manhattan Bridge (1909), and the Williamsburg Bridge (1903). The barely visible Queensborough Bridge (1909) crosses into midtown Manhattan over Roosevelt Island in the East River. Just South of the Williamsburg Bridge in Brooklyn is the Brooklyn Navy Yard, presently being redeveloped for industry.

This photograph clearly differentiates Manhattan's two concentrations of office buildings. "Downtown" is the Wall Street and financial district. "Midtown," between 34th and 59th Streets, is the concentration of corporate headquarters. (Photo courtesy of the Port Authority)

This is the Atlantic Basin along the Brooklyn waterfront. Port activity and industry in Brooklyn suffer from lack of adequate railroad linkages to the mainland, and thus freightcar ferries, as in this picture, ply between Brooklyn and the Bronx or New Jersey. (Photo courtesy of the Port Authority)

South Brooklyn and Bush Terminal, all along the East River and around Upper New York Bay. Originally waterfront activity based on imported raw materials—sugar, coffee, rubber, asphalt—spread into the backland of the docks and terminals. The banks of Newtown Creek between Brooklyn and Queens saw early industrialization, and it is estimated that that waterway today carries more freight than does the Mississippi River! Later transportation developments expanded the industrial areas: the

deepening of Gowanus Bay brought industry to South Brooklyn inland from the Upper Bay, and the Long Island and Brooklyn-Queens Expressways diffused manufacturing outward again.

With the exceptions of tobacco products and petroleum refining, all major industries are represented in this District's more than 5,000 establishments employing over 200,000 people.

About 25 percent of district workers are in apparel and textiles. The electrical equipment industry and food processing industry each employ an additional 10 percent, and about 7 percent of manufacturing workers are in the metal fabricating industry.

The Bronx

Bronx industrial development has spread inland from original concentrations along the East and Hudson Rivers. Today metal fabrication, machinery and electrical equipment account for about 26 percent of Bronx manu-

facturing jobs, and apparel absorbs another 22 percent. Total manufacturing employment is 40,000. The sorry state of the Bronx economy shows up in the low capital expenditure and the low value added per production worker.

Other Areas in New York State

Staten Island. Staten Island, New York City's fifth borough, remains suprisingly suburban. Development has been slowed by an absence of

Some 70,000 riders use the Staten Island ferry system each workday. It is about five miles from St. George on Staten Island to the ferry terminal at Manhattan's southern tip. Roundtrip fare for passengers is still only a dime, and so the service is a significant subsidy for Staten Island landowners. (Photo courtesy of the Port Authority)

The amount of telephone and other electronic equipment in the New York Region is so great that Western Electric Company operates a foundry in Nassau County. There lead and copper are reclaimed to be manufactured into new equipment. (Photo courtesy of Western Electric Company)

highway links integrating it with the Regional economy. Thus the island's industry has been limited to waterfront sites. Proctor and Gamble's waterfront plant at Port Ivory is the island's principal manufacturing enterprise, and there are petroleum and chemical establishments along Arthur Kill.

The Verrazano-Narrows Bridge, opened in 1964, and the Staten Island Expressway have overcome the island's principal transport problem, and now Staten Island, with major tracts of undeveloped land, is the site of both industrial and residential development.

Long Island. On Long Island beyond the New York City Industrial Districts a string of some

8,000 plants employing about 310,000 workers stretches through Brooklyn, Queens, and Nassau Counties into western Suffolk County. Historically, industry settled along the route of the Long Island Railroad, following the population east. More recently the Long Island Expressway has opened new areas to industrial settlement. Industrial settlement is not, however, continuous, but there are important industrial clusters. These include College Point and Jamaica in Queens, and Fort Green and East Flatbush in Brooklyn. Major industrial concentrations in Nassau are focused around Roosevelt Field in central Nassau.

Light industry predominates on Long Island.

The two major industries are apparel and transportation equipment, the former concentrated in Queens and Brooklyn, and the latter in Nassau and Suffolk. The transportation equipment industries are part of the important aerospace complex, which also absorbs a great share of the large electrical equipment and instruments industries. This total complex constitutes an impressive array of advanced technology production, and various companies in the District have recently turned their attention to such continuing growth industries as environmental monitoring and control, health and medical equipment, and learning aids. Cutbacks in federal space and defense expenditures are evident in Nassau County's decline in value added by manufacturing 1967-72. Suffolk County farther out Long Island, by contrast, showed continuing manufacturing growth.

Westchester and Rockland. The rugged topography of much of Westchester and Rockland Counties is key to understanding their industrial settlement patterns. The oldest established industrial sites are along the Hudson River, in Yonkers and Tarrytown. In the inland portions of Westchester County there are concentrations of light industry along the north-south valleys of the Saw Mill, Bronx, and Hutchinson Rivers. Westchester accounts for over 80 percent of manufacturing employment in the two counties; industrial settlement in Rockland County is confined to the County's southeast (*vide* the County's name). Leading industries are electrical goods and equipment, chemicals and drugs.

Settlement of central offices and laboratories of large manufacturing corporations are increasingly important, especially in Westchester, as a result of that county's close economic linkage with New York City and its early residential settlement by upper class and corporate elite. General Foods, IBM, and Pepsico, to name just three large corporations, are all headquartered in Westchester, in White Plains, Armonk, and Purchase, respectively. The office-laboratory function will probably expand in Rockland County too.

New York as a Transport Hub

Much of New York's prosperity has long been due to the excellence of its port and its connections to the continental interior. The port offers sheltered harbors, 45-foot depth in all main channels, a tidal range of only four and one-half feet, ice-free waters year round seldom hampered by fog, and miles of low-lying waterfront at the mouth of the second longest navigable river on the east coast of the continent. The route to the continental interior up the Hudson River and then west along the Mohawk provided a natural highway exploited first by the Erie Canal (opened in 1825) and then followed by the New York Central Railroad—the famous "sea level route." The lowland corridor gave New York an advantage over the other ports of the eastern seaboard, cut off from the interior by the Appalachian Mountains.

Still today New York is the nation's leading port, and port activities are important to the Regional economy. The port is served by 54 airlines, 15 railroads, 421 certified motor carriers, and 184 steamship lines, which can take anything or anyone anywhere, or bring any product or anyone to New York. Almost one-third by value of total United States waterborne commerce passes through the Port of New York, and New York's airports handle more than one-half of all United States air imports and exports. In the 1974 fiscal year New York customs duty receipts on imports by ship and air were 1.3 billion dollars, about one-third the national total, and more than three times those of Los Angeles, the next busiest port of entry. The port activity goes hand in hand with the Region's role as an important wholesaling center.

THE PORT AUTHORITY

Most important Regional port facilities are operated by the Port Authority of New York and New Jersey. Before creation of this special bi-state commission, New York and New Jersey had long quarreled over Regional port matters: boat licensing on the Hudson River, the exact location of their border in the Hudson, waste disposal, and competitive shipping rates. Already in 1917, however, the Interstate Commerce Commission noted that "historically, geographically, and commercially, New York and the industrial district in the northern part of the State of New Jersey constitute a single community." In that year the Commission charged the two states to study ways of better coordinating port activities, a need clearly demonstrated when traffic through the port was especially heavy during World War I.

Finally in 1921, upon the recommendation of a bi-state Joint Commission, New York and New Jersey created a public, self-supporting corporation known until 1972 as the Port of New York Authority, and since then called the Port Authority of New York and New Jersey. The Port Authority district radiates approximately twenty-five miles out from the Statue of Liberty, encompassing about 1,500 square miles with 750 miles of water frontage. The district includes 18 counties and almost 250 municipalities to which the Authority need not pay property taxes, but with which it cooperates closely. The Authority's responsibilities are to buy, build, lease and operate transportation or terminal facilities and other facilities of commerce within the district (Fig. 8-2); to promote the commerce of the port; to recommend helpful legislation to the state governments; and to petition governmental regulatory agencies at all levels. Port Authority facilities also play an important role in internal movement within the Region, discussed below.

The Port Authority has no taxing power of its own, nor can it pledge the credit of either state. Its income derives from charges on the use of its facilities, from borrowing on its own credit, and from its own bonds. Twelve unpaid commissioners serving overlapping six year terms oversee the Authority's operations, and they hire an Executive Director. Six commissioners are appointed by the governor of each state and approved by the respective state senates. The Commission reports to the state governors, either of whom can veto any Port Authority action, and any major new project requires bi-state legislative approval. The Port Authority maintains commercial offices in Chicago, Washington, Cleveland, Pittsburgh, San Juan, Tokyo, London and Zurich.

SHIPPING

Most Port shipping activity has shifted from Manhattan to other areas along Upper New York Bay and Newark Bay. The increasingly high rents in Manhattan and the problems of congestion drove pier activity away from the island, which is today fringed by mile after mile of abandoned piers. Only passenger ships regularly dock in Manhattan, but the great days of passenger shipping are over. Few passenger ships still ply the North Atlantic, and New York is second to Southern Florida as an origin of passenger cruises. Most cruisers would rather fly to Florida and spend their cruise days in the balmy Caribbean than cruise out of New York. Nevertheless, at the request of the City of New York, the Port Authority did open in November 1974 a new passenger ship terminal between 48th and 52nd streets on Manhattan's West Side. This terminal offers six new berths, and a remodeled Pier 40 at the west end of Houston Street to the south offers three additional berths.

The City is also currently developing commercial piers at the Hunts Point Deepwater Cargo Facility in the Bronx. That project, including a refrigerated warehouse, a new 1,700-foot pier and other development, hopes to capture about sixty-five percent of the nation's meat imports.

Newark Bay

The major development of Newark Bay since World War II demonstrates the importance to shippers of intermodal freight transfer facilities. In one 20 square mile area in Newark and Elizabeth, New Jersey, seaport, airport, railroad and highway facilities combine to provide unequalled convenience for smooth coordination of land, sea and air transport. The New Jersey

In the foreground here is New York's new passenger ship terminal at the West end of 48th Street in Manhattan. The facility, opened in November 1974, is owned and operated by the Port Authority.

The West Side Highway defines the shoreline. The grey, balconied skyscraper just a few blocks inland is a new public housing project, built by the City with a Federal interest-subsidy. To its right the white building without windows is ATT's long lines building. Between these two and beyond them the tallest skyscraper visible is the Gulf and Western Corporation's international headquarters at 59th Street and Central Park West. The huge dark square building in the far left distance is the Annenberg Building of the Mount Sinai Medical Center at 101st Street and 5th Avenue. (Photo courtesy of the Port Authority)

Even with the many excellent facilities in the port, ships must occasionally wait for berths, as these ships are waiting in the Narrows. The Verrazano-Narrows Bridge is in the background. In the far right distance the Navesink or Atlantic Highlands in Monmouth County reach out into the Atlantic. (Photo courtesy of the Port Authority)

Port Elizabeth is to the left, Port Newark to the right of the Channel in the center of the picture. Newark Airport is in the near background. Downtown Newark is in the right middle distance, and the north-south Watchung Mountain Range defines the horizon. Portions of this low mountain range in Middlesex, Union, and Essex counties have been set aside as public space: Watchung Reservation just to the South, on the left, South Mountain Reservation just about in the center of this photograph, and Eagle Rock Reservation farther north, to the right. (Photo courtesy of the Port Authority)

complex was never planned as such, but developed largely because Newark Bay provided both deep water for ocean ships and wetlands that could be reclaimed to provide acreage for new projects. The reclaimed land made possible both airport expansion and vast shore-based shipping facilities. There has never been an overall plan for developing the area, and even now there is no integrated plan for future growth. Interagency committees must coordinate the projects of the Port Authority, the New Jersey Turnpike Authority, the New Jersey Transportation Department, and the United States Bureau of Public Roads. All of these, plus

This picture shows the variety of transportation services on the west side of Newark Bay, which is on the bottom of the photo. The Elizabeth Port Authority Terminal area, covering the bottom left quarter of the photo, provides shipping services and offers freight and container storage and inter-modal transport facilities. The peninsular terminal area in the right center is Port Newark, with equivalent facilities. Some of the facilities to the right of Port Newark are U.S. Naval Reserve properties. Top center is Newark Airport's new terminal, with the old small airport to the right of that. The major north-south highway, from right to left through the center of the picture, is the New Jersey Turnpike (I95).

The highway along the right edge is Interstate 78. At the top cloverleaf it meets New Jersey highway 19; at the exchange below that intersects the New Jersey Turnpike, and then as the New Jersey Turnpike Extension, it crosses Newark Bay to Jersey City, eventually leading to the Holland Tunnel into Manhattan. Railroad lines lace all of these facilities. In few places in the world are such elaborate air, sea, highway, and rail services so mutually convenient, or are they coordinated so well. (Photo courtesy of the Port Authority)

The City of Newark, in the background here, did not develop Port Newark to the port's capacity. Large-scale development began only after Port Authority assumption of responsibility in 1948. Note the Japanese flag flying from the ship in the lower right corner. (Photo courtesy of the Port Authority)

several local agencies, exercise jurisdiction in the area.

Railroad freightyards actually developed the area first, and today the Penn Central and three smaller lines still operate major yards and storage facilities there. The railroad tracks come right up to the wharves and provide direct rail service to all of the Northeast, to the Midwest, and into the South.

The City of Newark established Port Newark in 1915 and the Newark airport in 1928, but the real impetus for growth came when the Port Authority leased both of these facilities in 1948. Since then the Port Authority has poured literally hundreds of millions of dollars into improvements.

The Elizabeth shipping terminals are especially significant as the world's largest containerport. Containerized shipping was first introduced in the early 1950s, when shipping companies began transporting what were basically truck-trailers on ocean-going vessels. The transportation of such large containers sealed from the shipper to the recipient, no matter how many freight transfers the shipment experienced, allowed for better packing at the shipper's plant, it reduced pilferage, and the mechanization of dealing with containers cut the time and cost of cargo handling. The Port Authority foresaw an inevitable revolution in shipping, and began to dredge the Elizabeth Channel and to prepare facilities for container handling. Containers and container-handling equipment have been improved steadily. In the 1950s it took six longshore gangs five days to load or unload a conventional 10,000 ton ship, but today 1,500 containers, each holding ten tons of cargo, can be loaded or unloaded in 24 hours. About 70 percent of the general cargo trade of the Port is now in containers. Container handling facilities can be found at Howland Hook on Staten Island, at Port Jersey in the Bayonne-Jersey City area, at Port Seatrain at Weehawken, and along the Brooklyn waterfront, where a new containerport is scheduled for opening in the Red Hook section in 1977.

This photograph reverses the view of the photograph on page 150. Newark Airport dominates the foreground, separated from Port Newark and Port Elizabeth by railroad lines and the New Jersey Turnpike. The New Jersey Turnpike Extension bridges Newark Bay, and across the Bay we can see Bayonne to the right and Jersey City to the left. Still farther away across the Hudson River lies Manhattan, and in the upper right corner, across Upper New York Bay, Brooklyn is just visible. (Photo courtesy of the Port Authority)

Giant cranes such as these at Port Elizabeth roll up and down the dock easily transferring containers from their truck chassis onto containerships. The sealed container never need be opened during the transport mode transfer, or indeed, ever between shipper and recipient. (Photo courtesy of the Port Authority)

The Port Newark and Elizabeth terminals, however, today handle 60 percent of total port tonnage.

In addition to excellent rail, air and ship facilities, the highway network around Newark Bay provides easy vehicle access. In 1952 the 118-mile New Jersey Turnpike was opened. Originally six lanes wide through the Newark-Elizabeth area, the turnpike divides into two separate six lane routes, one leading to the Lincoln Tunnel to midtown Manhattan, the other to the uptown George Washington Bridge. A six lane extension leads to the Holland Tunnel to downtown Manhattan. These bridges and tunnels are Port Authority projects. United States Highways 1 and 9, State Route 22, and the new Interstate 78 also enhance accessibility.

Container Rates

The Port's preeminence in containerized shipping can be sabotaged by the way railroads set freight rates moving between New York and the continental interior. Railroads historically tended to keep the ports they serve competitive in the handling of import-export cargo. Port equalizations or specific differential relationships have existed on rail traffic since the 1870s. Thus rates on most import-export traffic in conventional railroad equipment between Chicago, on the one hand, and eastern and southern ports are equal or only slightly different at all ports between Montreal and Brownsville, Texas, although distances vary substantially. These practices are upheld in the important Rail Rate Equalization Case which, after seven years of litigation, was decided by the Supreme Court in 1963.

Rates for carrying truck-trailers on flatcars,

known as "piggy-backing," were established in the 1950s before international containerization. These rates were based on mileage scales, in order to be competitive with trucking. With the development of containers, the railroads insisted that they receive containers as trailers, and the railroads applied mileage rates as on truck trailers. The application of mileage rates to containers, rather than the equalized rates as on conventional rail equipment, would tend to concentrate rail traffic to and from the Midwest through a few ports favored by mileage advantages. Obviously, New York's investment in container facilities and its competitive position would be enhanced if the railroads would

This high altitude photograph of La Guardia Airport in Queens shows its construction on landfill into Bowery Bay to the left, the East River to the top, and Flushing Bay to the right. The airport was built by the City between 1937 and 1939, but today it is operated by the Port Authority. Grand Central Parkway passes the airport. Shea Stadium is just off the picture's lower right-hand corner. The upper left corner shows Rikers Island, site of the city prison. (Photo courtesy of the Port Authority)

This photograph shows a portion of John F. Kennedy International Airport, looking almost directly east. United Airlines terminal dominates the foreground. In the middle distance we see the three chapels: Roman Catholic, Protestant, and Jewish. The long building with the arched central pavilion and the control tower behind the chapels is the International Arrivals Building. The seemingly winged building to the left is Eero Saarinen's Trans World Airlines Terminal, and the round canopied building in the upper right corner is Pan American Airways' building. (Photo courtesy of the Port Authority)

change their freight rate structures for containers.

AIRPORTS

The Port Authority assumed responsibility for major Regional airports in 1947. La Guardia Airport, built by the City in 1939, today handles most domestic passenger movement (Fig. 8-3). John F. Kennedy Airport handles more total domestic and international passengers than La Guardia, and is also the world's largest air cargo center. The more than one million tons of cargo moved there by over fifty cargo airlines represents about one-quarter of total United States air cargo shipments and more than one-half of United States air cargo imports and exports. Newark Airport, the Region's third major terminal, has seen tremendous expansion in the past few years—to two and one-half times its 1970 capacity. Both passenger and cargo movements are increasing at Newark.

The Port Authority bought Teterboro Airport in 1949, and that facility sees about 270,000 landings and take-offs of business, training, and personal flights per year. Pan American Airways operates Teterboro for the Port Authority. The Port Authority also operates two heliports in Manhattan, one on West 30th Street and one downtown in the financial district.

Here looking to the west we see over the chapels to the United Airlines and Delta Airlines facilities. The stained glass facade of the American Airlines Terminal is the largest in the world. Manhattan looms in the distance. (Photo courtesy of the Port Authority)

This high-altitude photograph of Kennedy Airport shows how the airport encroaches Jamaica Bay on landfill. Brookville Park, the darker, obviously undeveloped area here to the right above the airport, actually on its northeast edge, is also in Queens County in New York City, but all visible land to the east of the small lake, is in Nassau County. The carefully planned but irregularly patterned housing development on landfill in the top right corner, in Nassau, is obviously newer than the housing in Queens in the top left. Aqueduct Horse Race Track can be seen at the left edge of the picture. The Southern Parkway cuts through the picture from left center to top center, and Van Wyck Expressway intersects the Parkway to continue into the airport. The Van Wyck Expressway crosses Queens almost directly to La Guardia Airport. (Photo courtesy of the Port Authority)

This is the central terminal area of John F. Kennedy International Airport. The airport was built between 1941 and 1948, but has expanded its facilities and terminals continually since then. (Photo courtesy of the Port Authority)

THE WORLD TRADE CENTER

Undoubtedly the most spectacular of the Port Authority's projects is the World Trade Center on Manhattan's lower West Side. This building complex was designed to bring together in one place all the information and services needed by those engaged in international trade—exporters, importers, American and foreign manufacturers, freight forwarders, Custom House brokers, international banks, federal, state and overseas trade development agencies,

trade associations, and transportation lines. Six buildings are included in the sixteen-acre complex: twin 110-story office towers, two low-rise office buildings, a new United States Customs Building, and an as yet incompleted hotel. The total office space in these buildings is over nine million square feet, more than in all of downtown St. Louis in 1970. The World Trade Center was begun in 1962, and the Center's first tenants moved in in 1970. Due to weakness in the office market at the time, however, the State of New York occupied a number of Trade

The twin towers of the World Trade Center dominate the downtown westside skyline. The Woolworth Building's Gothic tower is to the left of the World Trade Center. To the right one can identify the big black box of the U.S. Steel Company; the tall thin black box behind that is Marine Midland Bank, and the taller grey box behind that is Chase Manhattan Bank. The next spire to the right is the Bank of Manhattan Company. (Photo courtesy of the Port Authority)

In this photograph, taken in July 1973, the twin 110-story towers of the World Trade Center have just been topped. The 23 acre landfill in the Hudson River behind them was earth dug out for the towers' foundations. This landfill area, deeded to the City, will become Battery Park City. In the middle distance across the Hudson we see Jersey City and Bayonne, with Newark Bay in the far distance. The Avenue visible in the foreground is Broadway, almost hidden along which is St. Paul's Chapel (1766), New York's only existing Pre-Revolutionary Building. It was designed by Thomas McBean, after his teacher James Gibbs' St. Martins's-in-the-Fields in London. The building in the foreground with the Gothic crown is architect Cass Gilbert's Woolworth Building (1913). (Photo courtesy of the Port Authority)

Center offices. It is hoped that the State will gradually be replaced with commercial tenants.

Originally the Port Authority favored an East Side location for the complex. When the New York and New Jersey legislatures approved the project in 1962, however, they linked its construction to the simultaneous purchase and modernization by the Port Authority of the bankrupt Hudson and Manhattan Railroad, which came under the Hudson River from New Jersey into Manhattan's lower West Side. Thus the West Side site was selected for the Trade Center, and the commuter railroad, modernized and renamed the Port Authority Trans-Hudson System (PATH) links the Center with commuter rail lines in New Jersey.

The more than 1.2 million cubic yards of earth and rock excavated for the Center was placed in the Hudson River to create 23.5 acres of new land on the lower West Side. This new land was deeded to the City, and it will ultimately become part of the Battery Park City housing project.

FREIGHT MOVEMENT

While the total amounts of freight moving in and out of the Region are enormous, the amount of freight moved per person per year is actually below the national average. Relevant figures are published by the Tri-State Planning Commission. The national average for both originated and terminated intercity freight is 27 tons per capita per year. For the Tri-State New York Metropolitan Region, however, the annual figures are about 11 tons per capita per year inbound and 5 tons outbound.

Two reasons help explain this relatively small bulk of freight movement in and out of the Region. One is that the specialized transportation, communication, finance and service industries of the Region generate little freight. Secondly, much of the Region's manufacturing is relatively light—apparel, light machinery, instruments and printing. These consume relatively little fuel and relatively low-weight raw materials, and their output, while of low bulk, is of high value. This is confirmed by the fact that 52 percent of the Region's outbound intercity tonnage moves by truck, contrasted to only 45 percent for the nation as a whole.

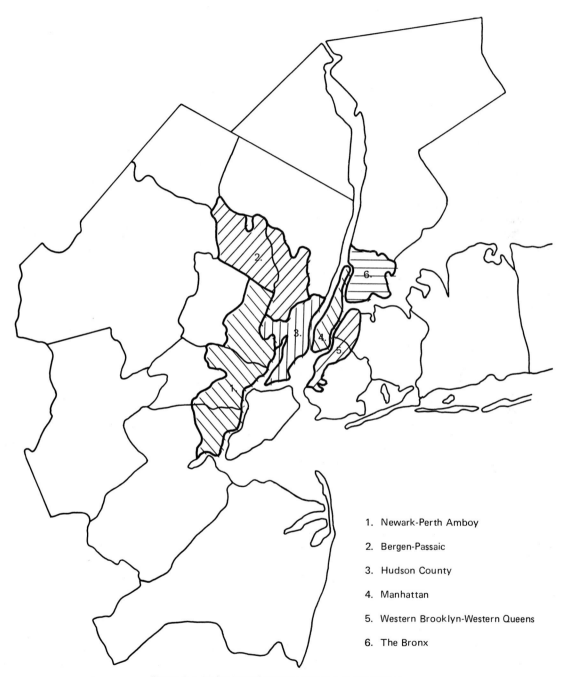

1. Newark-Perth Amboy

2. Bergen-Passaic

3. Hudson County

4. Manhattan

5. Western Brooklyn-Western Queens

6. The Bronx

Figure 8-1. Major Manufacturing Districts in the Region.

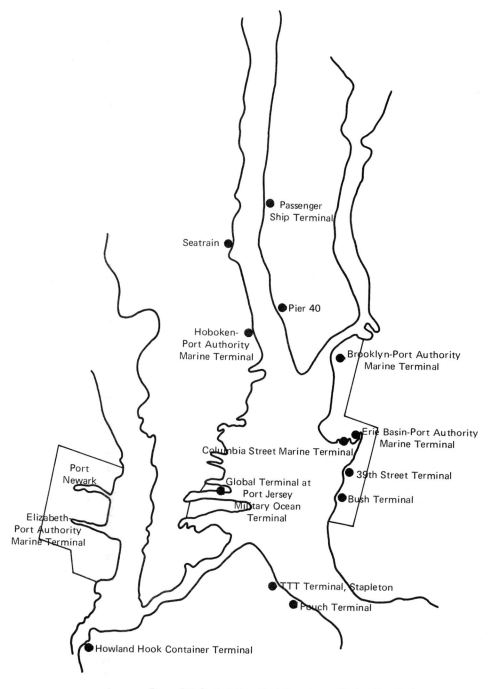

Figure 8-2. Port of New York-New Jersey Harbor Terminals.

Activity at Major Regional Airports (1973)

	Total	J.F. Kennedy	LaGuardia	Newark
Plane Movements	872,000	346,000	320,000	206,000
Passenger Traffic	42.252 million	21.389 million	14.028 million	6.835 million
Domestic	30.830 million	9.967 million	14.028 million	6.835 million
International	11.422 million	11.422 million	—	—
Tons of Cargo	1.236 million	1.011 million	.62 million	.163 million

Marine Activity (1972)

Vessel Arrivals

Passenger Ships	464
Tankers (Coastwise and Intercoastal)	2,891
All other	5,992
Total	9,347

Foreign Trade (Long Tons)

	Exports	Imports	Total
General Cargo	4,810,117	10,073,313	14,883,430
Bulk Cargo	829,615	44,821,734	45,651,349
Total	5,639,732	54,895,047	60,534,779

Figure 8-3.

Chapter Nine

THE ECONOMY
OF NEW YORK CITY

In 1970 the City of New York counted a resident civilian labor force of 3.3 million. An additional 617,000 workers commuted into the City—about 19 percent of all workers employed there—and three-fifths of these commuted from Nassau, Suffolk, Westchester, Rockland, or Putnam Counties. New Jersey sent 207,000 commuters, and Connecticut sent 23,000. Some 170,000 workers live in the City but commuted to jobs out of the City.

Industry Groups

In 1970 the service industries employed the greatest proportion of the City's resident jobholders, for the first time outranking manufacturing, the largest employer in 1960 (Fig. 9-1). The concentration of service industries is especially great in Manhattan, and so is the concentration of service industry workers. Over 40 percent of the borough's working residents hold jobs in service industries. Because these statistics record residence of jobholder, some confusion is inevitable between where certain sorts of jobs are, and where people who hold those jobs live. This confusion must be kept in mind when reading the statistics, but reduced somewhat by the fact that most people prefer to live near their jobs and interpreted in the light of what we know about journeys to work within the Region as a whole.

Manufacturing industries remained the second largest source of employment in New York City, accounting for about 21 percent of working residents. Brooklyn had the highest percentage of its residents working in manufacturing, about 23 percent, and Staten Island the lowest, only 14 percent.

Wholesale and retail trade employ almost one-fifth of New York's resident labor force. Retail trade claims by far the larger share of these workers, but the relatively high five percent of workers in wholesale trade emphasizes the City's role as a major distribution point for foreign and domestic trade. We noted earlier the external economies of concentrating wholesalers for visits from out-of-town buyers, who visit the City in the tens of thousands each year.

New York's prominence as a money capital is demonstrated by the 11 percent of the labor force in finance, insurance, and real estate. This is more than double the ratio for the nation as a whole. Transportation, communications, and utilities are also clustered in this economic center, employing about 10 percent of City residents, compared to seven percent of the national labor force.

THE DECLINE OF MANUFACTURING

Manufacturing industries have declined not only relative to the service industries in the City, but in actual numbers of jobs offered. The numbers of jobs in manufacturing have declined steadily since the early 1950s, when manufacturing employment peaked at 1,066,000 jobs. Most

of these jobs being lost are blue collar produc
tion jobs.

Reasons

Many factors, some already outlined, explain
the City's loss of manufacturing jobs. Traffic
congestion, particularly in Manhattan, raises
transportation costs. Manufacturing necessitates trucking facilities, and only industrial
parks in the outer boroughs can guarantee
easy highway access.

Secondly, energy costs can run two to three
times as high in New York City as elsewhere
(Fig. 9-2). Thirdly, large tracts of horizontal factory space are hard to find and even harder to
develop. Rents and taxes may be insupportable.

The types of manufacturing jobs found in the
City also affect employment trends. It is unlikely
that the City can advance in industries that are
declining nationally. Most of the nation's
growth in manufacturing is in durable goods;
most growth in manufacturing even in the New
York Region is durable goods. Durable goods
manufacturing is, however, least well
represented in the City itself. In 1973 the nation
as a whole had 11 million jobs in durable
manufacturing and 8 million in nondurables,
while in New York City the proportions are
reversed. Of the City's 658,000 manufacturing
jobs in 1973, 509,000 were nondurable and only
149,000 were in durables. The United States has
been buying more soft goods abroad, where
cheaper labor is an important saving. The dollar
devaluations of 1971 and 1973, plus the higher
inflation rates abroad have diminished this
foreign advantage, but it will probably continue
to be significant for several years.

Even compared with national average wage
scales, however, New York's are high. In apparel, the City's largest single manufacturing
industry, average hourly earnings in 1973 were
$3.46 in New York, compared with $2.61 nationally. In printing and publishing, the City's
second industry, the New York average rate was
$6.47 per hour; the national rate was $4.48. In
food processing the averages were $4.46 in New

York and $3.60 nationally. These three in-
dustries account for more than one-half of City
manufacturing employment. The higher wage
scales may reflect higher labor skills or productivity, or economies achieved in other costs connected with manufacturing in New York, such
as external economies. The promise of finding
cheaper labor elsewhere, however, has
undeniably lured many manufacturers out of the
City.

As listed above, the variety and level of taxes
levied in New York City are still additional factors discouraging the New York City industrialist.

The Garment Industry. The garment industry, New York City's leading industry,
typifies industries which rely on external
economies. It is competitive, uncertain, easy to
enter, low-capitalized, seasonal, fashion
oriented, and technologically sluggish. The
changeability of fashion dictates that energy is
spent in marketing, not in innovation in production methods.

New York seized the lead in the national garment industry in the mid-19th century, when
the invention of the sewing machine heralded
the replacement of custom clothing by ready-
made clothing. New York also had a near
monopoly on the importation of textiles from
1840 to 1860, when textiles constituted about
one-third of total United States imports. The
New York garment industry was launched with
the manufacture of sailors' uniforms, and expanded when producing military uniforms during the Civil War. The massive foreign immigration to New York in the mid and late 19th
century provided a low-wage but skilled labor
force for the mushrooming apparel industry,
and New York's lead in wholesaling acted as a
magnet for buyers from around the country. The
importance of external economies, as well as
bargaining and gossiping about fashion trends,
dictated extraordinary concentration of the industry. Manhattan's garment district lies between 34th and 41st Streets and 6th and 8th
Avenues. Seventh Avenue through the district
bears the official name Fashion Avenue.

Today the garment industry is suffering hard times. There is both a relative change in demand for New York's products, and a slip in New York's cost position. The trend toward suburban life and casual and sports clothes has weakened New York's fashion image and benefited the garment industries in southern and western centers such as Miami, Dallas, and Los Angeles.

Obsolescence of many important plant structures in Manhattan's garment district, truck congestion in the streets, and the City's high labor costs combine to drive out the industry. Particularly standardized clothing items are, as we have seen, abandoning the City for cheap labor areas in the American South or even abroad. Item 807 of the United States tariff schedule allows a manufacturer to begin production of an item here, ship the goods abroad for completion, and return them here for sale. This has allowed manufacturers to employ Latin American and Asian labor for pennies per hour. In 1961 only six percent of the clothing worn in the United States was imported, but by 1974 that figure had run to about 25 percent.

Thus jobs for New Yorkers are disappearing. In the six years from 1966 to 1972 the number of companies in women's and children's apparel fell from 8,683 to 6,415, and the number of employees from 238,000 to 182,000. Even in menswear, historically concentrated not in New York but in Rochester and Philadelphia, New York saw a decline in jobs from 42,000 in 1966 to 35,000 in 1972. The total number of 208,600 apparel, textile, and knitgoods workers in the City in 1974 was down 68,000 from just ten years earlier.

Printing and Publishing. Printing and publishing is the second largest industry in New York City. Job printing and newspaper printing and publishing is everywhere a local enterprise, although there are uncommonly large local markets for both in the New York Region. The City, however, also claims the concentration of national market printing and publishing of periodicals and books.

Nation-wide magazines developed after the Civil War, when the national transport system was sufficiently developed to allow national marketing and advertising; at the same time the cost of paper declined, popular magazines appeared, and magazines came to be financed by advertisers rather than subscribers. New York then offered and still offers not only a huge local market, but also all the external economies for national magazine publication. In New York are clustered the research facilities, libraries, subcontractors to supply photographs and pictures, artists, mailing lists, literary agents, cartoonists, intellectuals, and writers. New York is the center of news sources: financial, theatrical, musical, diplomatic, fashion, art, and of the foundations; and in New York are concentrated the advertisers and advertising agencies.

While magazine preparation and publishing are in New York, the actual printing has been moving out since World War I. The printing is a standardized procedure, and time and cost advantages in national distribution can be achieved from the Midwest. *Time* magazine, for instance, is written and edited in New York, but printed and distributed from Chicago.

Nontrade specialized books (e.g., religious, legal, medical) are published all over the United States, but the publication of trade books is concentrated in New York for reasons of the same external economies as periodical publishing is concentrated in the City.

Printing costs in New York are very high, but much printing remains in the City. This is because of high local consumption, because some printing jobs require frequent consultation with the officers of a corporation, law firm or so forth, or because the printing must be done to meet deadlines, as do many financial or legal papers. Long-run printing for the national market has generally moved away from the City.

Stopping the Losses

Many suggestions have been offered to staunch the City's loss of manufacturing jobs, but few of them in fact respond directly to the list of problems. Certainly the Traffic Bureau does what it can to ease congestion, and air quality preservation may dictate substantial thinning of vehicular traffic in Manhattan.

Manufacturers and real estate interests have suggested eliminating the tax on rents paid by manufacturing tenants, eliminating the City's corporate income tax, reducing the State corporation franchise tax, and freezing real estate taxes on manufacturing buildings.

The City's Economic Development Administration has been working to create four new industrial parks within the City, as well as nine industrial renewal areas and ten vest-pocket industrial projects (Fig. 9-3). Each would have plenty of space for horizontal manufacturing, plus good accessibility. The principal industrial parks include the ninety-six acre Flatlands Industrial Park in Brooklyn and the 265-acre College Point Park in Queens, which is convenient to the Flushing Airport. The 265-acre Brooklyn Navy Yard has excellent waterfront and rail facilities, but industrial park development is encumbered with obsolete buildings inherited from the Navy. Land for the fourth industrial park, near Fresh Kills on the far West side of Staten Island, is still being assembled. Development of a 700-acre industrial park and general aviation airport there await some resolution of the City's continuing present need for the site as a solid waste dump. A possible fifth major new industrial park may develop on the present 100-acre site of the Penn Central Railroad's Harlem River yards at the southern tip of the Bronx. This site offers excellent rail, ship, and highway connections in a job-starved part of the City, and the City government is negotiating purchase of the land from the railroad. Still other "surplus" railroad freightyards, such as several Penn Central properties along the Hudson River in Manhattan, may see development as industrial or residential-commercial properties.

Mayor Beame has suggested the physical renaissance of the garment industry by expansion to the West from its present concentration to the forty square blocks between 30th and 40th Streets, 8th and 12th Avenues. There existing loft buildings could be renovated or new facilities built. The State has created for the City an Industrial Development Agency, which enables the City to issue tax-exempt bonds to build or buy new factories and to offer tax abatements to private developers of industrial facilities.

Occupation Groups

An analysis of New York City occupational groups underlines the economic threat of a continuing loss of manufacturing industries. The City's leading occupational classification is clerical worker, some 27 percent of City workers. Professional and technical workers rank second, with 16 percent. Both of these categories are more important to the City than to the nation as a whole, where they account for 18 percent and 15 percent, respectively. Professional and technical employees are concentrated in Manhattan; one quarter of the borough's working residents hold such jobs.

The fourth largest occupational category is service worker, representing about 14 percent of the City's employed. The third and fifth ranking occupational groups in the City, operatives and craftsmen, are mostly employed in manufacturing. These two groups number 15 percent and 10 percent of total City employed.

These figures portray the economy of the City as predominantly white collar. Almost 60 percent of the jobs it offers are in professional, managerial, clerical, and sales positions. New jobs being created in the City are also mostly white collar. Fewer jobs in service occupations are opening, and blue collar jobs are in fact declining. All projections until at least 1985 indicate that employment in the City will grow slowly, but that white collar jobs will come to dominate the City's economy even more.

This imposes upon the City the special problem of bringing into its economy its large and growing population of poor blacks, Puerto Ricans, and other minorities. These groups are the fastest growing part of the City's population, making up 13 percent in 1970. From 1950-70 the City's white population declined by 1.5 million, while blacks, Puerto Ricans, and other minorities increased by 1.6 million. Assuming only marginal growth of the City's total resident labor force, and assuming continuing outmigration of whites, then blacks, Puerto Ricans and other minorities will total 46 percent of the City's resident labor force by 1985, compared to only 28 percent in 1968.

Traditionally factory work, which can be learned on the job, has been the path of upward mobility for such groups. Today, therefore, with factory work leaving the City, the skills of the City's resident labor force are lagging behind the needs of the City's economy. Only 52 percent of resident workers have white collar occupations, and recent increases in white collar skills among resident workers have been less than one-quarter of the increases in white collar jobs. Even the increases in simpler service skills among City resident workers have been less than one-fifth of the increases in new jobs in this category. The deficits have been filled by the virtual elimination of unemployment in white collar and service occupations, by increased double jobholding, and by commuters from the suburbs.

Whether City residents can capture the new white collar or service job opportunities in the City depends largely upon the upgrading of skills among City residents. Improved job placement programs organized at the Regional level could perhaps find some suburban jobs for City residents, but the City's disadvantaged are closed out of most suburban jobs by the lack of low income housing in the suburbs and by the high cost of commuting out of the City. Thus for the vast majority of City residents, opportunities for employment are and will remain within the City. Advancement of the City's lesser-skilled residents is most probable in jobs that can be entered without extensive formal schooling, that are expected to increase in numbers, and that are presently filled at least partly by commuters. These categories include clerical, service, and skilled blue collar jobs. If City residents can claim these jobs, it would at least shift some of the burden of Regional unemployment which now falls unfairly on the City.

Lesser-skilled white collar clerical and sales positions account for about one-half of City white collar jobs. The number of such jobs is increasing, and the excess of jobs over resident workers in these categories is about 150,000. The location of these jobs—particularly the clerical ones—is highly concentrated. About 40 percent of all clerical jobs in the SCA are in the Manhattan Central Business District, and 60 percent in a wider area drawing in the rest of Manhattan, the East River industrial band, downtown Brooklyn, and Newark.

Service jobs, too, are increasing, and the present excess of jobs over resident workers in the City is about 70,000. Some 40 percent of service jobs in the SCA are in the Manhattan CBD and 60 percent can be found by including central Brooklyn, the Bronx, and Queens.

The number of skilled blue collar jobs in the City is expected to decline, but at present the excess of jobs over resident workers is substantial, and many of these jobs are held by commuters. These job opportunities are quite dispersed. The area including the top 40 percent of these jobs includes not only the Manhattan CBD and vicinity, but also clusters in Harlem and in the South Bronx, in Long Island City and Corona-Flushing, a large area from Greenpoint to Bush Terminal in Brooklyn, and several small clusters in Bergen, Hudson, Nassau, and Westchester Counties.

The Office Industry

Many of the white collar jobs which so dominate New York City's economy stem from the City's role as *the* great corporate and financial center. New York City has 17.6 office occupations for each 100 people in the City's total population, a figure exceeded among United States cities only by Washington, D.C., with 20.4. The United States as a whole has 10.7. The concentration of offices in the Manhattan

Central Business District has led many to refer simply to the "Manhattan Office Industry." In fact, of course, Manhattan's white collar army is employed in offices of all the formally defined "industry groups": offices of manufacturing companies, wholesale and retail traders, service industries, finance, insurance and real estate, public administration, etc. As Figure 9-4 illustrates, the amount of office space in Downtown New York (the Central Business District) is greater than the amount of office space in the following six ranking cities combined.

We have already examined the great printing and publishing complex in New York City, but we must now take a closer look at New York's role as the nation's financial and corporate capital.

FINANCE CAPITAL

Philadelphia was the first economic capital of the United States, but financial activities migrated to New York as the City seized commercial preeminence. Today New York is unquestionably the nation's chief money market,

The American Stock Exchange is the country's largest securities market and the leading exchange for foreign securities. (Photo courtesy of the New York Convention and Visitors Bureau)

the term which covers the markets for securities, commercial paper, banks' acceptances, call money, federal funds, government securities, fiduciary services, and a vast array of other financial activities.

In the money industry external economies and the necessity for quick knowledge dictate clustering, and history has given New York the lead. All professionals in the money markets are attuned to a common market of facts—and hunches and surmises—on the basis of which financial commitments are made or avoided. The course of inflation or deflation, the fiscal and monetary policies of governments, the strengths of individual corporations, and public moods—all of these factors both domestic and foreign—are critical to the national and international economy. The actual business of financial transactions is increasingly recorded in computers and exchanged among computers, but vast quantities of paper still must physically move, and the work requires armies of clerks, stenographers, and messengers, all clustered around the real decision-makers, who probably number in fact no more than five thousand.

Financial activity remains focused on Wall Street and Lower Broadway at the southern end of Manhattan—downtown. There the stock markets, stock brokers, underwriters, investment houses, and banks remain concentrated, although the past twenty years have seen some migration of financial institutions to midtown Manhattan (42nd to 60th Streets), where corporate headquarters are clustered.

New York is home to six of the nation's ten biggest banks, but their dominance of national capital is not so great as it was twenty-five or thirty years ago. The relatively greater economic growth of the nation's South and West have pulled financial activities in those directions. Compounding this, large national corporations still tend to borrow in New York while their purchases and deposits rise elsewhere. This has drained the City's banks' liquidity, and they have met the challenge by veritably explosive growth in international money fields.

Standing on the steps of historic Federal Hall where he took the Presidential oath of office, George Washington looks across Wall Street to the New York Stock Exchange. In 1792, twenty-four brokers met here under a Buttonwood tree and created what is today the world's leading money market. Today a modern Buttonwood tree, just a few leaves of which can be seen along the left margin of the picture, marks the spot. (Photo courtesy of the New York Convention and Visitors Bureau)

INSURANCE HEADQUARTERS

The first insurance companies specialized in sea risks and in property insurance, thus necessitating their concentration with the banking and shipping complex in southern Manhattan.

Life insurance companies appeared later in the mid-19th century, and as actuarial knowledge improved these companies' business grew less and less risky. This loosened the life insurance companies' need for immediate personal communication with the finance community, and they began to migrate uptown. Life insurance companies' locational needs still today include the availability of a large clerical force and also prime exposure, that is, an outstanding location and building to associate the company with permanence and solidity in the public mind. These needs have so far kept insurance companies' head offices in the central city served by mass transit. New York Life, Equitable, and Metropolitan Life, to name just three of the largest, remain in Manhattan; Prudential's home office is in downtown Newark.

CORPORATE HEADQUARTERS

New York City is the nation's preeminent center for corporate main offices. In 1974 the New York Region hosted about one-third of the 500 largest manufacturing and mining corporations in the country. New York also has six of the top ten utilities. A large number of other major corporations have corporate headquarters elsewhere, but maintain large administrative offices in New York. Monsanto Chemical, for instance, a Saint Louis company, occupies one of Manhattan's largest skyscrapers.

The national concentration of corporate head offices came about with the separation of corporate office functions from the corporations' production facilities. This began to happen when the benefits of executives' exchanging information with offices of other firms became greater than the costs of executives' directing the production facilities of their own firms at a distance.

The clustering of corporate head offices can best be understood as a function of special external economies. The "product" which an executive makes is a decision, and the decisions executives must make vary greatly from hour to hour. The chief executive officer of a multinational conglomerate must be concerned with labor unrest in California, an advertising campaign in East Africa, the Peruvian railroad net, whether the Russian winter is slowing a construction project on the shores of the Volga River, a breach of patent suit against his corporation by a German company, and Wall Street rumors about the value of his corporation's stock. Thus decision-makers require access to diverse expertise, not all of which could possibly be maintained within the corporation. Access must be immediate, and, in most cases, face-to-face contact is essential.

Another important external economy is the convenience of Kennedy Airport, which offers regular direct flights to cities around the United States and the world. An executive can fly more places more easily from New York than from any other corporate headquarters.

The corporate elites agglomerate with the offices of the accountants, lawyers, advertising agencies, financiers, and others upon whom they draw for information. These services in turn pull those upon whom they depend: advertising agencies need artists, lithographers, publishing firms, radio and television networks; lawyers need printers and each other; accountants need lawyers.

New York's early lead in wholesaling and finance boosted its ascendency as national corporate headquarters, and since World War II the intricacies of world trade and finance have made it increasingly important for large corporations to be headquartered or represented in New York. Not only American corporations, but foreign corporations and financial institutions have felt the need. Thus a growing number of foreign firms have offices in New York, and the assets of foreign banks in the City count in the tens of billions of dollars. New York is quite literally the capital of the world economy, a role served by London in the past, but on a far smaller scale.

The thousands and thousands of workers in corporate headquarters in New York are not of course, all elite decision-makers. Those who handle fairly routine central office functions outnumber true decision-makers by at least fifty or one hundred to one. The standardized office functions (repetitive data processing, accounting, billing, tabulating, payrolls, sales orders, etc.) do not have to be in the Central Business District. They are concentrated there because the decision-makers usually do prefer immediate access to corporate records, and because a central location at the focus of mass transit provides a pool of office labor. A corporation might choose to keep its top executive offices in Manhattan, but move routine office procedures into the suburbs. Texaco Oil Company has done this; its executives are in Manhattan, but most clerical work is located in Westchester.

Whether New York City can retain the concentration of offices and office jobs will largely depend upon its ability to supply office workers. The future of the City's office industry and the advancement of the City's disadvantaged population must be tied together in the long run. Stepped-up training for white collar skills, broader access to university education through the City University's open enrollment, and a massive improvement in the quality of the public school system are essential. The City school system does not now regularly produce graduates ready for business jobs, whether the shortcomings are in the City school system itself, or in the qualifications and approach taken by the students. As a result, some large employers must run their own private school systems, at their own expense, to qualify employees in such basic skills as English and mathematics. This obviously discourages employers from locating or remaining in the City.

Suburban Headquarters

A number of corporate offices have abandoned the City for campuslike settings in the suburbs, but the reasons for this are unclear. Building a corporate office at a suburban site is usually more expensive than obtaining equivalent office space in Manhattan, partly because of the additional space required for employee amenities, to meet zoning laws, and to provide parking space. Lack of mass transit means that the employees must have their own automobiles, and thus employee wages often must be higher than in town. A qualitative difference in the work force is indefinite. Executive communication with other executives and with executive services suffers, although corporate officers can get into the City for a business lunch. A gain in corporate prestige is doubtful. In fact the only clear advantage suburban headquarters have ever demonstrated—whether in New York or in other metropolitan areas—has been a reduction in the journey-to-work for executives. Nevertheless, General Foods moved from New York City to suburban White Plains in the 1950s; IBM is today in Armonk, Pepsico in Purchase, and the list goes on. Movement of corporate headquarters to suburbs does not necessarily mean abandonment of the City. IBM, for instance, still has a labor force of over 5,000 in the City, but the employment in the City usually stabilizes, and new office jobs are created in the suburbs.

Total Jobs

We have seen the sharp declines in jobs in the manufacturing industries in New York City. Until 1969 these job losses were more than offset by gains in office work, services, and government. Since 1969, however, the City has suffered net losses of jobs each year. From 3,844,600 jobs in June 1969, the number shrank to 3,528,100 in June 1974, a loss of 316,500 jobs.

This is not unique to New York among United States metropolitan areas, as Figure 9-5 shows. Most central cities are losing in total population as well. It is the loss of manufacturing production jobs—blue collar labor force entry jobs—and the delays of central city residents in upgrading their skills to capture the better-paying skilled blue collar and white collar jobs, which makes central city job losses such an economic and social burden to the central cities.

New York City's share of jobs within its Region has naturally declined as suburban areas have developed. As the population spreads across the countryside, certain consumer services necessarily follow. Thus the *number* of central City jobs in these occupations may not decline, although the City's *share* does. Grocery stores, department stores, beauty parlors, local banking and insurance offices all appear

The headquarters of the United Nations occupies eighteen acres between 1st Avenue and the East River, from 42nd to 48th Streets in Manhattan. This land, known as Turtle Bay, was occupied by slaughterhouses as late as 1946, when John D. Rockfeller, Jr., donated the site to the new international organization. Today it is not strictly speaking a part of New York City, or even of the United States.

In this view from the south we see the Dag Hammarskjold Library, the slablike Secretariat, and the domed General Assembly Building. The City diverted 1st Avenue through traffic into a tunnel under United Nations Plaza. (Photo courtesy of the New York Convention and Visitors Bureau)

wherever there is new residential settlement, and if we know where the consumers are, we can fairly well predict where these consumer-service jobs will be. Most areas generally count 96 food store employees, for example, for each 10,000 of local population.

More highly specialized services such as opera, museums, theatre, fine jewelry stores, and others for which the population threshold of demand is high, remain concentrated in the central city. There they gain the advantages of centrality and of the City's constant stream of out-of-town visitors. Middle-quality department stores can be found almost anywhere, but there is only one Fifth Avenue in all the world.

The United Nations

The economic value to the City of the United Nations headquarters is difficult to measure. In addition to the thousands of foreign representatives it brings to the City, it attracts many people and businesses who have dealings with those foreign countries. It is also important to the news media concentrated in New York—a factor keeping some of them in the City. The United Nations is a tourist attraction, and certainly it is prestigious.

New Yorkers, however, seem to grumble incessantly about the presence of the United Nations. Diplomats' cars receive diplomatic immunity, and diplomats do park with infuriating impunity. They double-park, triple-park, occupy bus stops, and block driveways and loading zones on congested Manhattan streets. Also, since the City receives no subsidy from the federal government to host the United Nations, the costs of protecting diplomatic visitors fall on New Yorkers alone. These costs are not small; the brief visit of Palestine Liberation Front leader Yasir Arafat in the fall of 1974, for instance, cost the City some three hundred thousand dollars in policemen's overtime pay.

Despite these two native gripes about the United Nations, the organization's presence clearly benefits the City, and most New Yorkers are proud of it.

Viewing the United Nations complex from the East River, the tall rectangular building on the left is the Secretariat, and the General Assembly is the low structure with the domed roof to its right. The Conference Building extends over Franklin D. Roosevelt Drive, out of sight from United Nations Plaza.

The tallest buildings in the background from left to right are the Empire State Building, the Chrysler Building, and the Pan Am Building, which is the largest commercial office building in the world. (Photo courtesy of the New York Convention and Visitors Bureau)

The Metropolitan Museum of Art, on 5th Avenue facing 82nd Street, is one of the greatest museums in the world, and New York's number one tourist attraction. Its collections span the history of art of all ages from around the world. Farther north on Manhattan's upper west side overlooking the Hudson, the Metropolitan also operates the Cloisters, a museum of medieval art which is itself composed of parts of medieval buildings brought from Europe and reassembled, stone by stone. (Photo courtesy of the New York Convention and Visitors Bureau)

Lincoln Center for the Performing Arts is a complex of buildings dedicated to the teaching and presentation of music, drama, and the dance. The fourteen acre project built on Manhattan's upper West Side between 1962 and 1968 is the permanent home of several of the City's most renowned organizations in the performing arts.

Here we face the facade of the Metropolitan Opera House; that of the New York State Theatre is on the left, and that of Avery Fisher Hall (formerly Philharmonic Hall) is on the right. Other Center facilities not shown include the Vivian Beaumont Theatre, the Library—Museum of the Performing Arts, the Julliard School of Music, Alice Tully Hall, and Damrosch Park with its bandshell for outdoor concerts. Plazas with plantings and reflecting pools connect the buildings. (Photo courtesy of the New York Convention and Visitors Bureau)

Visitors

Visitors come to New York City not only as wholesale buyers or diplomats, but as conventioneers and tourists. The City's many fine hotels and other convention facilities, plus its unique variety of shopping opportunities, museums, musical life, art galleries, stage shows, professional sports, zoos, and other amusements attract each year about sixteen million tourists and convention delegates who spend an estimated one and one-quarter billion dollars. Thus the visitor industry is one of the biggest in the City, although its financial impact is difficult to measure as such.

The City is currently developing a new Convention and Exhibition Center. This four-level forty-acre facility is to be built along and extending over the Hudson River between 43rd and 47th Streets, and its completion ought to attract still more than the over 800 conventions which meet in the City each year now.

Manufacturing	20.6
Wholesale Trade	5.0
Retail Trade	14.3
Agriculture	0.2
Mining	0.1
Construction	3.5
Business, Repair Services	5.3
Personal Services	4.5
Professional, Related Services	18.8
Entertainment and Recreation	1.3
Finance, Insurance, and Real Estate	10.7
Transportation, Communications, Utilities	9.9
Public Administration	5.7

Figure 9-1. New York City Labor Force Percentage of Employed Persons by Industry Group (1970).

City	Demand Charge (1,000 kw)	Use Charge (400,000 kwh)	Fuel Adjustment	Taxes	Total
New York	$6,960	$7,904	$7,374	$3,244	$25,482
Newark	2,340	5,474	6,800	none	14,614
Atlanta	4,350	1,600	2,664	345	8,959
Chicago	2,317	4,641	1,688	178	8,824
Denver	1,820	4,186	870	447	7,323
San Francisco	1,500	3,426	1,892	none	6,818
Dallas	1,732	2,915	1,308	none	5,955

Data courtesy of the Fantus Company, Location Consultants.

Figure 9-2. Monthly Cost of Electricity for a Medium-Sized Textile or Metal-Working Plant Employing 300 to 400 Workers (December, 1974).

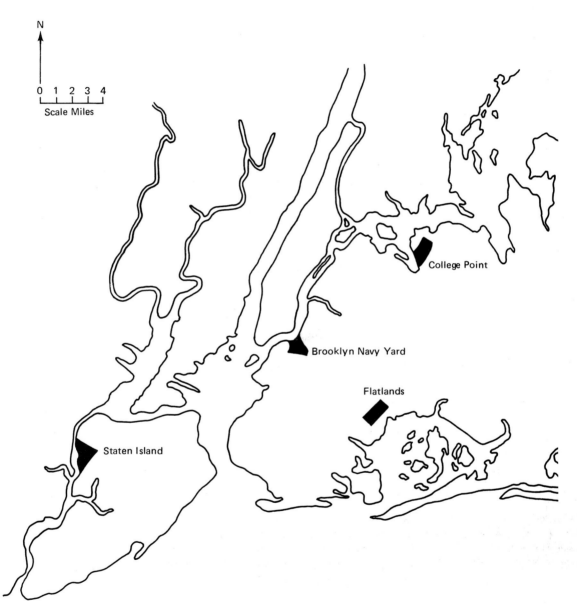

Figure 9-3. New York City Economic Development Administration's Four Major New Industrial Parks.

	1960	—	1970		1960	—	1970
New York	179		247	Newark	12		14
Chicago	47		63	Milwaukee	12		14
Washington, D.C.	36		54	Minneapolis-St. Paul	10		12
Los Angeles	16		35	Cincinnati	10		12
Philadelphia	26		34	Cleveland	8		11
Boston	24		34	Kansas City	6		9
San Francisco	16		26	St. Louis	4		8
Detroit	16		23	Wilmington	2		3
Dallas	16		22	Paterson	1		1
Pittsburgh	15		22				
Houston	13		22	**Total**	477	—	681
Atlanta	8		17				

Figure 9-4. Downtown Office Space (millions of square feet).

1969-1973 in Percentage

Detroit	−19.4	San Francisco	−6.8
Baltimore	−11.8	New York	−6.4
Dallas	−11.3	Chicago	−6.0
St. Louis	−9.7	Los Angeles	+4.4
Milwaukee	−8.9	Houston	+11.3

Figure 9-5. Net Job Loss (−) or Gain (+) in the City.

Chapter Ten

DEMANDS
ON THE ENVIRONMENT

Regional Air Quality

Air pollution is a widespread annoyance in the New York Region, as it is throughout the country, but there are many kinds of air pollution, and we have only crude estimates of air pollution damage. In the air are nitrogen oxides and carbon monoxide, acids and lead from cars, sulfur dioxide from electric generator smokestacks, soot, dust, and gases from incinerators and furnaces. Each inflicts a different amount and kind of damages or discomfort, and the degree depends upon the weather, the time, the place, peoples' idiosyncrasies, and more. We do not yet fully understand what to look for in polluted air, nor what, in order of priority, we must cleanse out. Carbon monoxide, for example, is the number one man-made pollutant (61 percent by weight), but our knowledge of what constitutes a dangerous concentration and of what actual damage is done remains inconclusive.

Unlike sewage or refuse, air cannot be collected and treated at a central facility. Air pollution must be attacked at its source, and because air pollution drifts freely across all political borders, it must necessarily be a Regional concern. The construction of new incinerators in the Hackensack Meadowlands, for instance, suggested as a possible solution to Regional solid waste disposal problems, is denounced by New Yorkers for the incinerators' presumed degradation of New York City's air quality. Winds generally blow from West to East across the Region.

In all studies the automobile emerges clearly as one chief source of air pollution. In Figure 10-1, which shows estimated sources of major air pollutants in the Region, transportation is a major contributor of each contaminant. The spread of development in the New York Region, with the private car the indispensable means of transportation in the suburbs, has thus multiplied the number of these pollution sources. Today emission controls are standard on new models, but these controls are by no means perfect, and it will be years before all cars on the road have them. Development of an alternative to the internal combustion engine is not foreseen in the immediate future, and so every way that car pools or use of mass transit can be encouraged helps save energy and preserve air quality too.

The Region's cities have moved to prohibit burning of high sulfur fuel for electricity generation or for heating, and to require stack emission control devices. In 1966 New York City required that all heavy fuel oil burned in the City contain less than one percent sulfur, and a 1971 air pollution code cut that further to less than 0.3 percent sulfur while also restricting emissions of nitrogen oxides and particulates. This did much to improve New York City air quality, but the cost of switching to low sulfur fuel was partly responsible for an escalation of electricity rates. Unfortunately, all envisioned means of air pollution reduction are expensive.

An attack on incinerators as sources of air pollution demonstrates the connection between air quality and the disposal of solid waste. In 1966 the City tried to ban the many private incinerators in old apartment houses, but the City found it could not collect all the additional refuse, nor could it find adequate sites to use the refuse as landfill. Thus today many private incinerators are still in operation. All furnaces and incinerators are supposed to be inspected for efficiency periodically, but the City Department of Air Resources has never been sufficiently manned to carry out the inspections.

At the Regional level, most incinerators are admittedly old and inefficient; many have been cited again and again for environmental pollution. Until the entire Region decides where responsibility for refuse disposal is to be, however, whether with the cities, counties, or some new Regional agencies, and whether landfill, incineration or some new method will appear in the near future, little money is being spent to upgrade existing incinerators.

Most of this sounds pretty glum, but, due to the combined efforts mentioned, the quality of air in New York City has in fact improved markedly over the past decade. When the City's first air pollution code was passed in 1966, air quality was widely recognized as a serious health hazard. The improvement of air quality in the early 1970s can be seen in Figure 10-2, showing daily air quality as measured by the City's Department of Air Resources. Most days of poor quality occur in the summer, when incoming solar radiation is greatest, and photochemical action is thus greatest (Fig. 10-3).

The Federal Clean Air Act of 1970 required the Environmental Protection Administration to establish standards of air quality for major pollutants, and required the New York State Department of Environmental Conservation to propose a plan to improve City air quality. Statement of a plan has been hampered by political jockeying between New York City and the State, but major concepts so far considered included a ban or limit on midtown taxi cruising, tolls on the East River and Harlem River crossings, a reduction in parking in the Manhattan Central Business District, improvement of commuter bus service, stepped-up emmission inspections of cars and trucks, and scheduling of more commercial deliveries during the night. Clearly the automobile is the focus of concern, and some program incorporating some or all of these attacks will probably be adopted in the 1970s.

Water Needs

With numerous rivers, bays, the adjacent ocean and forty inches of annual rainfall well distributed through the seasons, lack of water does not threaten as a major problem of the Metropolitan Region. At present Regional needs are met from a number of sources, some of which extend well outside the area. West of the Hudson River the major water supplies are derived from the surface waters and basins of the Delaware, Passaic, Hackensack and Raritan Rivers, supplemented by intensive development of ground water resources. East of the Hudson the New York City system reaches far into New York State to draw from the Hudson and Delaware Rivers, and from the City's extensive reservoir system in the Catskill Mountains. Groundwater is the main source for most of Long Island, including parts of Queens County.

About 70 percent of the Region's drinkable water is provided by municipalities, and another 24 percent by investor-owned utilities. Reliance on individual wells is largely confined to the Region's fringe counties. Thus the northern halves of Passaic and Westchester counties and the outlying portions of Union, Monmouth and Suffolk lack complete water service coverage.

Most of the area's requirements are met by about a dozen large purveyors, by far the largest of which is the New York City system. As early as 1840 New York reached out to develop reservoirs along the Croton River in Westchester County, and today the City owns eighteen reservoirs plus four controlled lakes in 1,950 square miles of watershed in nine upstate counties. Within the City there are four local reservoirs and numerous major interborough tunnels, with still another under construction. Over 6,000 miles of pipe distribute the water to users within the City. The New York City system is required by State law to supply distributors in Westchester, Putnam and Orange Counties. Its present deliveries amount to well over 1.5 billion gallons of water per day, which includes up to 75 percent of Westchester County's needs. For several years the City has battled State schemes to create an entirely new Regional water supply corporation. Upstate areas charge that the City takes too much water and wastes it, while the City fears that a New York State regional system could not guarantee the City's future needs.

Only about 10 percent of current Regional deliveries of water are consumed by manufacturing industries. This contrasts sharply to the national norm, in which manufacturing takes between a quarter and a third of total supplies. A sizeable portion of industrial requirements in the New York Region, particularly in New Jersey, is drawn from private sources, either fresh or brackish surface water or wells.

THE FUTURE

On a minimum safe-yield basis, the reliable output of present metropolitan water sources is estimated at 2.6 billion gallons per day. With present use about 2.2 billion gallons, the Region has a current daily surplus of 0.4 billion gallons. While there is little likelihood of an absolute shortage of water, increasing demand may pose problems of Regional distribution. The famous "drought" of 1965 was in fact the result of inadequacies in the system of Regional distribution, rather than from an actual scarcity of water. Several large-scale projects have been proposed to meet expected demands and to guarantee adequate supplies throughout the Region through the year 2000. Some of these projects are scheduled for completion in the 1970s, others in the 1990s.

For the needs of New York City and adjacent counties, the largest proposed project is to tap the Hudson River at Hyde Park in Dutchess County and to build an aqueduct thence to Kensico Reservoir in central Westchester County (Fig. 10-4). This would provide additional water for the City and for Dutchess, Putnam, Westchester, and Nassau Counties as well. On Long Island additional supplies can be obtained by expanding the use of local groundwater, but this must be accompanied by extensive sewerage to preserve the quality of the island's groundwater.

Northeast New Jersey now relies on the Passaic and Hackensack River basins. The Passaic, however, can supply little more than it does now, and the Hackensack no more. The future here will necessitate tapping the underutilized Raritan Basin and the midsection of the Delaware River. These sources could supply Northeast New Jersey and also Central New Jersey, which is reaching the limit of usable groundwater supplies.

The largest of these water supply projects cannot be launched by local communities, but require State or Regional action. The Delaware River is already the object of Tri-state planning. The River has its source in New York and thence flows through New Jersey and Pennsylvania. These three states are concerned with its use, and in the past New Jersey even went to court to prevent New York City from diverting Delaware River water. In 1961 the three states, with Congressional approval, set up the Delaware River Basin Commission to plan, regulate and coordinate the River's use. One ambitious scheme authorized by Congress in 1962 was the construction of a dam at Tocks Island just above the Delaware Water Gap. The dam would create a 37-mile lake from Tocks Island to Port Jervis, New York, flooding about 12,000 acres along the New Jersey and Pennsylvania shorelines. Its purpose would be to control floods and to provide water, hydroelectric power and recreational facilities. Squabbling among state and local officials of the three states has so far held up the project.

Another ambitious large-scale Regional project would be the inter-connection of the Naugatuck River and Housatonic River water supply systems in Connecticut with New York and New Jersey systems. The Tri-State Regional Planning Commission has supported this idea. Its purpose would be, again, not so much to increase the generous total water supplies in the greater Region, but to improve intra-Regional distribution.

Sewage Disposal

The disposal of sewage presents three related problems. One is getting the sewage away from people. The second is keeping the sewage away from water supplies, and the third is treating the sewage so as to preserve the environment.

The earliest sewer systems in the Region carried both rainwater and human waste to adjacent waters without any treatment. Such "combined" sewers still prevail in several of the Region's older cities. Some 70 percent of New York City's 6,500 miles of sewers, for instance, are still combined, and when a storm causes an overflow, sewage flows directly into the adjacent waters.

Only in the early 1900s did developing areas first separate storm sewers from sanitary sewers, and local communities began to provide at least primary sewage treatment. Primary treatment means simply screening or filtering the sewage, and then letting it stand some time in large settling tanks.

By the early 1960s nearly 85 percent of Tri-State Regional sewers were connected to treatment plants, although new suburban communities continued to be built relying on private cesspools. Increasing population densities in these areas made eventual groundwater contamination inevitable, betraying the short-sightness of early reliance on cesspools. Pollution of groundwater supplies has been and remains a serious threat in Nassau and Suffolk Counties on Long Island. Today all new developments in the Region must have sewerage, and the treatment provided by the systems in the new areas, as in some of the old, is now commonly secondary treatment. Second-

ary treatment combines settling tanks, aeration, and bacterial attack, and it usually removes some 90 percent of organic pollutants. Tertiary treatment, which is a very expensive method of concentrating on the removal of inorganic pollutants, is not considered necessary in the Region, because there is supposed to be little industrial waste in Regional sewage. Regional industries are required to pretreat their sewage, although governments in the Region do not police this as closely as they might.

CONTINUING PROBLEMS

Despite these sewerage and treatment facilities, the Region still discharges the raw sewage equivalent of about eleven million people into adjacent waterways. This comes from untreated effluent, the inadequately treated effluent of old and overloaded plants, plus industrial waste. Floating debris and oil contribute direct pollution to Regional waterways.

The problem of cleaning up these waterways requires first Regional organization and definition of water quality goals. A New Jersey-New York-Connecticut Interstate Sanitation Commission has existed for more than 25 years, and in 1967, in cooperation with the Federal Water Pollution Control Administration, it did establish class standards and a goal for quality for each Regional waterway (Fig. 10-5). Class One waters were to be acceptable for water supply, swimming, and shellfishing. Class Two waters would be acceptable for fishing and boating, but not for swimming. Class Three waters would be suitable only for navigation and for industrial water use. The criteria set for categorization were oxygen loss, coliform bacteria, suspended solids, temperature increase, and acidity and alkalinity. The damage caused by any pollutant is a function of water oxygen content, speed of the current, the amount others are dumping in the water, and water temperature. It is difficult to define precisely how clean we want adjacent waters, especially because that relates to what we are willing to pay. If, for example, we are willing to pay ten million dollars to remove 80 percent of water pollutants, is it worth twenty million dollars to remove 90 percent or thirty million dollars to remove 95 percent?

The original timetable targeted 1972 for achievement of the designated waters' class standards. Lack of adequate funding for sewage treatment, however, now makes that optimism rather pathetic in retrospect.

The Region as a whole does not yet plan sensibly. A new Westchester-Yonkers treatment plant, for instance, will improve the Hudson River above Spuyten Duyvil, but the water there is relatively clean now. The Raritan Bay, on the other hand, is polluted, and the shellfish industry closed. This area is a potential recreation resource for the whole Region, but key sewage treatment plants await federal funds. Under the terms of the 1972 Federal Water Pollution Control Act, this Region would be eligible for up to 75 percent federal aid for sewage treatment projects. Federal decisions to grant or withhold these sewerage subsidies in particular areas can actually direct Regional development patterns. On the basis of confidence in forthcoming federal funds New York State and Connecticut voted to bond themselves to prepay the federal share so that work would get started on projects. New Jersey has not done so, and, as a result, over 100 of the 576 communities in the state were forced to ban new construction sometime in 1973 or 1974 because of inadequate sewerage. Many of these communities were in the New York Metropolitan Region. The Nixon Administration impounded for years money authorized by Congress to assist in financing sewage treatment projects. The status of federal financial assistance is still unclear.

Under the forms of other federal legislation, public sewage treatment plants must provide secondary treatment by 1977 to eliminate 90 percent of the BOD (Biochemical Oxygen Demand rate—a measure of pollution) and suspended solids. Manufacturers dumping into public waters must use the "best practicable control technology currently available" by 1977 and the "best technology economically achievable" by 1983.

THE CITY

New York City currently has twelve sewage treatment plants providing secondary treatment to 1.1 billion gallons of sewage per day (Fig. 10-6). The City is upgrading treatment at these plants, and building new plants. By the 1980s, it is hoped, there will be a 90 percent reduction in water pollution from the City's raw sewage.

Two large new plants are under construction. A new Red Hook Water Pollution Control being built in Brooklyn will provide secondary treatment for the last major untreated discharge from Brooklyn, some 70 million gallons per day. The sludge from this plant will be treated for acceptability as landfill.

The City's second major project extends out into the Hudson River from 137th to 145th Streets on Manhattan's West Side. It is the North River Water Pollution Control Plant project. Ever since Manhattan's first sewers were laid in the 18th century, the island's West Side has emptied untreated sewage into the Hudson. This now amounts to 220 million gallons per day. The new plant, scheduled for opening in 1981, will provide secondary treatment to that sewage and also provide a new public park on the plant's 30-acre roof.

The City also plans to build a number of separate storm water treatment plants in the 1980s. One such demonstration plant opened on the north shore of Jamaica Bay in 1972. The Bay, a 25 square mile wildlife refuge and recreation resource, is presently polluted, and it has been a focus of public concern.

DUMPING SLUDGE

For forty years several Regional jurisdictions have barged out to sea and dumped the sludge remnant of secondary treatment in a fourteen square mile area about twelve and one-half miles south of Rockaway Point, Long Island and ten miles east of Sandy Hook, New Jersey. Of the 5.591 million cubic yards of sludge dumped there in 1973, New York City dumped 59 percent. New Jersey, Nassau, and Westchester counties added the other 41 percent. Controversy has recently arisen over whether this sludge may be drifting in toward the southern shores of Long Island, but contradictory studies are so far inconclusive. Treatment of sludge for use as landfill will be possible, of course, only if the Region can find more potential landfill sites!

Refuse

Through most of the 19th century the disposal of refuse and solid waste posed little problem for the Region's residents. Plenty of open land existed for dumping. Already in 1900, however, the population had so grown and spread that the city governments assumed responsibility to pick up refuse and cart it away. It was either dropped at municipal dumps or used for landfill. Burning trash was another way of getting rid of it. Open burning was banned throughout the Region by the 1960s, but large incinerators are still necessary.

The amounts of solid waste generated in the Region are staggering—about one ton per person per year. This amount has been rising faster than population increases, as our affluent society has consumed ever more materials in disposable products, packaging, and so forth. The City produces 50 percent more refuse today than ten years ago, with about the same population. Waste generation escalates at about four to six percent per year, so that while today the City must dispose of 30,000 tons of waste per day, by the mid-1980s the City is expected to have to dispose of 40,000 tons per day.

For the Tri-State Region as a whole about 50 percent of solid waste goes into sanitary landfill, and another 40 percent is burned in incinerators, but the amount of garbage we generate threatens to bury us. Areas suitable for landfill close to populated areas are increasingly scarce, and there are pressures to save those areas for ecological sanctuaries or for recreation. Many of the incinerators in the Region are old and inefficient, and burning refuse in them in effect substitutes an air pollution problem for a solid waste problem.

At present about 22 percent of the City's waste is burned in seven large incinerators, the residue from which is used to cover sanitary landfill sites. Another 42 percent is trucked to five medium-sized landfills areas in the City, and 36 percent is trucked or taken by barge to Fresh Kills, a 3,000 acre landfill operation on the far West Side of Staten Island. Years ago it was planned to stop dumping at Fresh Kills in the mid-1970s, to build a new small airport there, and to develop a large industrial park on the site. These plans have had to be put in limbo, because the City is running out of landfill space elsewhere. An important landfill site at Pelham Bay in the Bronx is scheduled for closure in 1975, and so the City has to keep mounding the waste higher and higher at Fresh Kills. The City hopes that by mounding over one hundred feet high at Fresh Kills, the site will be serviceable until 1985.

Debris from demolition sites is different from refuse garbage; it does not release gases, nor does it settle so much in compaction. Thus the City has successfully used demolition debris to create new landfill parks. The debris is covered with light soil, earthworms are imported, and vegetation is planted. The 110-acre Pennsylvania Park on the north shore of Jamaica Bay is an example, and similar projects are going ahead. Parts of La Guardia and Kennedy airports, and other large areas of waterfront around Manhattan and the other boroughs have been created by landfill.

THE FUTURE

The City is publicly considering a number of potential solutions to the refuse problem, but has been frustrated in effecting most plans. The City could build more incinerators, but more incinerators would be expensive, and could add to air pollution. Pyrolysis is being investigated, a process of burning refuse with insufficient oxygen at very high temperatures, thus converting organic trash to oil or gas and giving off very little pollution. Some refuse might be mixed with oil or gas and itself used to fuel power production. This has already proven successful in St.

Louis and elsewhere. Recycling is an attractive possibility the City is just beginning to explore. Some bulk metals, such as refrigerators and stoves, have been consigned to a private shredder on Newtown Creek in Brooklyn, but this amounts to only one or two hundred tons per month. The City has been more successful with junked cars. Some seventy to eighty thousand cars are abandoned on the City's streets each year, and while just a few years ago the City had to pay to pick them up or have them picked up, the steadily rising price of scrap has enticed dealers to pick up these cars and pay the City for the privilege.

Shipping refuse by rail to abandoned mines in Ohio has been investigated, but social opposition stymied that program. Pennsylvania law prohibits transit of refuse across the State, although a New York City commissioner threatened to drive a garbage truck to Ohio in order to test that Pennsylvania law in the courts.

New York State has created an Environmental Facilities Corporation with power to plan, finance, construct, acquire and operate sanitary facilities for state agencies and municipalities, and to lease equipment to sanitary landfill operators. The agency has been studying in particular the problems of Westchester County. That County's large Croton Point landfill is nearing capacity, and all eight incinerators in the County have been cited for environmental pollution violation. The Corporation might assume responsibility for hauling Westchester refuse upstate, or under another plan, the County government might assume county-wide responsibility. The County would take over and improve existing incinerators, and build new ones to provide power and heat to County institutions. Lack of cooperation from the city of Yonkers, which represents one-quarter of the County population, has so far prevented execution of this plan.

The most built-up parts of New Jersey rely heavily upon landfill in the Hackensack Meadows. In 1968 the State created a Hackensack Meadowlands Development Commission to prepare a masterplan for the 20,000 acre area, but it required the Commission to guarantee continuing facilities for the 122 municipalities then using the area for landfill. That the Meadowland can in fact continue to serve so many municipalities is doubtful. New Jersey is already considering stopping the hauling of demolition debris from New York City to the Meadowlands.

Connecticut is going ahead with an ambitious Statewide plan. By 1985 Connecticut hopes to have eleven solid waste zones. Within each zone steel, glass, and aluminum will be recovered from refuse by air, water flotation and magnets. Remaining trash will be burned in eleven large incinerators to provide, it is hoped, ten or eleven percent of the State's total energy needs by 1985. One of these large zones includes Bridgeport and surrounding towns on the northern fringe of the New York Metropolitan Region.

The disposal of solid waste is a problem which might better be approached by the creation of some Regional authority. Such an agency could centralize responsibility, achieve economies of scale and lower pollution in large incinerators or in recycling efforts. Funding such an agency, however, would be a source of intergovernmental quarreling, and if the authority had power to override local objections in choosing locations for its facilities, the local publics would undoubtedly protest vehemently.

Energy

Any attempt to prophecy future energy needs or sources for the Region would be foolhardy. The national economic and political scene and international events combine to make the changing energy picture a daily news item. The dangers of prophecy are well-illustrated by a June 1968 official energy report of the Tri-State Regional Planning Commission, which then assured us that "all fuels will be available in plentiful quantities to 1985 and beyond to meet the requirement of the public utility industry, as well as for other uses." At best we can describe the situation at present and indicate what plans are being laid to assure future supplies.

Demands

In 1970 the Tri-State Region consumed about 4 trillion BTU's of energy. Of that, 37 percent went for homes and business heating and cooking, 27 percent for fuel for vehicles of all types, 24 percent for generation of electricity, and 12 percent for industry and miscellany. In keeping with national norms, the use of energy has been rising much more rapidly than has population. Our national way of life has long taken ever-increasing supplies of cheap energy for granted. The greatest increases have been in the use of fuel for private vehicles, as cars have become indispensable to suburban life and their mileage per gallon decreased, and in the demand for electricity.

Consolidated Edison Corporation's customers in New York City and Westchester County have doubled electricity consumption about every fifteen years. Public Service Gas and Electric Company, which serves most of metropolitan New Jersey, doubled its electricity output in the 1960s. Long Island Lighting had to increase its output two and one-half times from 1960-1970, and Orange and Rockland Utilities, Inc., which serves northern Bergen and most of Passaic Counties as well, increased its production well over three times. All projections have routinely assumed continuing escalation of energy consumption, but within the past few years many Regional utilities have replaced advertisements to sell electricity with admonitions to save it.

SUPPLIES AND COSTS

Increasing use of cars and trucks, but also a shift from the use of coal to oil to generate electricity have made us increasingly dependent upon petroleum. In the Tri-State Region in 1965, 57 percent of fossil fuel generation of electricity was by coal and 37 percent was by oil. By 1971 the shares had switched to 14 percent coal and 75 percent oil. Oil was cheaper for the Region in the late 1960s, and also oil-fired electrical generators were less air-polluting.

The source for a great share of the Region's petroleum supplies was the Near East—a larger share, in fact, than for the nation as a whole. This was because of the convenience of Regional port facilities and the Region's distance from the United States oil-producing areas. In 1970 the United States consumed fifteen million barrels of oil per day, and projections of increasing national consumption estimated that the country would have to import as much as 40 percent of its oil needs by 1980. In 1970 the New York Region, however, was already importing from abroad about 40 percent of its total petroleum needs. This imported oil represented about one-third of *total* Regional energy sources. With the Arab oil embargo in late 1973 and the subsequent escalation of world petroleum prices, the New York Region was particularly hard hit. The federal government has failed to enact national petroleum price equalization legislation, and distribution of price-controlled domestic petroleum has been confined to the Western and Southwestern states and to users of petroleum distillates. Thus energy rates in the New York Region are particularly high compared to national norms.

Most of the economic activities located in the Region are not heavy users of power, but heavy users probably could not afford to locate in the Region. Oil, gas, and electricity are all expensive in the Region, and even within the Region, costs in New York City are particularly high (Fig. 9-2). Power costs represent about three percent of the total value of shipments for New York manufacturers, in contrast to a national average of less than one percent. Unless the New York producer can raise his prices to overcome the disadvantage, he suffers a corresponding cut in profits.

Most important new energy legislation will have to come at the federal level. To achieve some release from dependence upon imported oil, the nation may concentrate on the use of domestic coal for heating and for electricity generation. The nation has enormous supplies of coal, but coal is a dirty fuel, most low sulfur varieties are in the American West, and air pollution regulations have all but eliminated coal as a fuel in the New York Region. Total Regional consumption was less than 8 million tons in 1970, and about 2 million tons in 1973. In his economic address to Congress, on October 9, 1974, President Ford proposed "that we, together, set a target date of 1980 for eliminating oil-fired plants from the nation's base-loaded electrical capacity." If we are to return from oil-fired to coal-fired plants, much research is needed on coal stack antipollution devices. Coal-fired electrical plants generating power for mass transit can provide an alternative to present dependence upon petroleum-fueled vehicles. New York is particularly lucky in this regard, because it has a mass transit system—a system which is already the Region's largest user of electricity.

The manufacture of substitute natural gas from coal seems promising for the future, considering the enormous national coal supplies, but only experimental projects are yet operating. In 1970 the Region had to import 617 billion cubic feet of natural gas by pipeline (4 lines from Texas and Louisiana and one from Lambertville, New Jersey). The importation of liquified natural gas from Arab states has been negotiated in the early 1970s, but those deals may collapse for any number of political or economic reasons.

It is obvious that the nation must for some time continue to import energy, but we must also develop our own resources and conserve where we can. Many decisions can be made only at the national level, but regional and local actions can make a difference. Significant quantities of oil may lie in the Region's offshore waters, particularly in Long Island Sound. Drilling for offshore oil there within the three-mile limit would be largely state-regulated. Regional energy conservation practices would include better insulation of buildings, reduction of lighting (which would reduce air conditioning, because most office building air conditioning is only to balance the heat of lighting), manipulation of thermostats up in summer and down in winter, and improvement of some older relatively inefficient electricity generators. Encouragement of use of the Region's uniquely fine mass transit—or even of car pooling—might achieve significant reductions in Regional energy use.

Any preference of mass transit facilities over private cars lowers net fuel consumption, and has the important geographic side effect of favoring the central city focus of mass transit over suburban locations for residence, economic activities, or even leisure and recreation.

CONSOLIDATED EDISON

For New Yorkers "energy" is almost synonymous with Consolidated Edison Company, which provides electricity, gas and steam to nine million people in the City and in Westchester County. The company is fighting a losing battle to stop rises in rates which are already the highest in the nation and going up. Public discontent focuses not only on bills, but unreliability, environmental pollution, and streets torn up to repair electric cables. Because Consolidated Edison is the largest utility in the nation, and because of certain local legal restrictions, some of Consolidated Edison's problems are unique. Many of the financial and public pressures which are squeezing the Company, however, are only the best examples of pressures on utilities around the nation.

Financial pressures derive both from high capital expenditures and from high operating costs. The famous Northeast blackout of 1965 led to restructuring and new management for Con Edison. Since then between 1967 and 1975 the Company has retired 90 percent of its old generating capacity. With modern facilities, the Company is today generating 160 percent as much power as ten years ago, but with the same number of employees. Actually two-thirds of the Company's capital needs are for transmission lines and for its local distribution system. Ninety percent of the Company's power passes through underground cables that cost about eight times as much to install and repair as do overhead cables. Consolidated Edison has 75,000 miles of wire beneath New York's streets.

The 1971 air pollution code which forbade burning oil with a sulfur content greater than one percent forced the Company to cancel long term contracts for delivery of one percent sulfur oil at two dollars per barrel, and costs for low sulfur oil have since been as high as $15.50 per barrel. Consolidated Edison pays heavy taxes to both New York City and to the State—taxes unknown in Connecticut or New Jersey.

In 1972 it became evident that Consolidated Edison needed outside financial assistance. The State government stepped in and made the State Power Authority responsible for the future "bulk power supply" of the Metropolitan Transit Authority's subways and of the Region's commuter rail lines. The Authority took over the Astoria-6 oil-fired generator in Queens and also assumed responsibility for completing the Indian Point nuclear generator south of Peekskill on the Hudson River. The Authority has since announced additional plans and projects for power supplies, but these have all met the same public resistance that Consolidated Edison projects met.

One continuing problem is the siting of power plants. Everyone wants more power, but no one wants it generated nearby. Since 1962 Consolidated Edison has been trying to build a pumped storage plant at Storm King Mountain on the Hudson River, but conservationists' court suits have blocked construction. The facility, they contend, would deface the mountain and perhaps damage fish life in the river. Similarly, when the State Power Authority announced in December of 1974 that it intended to build a new generator by Fresh Kills in western Staten Island, and that the plant would burn over 2,000 tons of refuse each day to supplement fossil fuels, a barrage of protest arose from island residents. Air quality monitors of every governmental level joined the chorus of doubt that the new facility could meet environmental standards.

Even with the State Power Authority's assumption of some responsibility, Con Edison, in a move that shocked utilities' stockholders and financial markets around the nation, for the first time skipped a quarterly dividend in April 1974.

Electricity costs continue to climb, and Con Edison's financial future is increasingly obscure. It is not wholly impossible that the State or some Regional governmental agency will have to assume responsibility for power supplies.

Recreation

It is very difficult to set aside land for public recreation in a rapidly growing metropolitan area. Public acquisition of large recreation spaces requires planning on the outer fringes of advancing settlement. Recreation lands must be reserved early, or else the whole area is given over to other economic uses and thus lost. Small neighborhood playgrounds and "vest-pocket" parks can be shoehorned into built-up areas, but developing new large recreation facilities in an already built-up metropolitan area is almost impossible.

LOCAL FACILITIES

We can differentiate two different scales of recreation facilities. Subregional or local facilities are thought of as those within twenty minutes travel time of the population served—usually within the county—and designed for part-day use. Local facilities are best planned and maintained by local agencies. Unfortunately, the core developed counties of the New York Metropolitan Region contain precious few acres of local recreation land for their great populations. The Tri-State Regional Planning Commission suggests an ideal of 18 acres of local recreation space per 1,000 of population, but Figure 10-7 shows how far behind this recommended acreage some of the Region's most populous counties fall. The intense present development of these counties makes it altogether unrealistic to think that the ideal recreational acreages will ever be achieved in these core counties. New parks might continue to be created out of landfill, or donated by generous citizens, but it is doubtful that these new gains could possibly total the ideal acreages.

Regional Parks for New Yorkers

The second scale of facility is the regional park, which is usually a goal of a day-long outing. The Regional Planning Commission recommends that twelve acres of regional park—in addition to eighteen acres of local park—be set aside for each 1,000 of regional population. The Tri-State Metropolitan Region as a whole is presently 226,000 acres short of this ideal acreage, but sufficient undeveloped land exists in the outer counties so that the goal is not unrealizable. Large regional parks in the outer counties can serve as a partial substitute for local parks in the core, thus imposing higher time and travel costs on park users, but avoiding

Bethesda Fountain is a popular gathering spot in the middle of Manhattan's great Central Park. The 840 acre Park, designed by Frederick Olmsted and Calvert Vaux, was begun in 1856, and not completed for almost twenty years. After the City acquired the land, squatters were forcibly driven off, bone-boiling works and swill mills were torn down, swamps were drained, and the Manhattan schist blasted to form the Park's magnificent landscaping. The Terrace area here was the only formal architectual element of the original Olmstead-Vaux plan. The Ramble, an area of dense foliage beyond, is a favorite spot for the City's birdwatchers.

The Beresford Cooperative Apartment building on Central Park West looms in the left distance. (Photo courtesy of the New York Convention and Visitors Bureau)

the impossibly high land acquisition costs in the core.

Site selection and reservation of regional facilities requires some regional executive agency; otherwise outer-county residents see no profit in setting aside disproportionate shares of their lands for residents of other jurisdictions. The Regional Planning Commission can identify priority sites for reservation of lands, but as yet no existing regional authority can acquire and operate the necessary parks.

Sites designated as priority lands for acquisition for recreational use include the Navesink Highlands in Monmouth County, New Jersey, and other areas along the Raritan and Passaic Rivers in that State; in New York, wetlands in Nassau County and up-county highlands in both Westchester and Rockland Counties, and, in Connecticut, rolling hills sections of the State's southwest.

Waterfront sites in the Region are already so valuable that some studies have recommended the construction of park islands in Long Island Sound out of dredge spoils and construction debris. This would perhaps be cheaper than public purchase of valuable waterfront sites, although how the islands would be reached would be an entirely new problem.

Regional Parks for New Yorkers

The historical problem of providing parks for New Yorkers well illustrates the difficulties of setting aside space in a growing urban area. The battle to preserve parklands for New Yorkers was joined only in the 1920s, and by that time the City itself (excepting Staten Island) was largely developed.

To the North Westchester County had parks, but they were closed to nonresidents. The 2,500 acres of trees and meadows surrounding Kensico Dam were public reserve, but that was fifteen miles from the City, almost a whole day's drive on poor roads. To the West the Palisades Interstate Park was already probably the finest in the country. This park was founded in 1900 by the Rockefeller and Harriman families, who each year added to and improved the park's

splendid recreational facilities. Palisades Interstate Park is still often called New York City's backyard. Today its 50,000 acres offer a full range of recreational opportunities. There are actually seven sections to the park in Rockland and Orange Counties in New York State, and in Bergen County in New Jersey. Back in the early 1920s however, this park was almost inaccessible to most New Yorkers. At that time there were no vehicular bridges or tunnels to cross the Hudson River—the Holland Tunnel opened in 1927—and the ferries across the Hudson were inadequate to the traffic demand. The East River was easier to cross. It was already spanned by the Williamsburg, Queensborough, Manhattan, and Brooklyn Bridges. Once across the River, the Northern, and Conduit, and Queens Boulevards led out to relatively sparsely settled Nassau and Suffolk Counties. In 1920 those two Counties had a combined population of only 250,000.

Long Islanders, however, did not want City visitors. Almost the entire North Shore was already by 1920 in private estates through Nassau and out into Suffolk County. The fisherman and residents of the small villages along the South Shore kept out City residents, and the farmers in the central portions of the counties were set against parks for invaders from the City too.

One man, however, Robert Moses, decided to fight for regional parks for the New York City residents. He envisioned a system of *State* parks on Long Island linked together and to the City by a network of landscaped roads that would themselves be parks. He actually wanted a system of parks throughout the entire State, a system in which conservation would be combined with permanent improvements and facilities for recreation. To achieve this he politically engineered the definition of ten state park regions, each with a Commission, the presidents of which would form a State Council of Parks. In political alliance with Governor Alfred E. Smith, Moses was able to get the State Legislature to create such a State Park System in 1924, and Moses became himself the President of the Long Island Regional Commission.

Jones Beach State Park, fronting the Atlantic Ocean south of Nassau County, is one of the most popular public beaches on Long Island. (Photo courtesy of the Long Island State Park and Recreation Commission)

The story of how Moses built up the State Park System, so that by the time he resigned as Chairman of the System in 1962 New York State boasted 43 percent of the total acreage of state parks in the country, is tangled but fascinating. Here we will relate only—and briefly—how he established the Long Island system.

Moses' first coup was the discovery, in five tracts scattered through Nassau County, of 2,200 acres of untouched land already owned by the City of New York. Brooklyn had purchased these properties when it was a separate city back in 1874, in order to insure a city water supply. To launch the Long Island Park System, the City of New York yielded these tracts to the new Long Island State Park Commission. Then, by exercising eminent domain, by buying up abandoned properties, and with careful planning, Moses built up a total of 40,000 acres of state parks on Long Island. He also linked them and the City by a network of state parkways. All this was accomplished by 1929.

New York's parkways express a romance all their own. These roads, still among the most beautiful in the world, do not cross or highlight a beautiful environment, as California's Coast Highway does. They are in themselves a beautiful environment, and as such, played a role in defining what has since become a basic American experience: driving as an end in itself.

Today both inland parks (Bethpage, Hemstead Lake, and more) and splendid beaches (Jones Beach, Robert Moses State Park, and others) on Long Island provide recreational opportunities for City and Long Island residents. The State, the counties, and the local jurisdictions have added parks to the system begun by Moses.

Federal Parks

The federal government has recently taken a hand in providing parks for residents of the nation's largest urban area. Gateway National Recreation Area is actually America's first national park in an urban region. The park is an aggregation of former state and local governmental lands, including parks, but federal assumption of title has meant new funds for park facilities and maintenance. Intergovernmental squabbles have long delayed complete assembly of park properties, but this national park will eventually total 26,000 acres.

Jamaica Bay is an especially interesting unit of the park. The Bay was a City wildlife refuge until surrendered to the federal government in 1974. The National Park Service is now planning how best to maintain the 13,000 acres as a wildlife sanctuary, while also providing new beaches, picnic areas, camp grounds, and boating opportunities.

In 1964 Congress designated a long sand reef off the southern shore of Long Island the Fire Island National Seashore. The act recognizing the Seashore allowed landowners to stay as long as adequate zoning kept their properties compatible with the purposes of the National Seashore. Disputes over private rights and zoning powers have simmered for years, but much of the natural beauty of this reef has successfully been preserved for public and private recreation facilities.

New Jersey Parks

The New Jersey side of the Metropolitan Region offers a few state parks, plus private recreational facilities along the oceanfront. The Watchung Reservation, South Mountain Reservation, and Eagle Rock Reservation have been set aside in the Watchung Mountains running North-South through Middlesex, Union, and Essex Counties. The 8,000 acres of the Great Swamp in Morris County, one of the largest unspoiled natural wetlands between Maine and Virginia, is being turned into a wildlife refuge and nature study center.

The Hackensack Meadowlands in New Jersey offer the last great undeveloped space within the heart of the Metropolitan Region. This area stretches seven miles north from Newark Bay between the Hudson River Palisades and the Watchung Foothills to the west. Of the Meadowland's 20,000 acres, more than one-half are still quite empty, as little as three miles from midtown Manhattan (Fig. 10-8).

The fourteen towns which divide the Meadowlands have long thought the Meadows suitable only for dumping—about 50,000 tons of solid waste are dumped in the six authorized areas each day—with occasional development on landfill areas. In 1968, however, the State of New Jersey vested new responsibility in a Hackensack Meadowlands Development Commission, charging the Commission to plan and oversee orderly development of the area. By 1980, it is hoped, the entire area will be closed to dumping, and solid waste will be dealt with in recycling operations and in huge incinerators providing clean power. The Commission has planned to allocate 3,000 of the 20,000 acres to residential construction, with the concomitant shopping, cultural, and health facilities. A vast new sports complex, including a race track and a stadium, will be open on a 588-acre site in East Rutherford in 1976. The New York Giants' announcement of intention to make the stadium their home aroused cries of outrage in the City, but the new stadium is actually only one-half mile farther from Times Square than is Shea Stadium in Queens. Another 10,000 acres will be dedicated to industrial, commercial, and transport development. The rest of the Meadowland will be open space, including both recreational facilities and protected wetlands. The marshes, once seen as pestilential, are today appreciated as coastal marine and bird life sanctuaries. Marsh preserves and waterfront recreation sites will be located along the Hackensack and tributary creeks.

A key aspect of the Meadowlands development is, of course, the diminution of pollution in the Hackensack River and Berry's Creek. The Commission has been imposing strict new anti-pollution regulations and policing carefully, and these efforts have been successful. Complex marsh grasses such as Spartina, and fish such as striped bass have reappeared in the area, both sure signs of the rehabilitation of the habitat.

Pollutant	Space Heating	Power Generation	Transportation	Industry	Incinerators
Sulfur Dioxide	50	42	5	2	1
Particulates	30	10	24	5	31
Carbon Monoxide	1	—	98	—	1
Nitrogen Oxides	30	34	33	3	—
Hydrocarbons	2	1	67	28	2

Figure 10-1. Sources of Major Regional Air Pollutants (by percentage contribution).

Air Quality in New York City

Number of Days Air Was	1969	1970	1971	1972	1973	1974
Good	0	0	61	58	48	108
Acceptable	38	86	198	252	229	193
Unsatisfactory	209	196	80	48	65	27
Unhealthy	114	79	26	7	23	36

Figure 10-2.

Month	Temperature in Fahrenheit	Precipitation in Inches
January	33	3.3
February	33	2.8
March	41	4.0
April	51	3.4
May	62	3.7
June	71	3.3
July	77	3.7
August	75	3.4
September	69	3.9
October	58	3.1
November	47	3.4
December	36	3.3

Figure 10-3. Monthly Normal Temperature and Precipitation Based on the Thirty-Year Period 1931-1960, Inclusive.

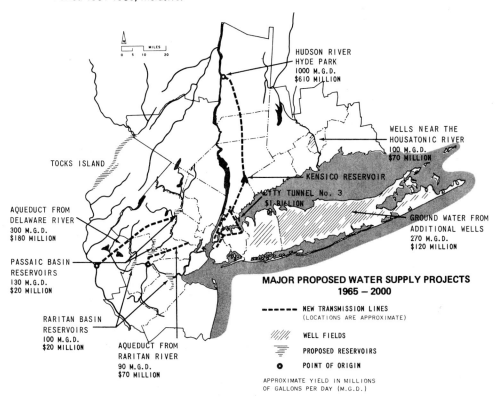

Figure 10-4.

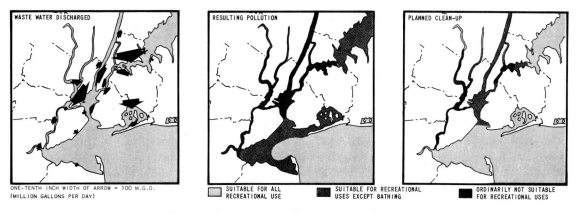

Figure 10-5. Improving the Quality of Central Waterways.

1 North River*
2 Wards Island
3 Hunts Point
4 Bowery Bay
5 Tallman Island
6 Newtown Creek
7 Red Hook*
8 Owls Head
9 Coney Island
10 26th Ward
11 Jamaica
12 Rockaway
13 Port Richmond
14 Oakwood Beach

(*under construction)

Figure 10-6. Existing Water Pollution Control Plant Locations.

New York	22,790
Bronx	22,430
Kings	39,580
Queens	28,950
Nassau	6,490
Bergen	10,440
Essex	6,330
Hudson	9,070

Figure 10-7. Theoretical Additional Acreage of Local Recreation Space Needed by County (1970).

Figure 10-8.

Epilogue:

The Region in the Future

The New York Metropolitan Region in the future will be much the product of decisions being made today. Public capital construction projects such as highways or mass transit facilities, refuse incinerators, sewerage, water pollution control plants, and aquaducts take years to plan and to construct. Throughout the book we have mentioned and mapped several such public investments, some of which will not be completed until the end of the present century, and all of which will play a role in shaping the Region in the 21st century. The distribution of new private capital construction such as factories and warehouses, shopping centers and offices is largely a function of the placement of the public capital projects. Intelligent public planning and applying land use controls can help shape the Region in the future. Regional level planning responsibility lies with the Tri-State Regional Planning Commission, although that agency has no executive authority. Homes and apartments, power plants and power grids can be either public or private investment responsibilities, and a polity obviously must decide whether these responsibilities are to be public or private before the facilities can be built or even planned. Innovative and imaginative public and private cooperative programs are being introduced in the New York Metropolitan Region to attack these questions: in the various schemes of government-subsidized housing, and in State assumption of responsibility for providing power to the New York City subway system, for example.

Here we must return, however, to a point made in the Prologue and brought up again and again throughout this book: there is no such thing as a Metropolitan New York polity, no existing legal or political framework allowing all people in the Region to come together to reach decisions and to take action for the Regional welfare. The dilemma is highlighted by the decision of the New Jersey State Supreme Court in April 1975 that local zoning regulations must consider the Regional welfare. Who, one might well ask, is to speak for the Regional welfare? However unified and bound the Region may be socially and economically, it is fragmented politically, and this frustrates the achievement of the common welfare, or even its definition.

When there is no action at the Regional level—and certainly everyone agrees that certain issues such as water supplies and refuse disposal are *Regional* problems requiring *Regional* solutions—then decision-making power shifts out of the hands of local citizens and governments. First the power shifts up to the State government level, and the State governments in the Tri-State Region have taken significant initiatives toward solving Regional problems. In many cases, however, power has shifted to Washington. If the Region does not act when something must be done, then the federal government determines what is best for the Region, and imposes its solution. The Tri-State Regional Planning Commission has what "muscle" it has largely by virtue of its federal support. The federal government determines often where new development can or cannot take place by granting or withholding subsidies for sewerage, which the federal government requires. The federal government is taking an increasingly active role in determining vehicle use by moving to protect air quality and by subsidizing mass transit. The federal government grants or withholds housing subsidies, poverty funds, sewage treatment subsidies, and other forms of aid. All this is to encourage planning, and certainly intelligent planning is becoming more and more important in the New York Region, as it is throughout the nation. One issue to watch in all metropolitan areas in the coming years is the question of what levels of government will carry out those plans, or what new forms of intergovernmental cooperation will—will *have* to—appear.

Economic Forecasts

The most complete economic forecasts for the 22-County Tri-State Region to the year 1990 have been prepared by the Port Authority, and those deserve our attention in the light of what we have already seen to be the major trends in the Region since the Second World War. The forecasts in the following paragraphs are based on the assumption of continuing national growth overall. Such current problems as energy and material shortages, environmental pressures, inflation, and productivity concerns have been recognized, but it is assumed that the severity of such dislocations can be tempered.

POPULATION

The population of the Tri-State Region is expected to increase to slightly over 20 million in 1990. This represents a significant deceleration of past growth rates, and assumes that there will be no continuing net in-migration to the Region and that fertility rates will remain low. Regional birth rates are generally ten percent below the national average, and the Region actually registered a "zero population growth" level in 1971, a year before the nation as a whole.

MIGRATION PATTERNS

The Region has historically been a magnet for in-migrants, registering a net inflow of 298,000 people from 1960 to 1970. In the period forecast to 1990, however, net in-migration is not expected. In-migration normally occurs when job opportunities exceed the available labor supply, and the Regional labor market is expected to be saturated until 1990 by the coming of age of those born during the "baby boom," 1947 to 1964. Zero net migration in the Region should be achieved through a balance of inflows of working age population 20-39, and outflows of persons over 40 and under 20.

DISTRIBUTION

Lowering fertility rates should affect the pattern of Regional settlement. There will probably be a greater proportion of singles, childless couples, and small families; they will opt for apartments in suburbs or small cities, thus creating a more densely populated area. Out-migration from the cities to the suburbs should continue, and no absolute growth in central cities' populations is expected, but the expected result is a retardation of the rapid suburbanization which occurred from 1950 to 1970.

New York City should maintain constant in population. The New York and New Jersey suburbs should each gain one million people. Thus the City's share of total Regional population will fall to 39 percent (Fig. E-1).

LABOR FORCE

While the total population in the Region is expected to increase by 12.6 percent between 1970 and 1990, population in the age group over 15 will grow by 19 percent. This should lead to intense competition for jobs, despite substantial job growth; relatively high unemployment rates at least until the 1980s; and decreasing rates of participation of workers 62 and over. More will probably take early retirement. The effect of the women's liberation movement on the numbers of women in the labor force is difficult to predict, but it will have to be watched closely. The need to generate new jobs to absorb the growing work force will present the Region with a formidable challenge.

JOBS

Total jobs in the Region are expected to increase 17.6 percent, to 9.5 million in 1990. The long-term outlook will, of course, be influenced by the course of the national economy, but the Region's competitive position looks strong. The Region should continue to be the nation's principal center for finance, communications, corporate headquarters, culture, fashion, and manufacturing.

New York City's total job level should match its 1969 peak by the late 1970s. Total jobs in the City are expected to reach 4.25 million in 1990, a gain of 5 percent over 1970. The generation of these jobs, and the question of whether City residents will be able to capture these jobs, depend upon the City's ability to assimilate and educate the waves of recent migrants to it, as it has always done so successfully in the past.

Most job growth from 1970 to 1990 will occur in the suburbs. The nine New Jersey counties should experience a 30 percent growth of jobs, and the seven suburban New York counties outside the City a 32 percent increase (Fig. E-2).

INDUSTRY DISTRIBUTION

Office activities will generate most new jobs, particularly in the services industry, which is expected to grow by 51 percent, and in the finance, insurance and real estate industries, expected to grow 25 percent by 1990. Wholesale and retail trade job growth will be related to recent population growth in the suburbs; the construction and transportation sectors of the economy will probably remain steady in total employment. No long-term growth in manufacturing jobs is expected over 1970 levels. Government employment growth should slow down from the rapid increases of the 1960s, but still climb 33 percent from 1970 to 1990.

We have seen the collection of colonial settlements in a radius of seventy-five miles from Manhattan fuse into the New York Metropolitan Region during the last 350 years. Since 1625 the Region has emerged from a raw material-producing outpost of a few hundred settlers as the nation's economic and cultural leader, housing nearly 20 million people.

New York City, the Region's heart, continues to dominate the Region's activities. Without New York City the Region as we know it would be unthinkable. The City has shaped the Region; it is the focus of the Region's internal links, its employment concentration, and its cultural activities.

The Region's vitality will continue to be linked to the City's well-being. The New York Metropolitan Region will, in turn, be affected by the vicissitudes of national and international developments. This will be even more true in the future than it has been in the past, for the Region has itself become a "city" within the larger urban region of America's East Coast. In an increasingly interdependent world, the future role of this Megalopolis may well be similar to the functional role of the New York City Region within the nation today.

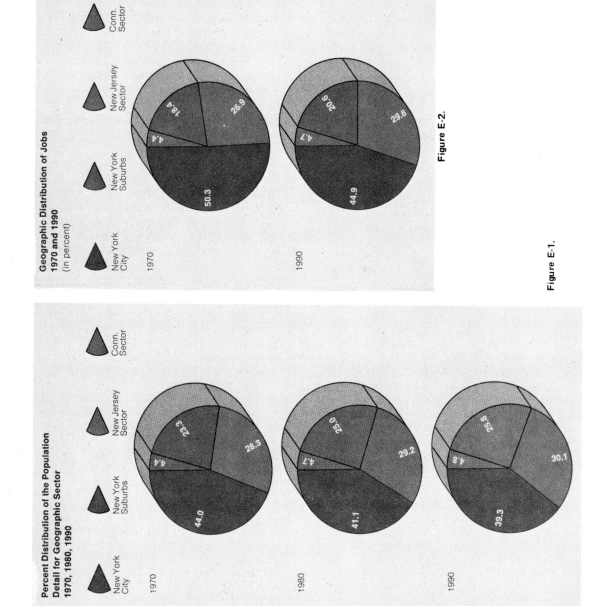

Percent Distribution of the Population
Detail for Geographic Sector
1970, 1980, 1990

New York City | New York Suburbs | New Jersey Sector | Conn. Sector

1970
44.0
23.3
4.4
28.3

1980
41.1
25.0
4.7
29.2

1990
39.3
25.8
4.8
30.1

Geographic Distribution of Jobs
1970 and 1990
(in percent)

New York City | New York Suburbs | New Jersey Sector | Conn. Sector

1970
50.3
18.4
4.4
25.9

1990
44.9
20.6
4.7
29.8

Figure E-2.

Figure E-1.

202

Selected Bibliography

The number of books and articles published about the geography of the New York Metropolitan Region is positively staggering. The number of excellent studies published regularly by just three agencies alone—the Port Authority of New York and New Jersey, the Tri-State Regional Planning Commission, and the Regional Plan Association—would fill a library. This bibliography is, therefore, restricted to a few titles which we feel are and will continue to be of special value. The reader's familiarity with the basic federal statistical sources, several of which are reproduced in tables in the text, is assumed. Almost every individual city and county in the Region has a planning board or commission, the publications of all of which could not possibly be included here.

Adams, Thomas *et al., The Building of the City.* New York: Regional Plan of New York and Its Environs, 1931. This is the second volume of the monumental *Regional Survey of New York and Its Environs,* published eight volumes in ten, 1927-1931.

Albion, Robert, *New York and Its Rivals, 1815-1860.* Cambridge: Harvard University Press, 1931.

———,*The Rise of New York Port.* New York: C. Scribner's Sons, 1939.

Alexander, L.M., *The Northeastern United States.* Princeton, New Jersey: Van Nostrand, 1967.

Bahrenburg, Bruce, "New Jersey's Search for Identity," *Harper's Magazine.* April 1964, pp. 87-94.

Bebout, John and Ronald Grele, *Where Cities Meet: The Urbanization of New Jersey.* New York: Van Nostrand Company, 1964.

Blake, Peter, *God's Own Junkyard: The Planned Deterioration of America's Landscape.* New York: Macmillan, 1964.

Bridenbaugh, Carl, *Cities in the Wilderness: The First Century of Urban Life in America, 1625-1742.* New York: Capricorn Books, 1964. Originally published in 1938.

———, *Cities in Revolt: Urban Life in America, 1743-1776.* New York: Alfred Knopf, 1955.

Brush, John, *The Population of New Jersey.* New Brunswick, N.J.: Rutgers University Press, 1956.

Bryant, William Cullen, ed., *Picturesque America.* Original edition, 1874; Centenniel Edition, Secaucus, New Jersey: Lyle Stuart, Inc., 1974.

Caldwell, William, ed., *How to Save Urban America.* New York: New American Library, 1973.

Carman, Harry, *The Street Surface Railway Franchises of New York City.* New York: Columbia University Press, 1919.

Caro, Robert, *The Power Broker.* New York: Knopf, 1974.

Chinitz, Benjamin, *Freight and the Metropolis.* Cambridge: Harvard University Press, 1960.

Chinitz, B., "New York: A Metropolitan Region," *Scientific American.* Sept. 1965, p. 134.

Conklin, Groff, *All About Subways.* New York: J. Messmer Inc., 1938.

Costikyan, Edward and Lehman, Maxwell, *New Strategies for Regional Cooperation.* New York: Praeger, 1973.

Cranmer, H. Jerome, *New Jersey in the Automobile Age: A History of Transportation.* New York: D. Van Nostrand Company, 1964.

Duffus, R.L. *Mastering a Metropolis; Planning the Future of the New York Region.* New York: Harper and Brothers, 1930.

Eiberson, Harold, *Sources for the Study of the New York Area.* New York: City College Press, 1960.

Erskine, Helen, *Round Manhattan's Rim.* Indianapolis: The Bobbs-Merrill Company, 1934.

First National City Bank, *Profile of a City.* New York: McGraw-Hill Book Co., 1972.

Gabriel, Ralph, *The Evolution of Long Island; a Story of Land and Sea.* Port Washington, N.Y.: I.J. Friedman, 1968.

Ginzberg, Eli, *New York is Very Much Alive: A Manpower View.* New York: McGraw-Hill, 1973.

Glazer, Nathan and Daniel Moynihan, *Beyond The Melting Pot: The Negroes, Puerto Ricans, Jews, Italians and Irish of New York City.* Cambridge: M.I.T. Press, 1963.

Gottmann, Jean, *Megalopolis: The Urbanized Northeastern Seaboard of the United States.* Cambridge: M.I.T. Press, 1961.

Hall, Max, ed., *Made in New York.* Cambridge: Harvard University Press, 1959.

Hall, Peter, *The World Cities*. New York: McGraw-Hill, 1966.

Handlin, Oscar, *The Newcomers: Negroes and Puerto Ricans in a Changing Metropolis*. Cambridge: Harvard University Press, 1959.

Hoover, Edgar M. and Raymond Vernon, *Anatomy of a Metropolis*. Cambridge: Harvard University Press, 1959.

Jacobs, Jane, *The Death and Life of Great American Cities*, New York: Random House, 1961.

———, *The Economy of Cities*. New York: Random House, 1969.

Johnson, James Weldon, *Black Manhattan*. New York: Atheneum, 1969. Originally published 1930.

Kenyon, James, *Industrial Localization and Metropolitan Growth: The Paterson-Passaic District*. Chicago: The University of Chicago Press, 1960.

Kouwenhoven, John A., *The Columbia Historical Portrait of New York*. New York: Doubleday and Co., 1953.

Lewis, Harold MacLean, *Transit and Transportation, and a Study of Port and Industrial Areas and Their Relation to Transportation*. New York: Regional Plan of New York and Its Environs, 1928.

Lichtenberg, Robert, *One-Tenth of a Nation*. Cambridge: Harvard University Press, 1960.

Lubove, Roy, *The Progressives and the Slums: Tenement House Reform in New York City, 1890-1917*. Pittsburgh: University of Pittsburgh Press, 1962.

Lyman, Susan, *The Story of New York, An Informal History of the City*. New York: Crown Publishers, 1964.

McKay, Richard C., *South Street: A Maritime History of New York*. New York: Putnams, 1934.

McKelvey, Blake, *The Urbanization of America, 1860-1915*. New Brunswick, New Jersey: Rutgers University Press, 1963.

———, *The Emergence of Metropolitan America, 1915-1966*. New Brunswick, New Jersey: Rutgers University Press, 1968.

Murphy, Robert, *Fish-Shape Paumanok; Nature and Man on Long Island*. Philadelphia: American Philosophical Society, 1964.

Nevins, Allan and John Krout, eds., *The Greater City: New York, 1898-1948*. New York: Columbia University Press, 1948.

New York City Guide. Copyright 1939 by the Guilds' Committee for Federal Writers' Publications, Inc. New York: Random House, 1939.

O'Hara, Clifford B., "International Container Movements." Speech delivered before the American Society of Traffic and Transportation, 23 August, 1974.

Osofsky, Gilbert, *Harlem: The Making of a Ghetto*. New York: Harper and Row, 1963.

Port Authority of New York and New Jersey. *The Story of the Port of New York Authority*, 1970. *The New York-New Jersey Metropolitan Area Industrial Development Guide*, 1971. *World Trade Services Directory*, 1972. *People and Jobs*, 1974.

Pratt, Edward, *Industrial Causes of Congestion of Population in New York City*. New York: Columbia University Press, 1911.

Regional Plan Association. *The Region's Growth*, 1967. *The Potential of Paterson as a Metropolitan Center in Northern New Jersey*, 1972. *Transportation and Economic Opportunity*, 1973.

Riis, Jacob, *How the Other Half Lives; Studies Among the Tenements of New York*. New York: Dover, 1971. Originally published in 1901.

Robbins, Sidney and Terleckyj, Nestor, *Money Metropolis*. Cambridge: Harvard University Press, 1960.

Roniger, George, *Metro New York, An Economic Perspective*. New York: First National City Bank, 1974.

Rosenberg, Terry, *Residence, Employment and Mobility of Puerto Ricans in New York City*. Chicago: The University of Chicago Press, 1974.

Rodgers, Cleveland and Rebecca Rankin, *New York: The World's Capital City, Its Development and Contributions to Progress*. New York: Harper and Row, 1948.

Rosenwaike, Ira, *Population History of New York City*. Syracuse: Syracuse University Press, 1972.

Row, Arthur T., *A consultant's Report to the Tri-State Transportation Committee on a Reconnaissance of the Tri-State Region*. New York: Tri-State Transportation Committee, 1965.

Scheiner, Seth, *Negro Mecca: A History of the Negro in New York City, 1865-1920*. New York: New York University Press, 1965.

Schoener, Allan, ed., *Portal to America: The Lower East Side 1870-1925*. New York: Holt, Rinehart and Winston, 1967.

Segal, Martin, *Wages in the Metropolis*. Cambridge: Harvard University Press, 1960.

Silver, Nathan, *Lost New York*. Boston: Houghton Mifflin, 1967.

Sobin, Dennis, *Dynamics of Community Change; the*

Case of Long Island's Declining "Gold Coast." Port Washington, N.Y.: I.J. Friedman, 1968.

State Study Commission for New York City. *The Neighborhoods, the City and the Region,* Jan. 1973. *New York City: Economic Base and Fiscal Capacity,* April 1973. *Final Report,* April 1973.

Stevens, John Austin, *Physical Evolution of New York City.* New York: 1907.

Still, Bayrd, *Mirror for Gotham: New York as Seen by Contemporaries from Dutch Days to the Present.* New York: New York University Press, 1956.

———. *New York City. A Students' Guide to Localized History.* New York: Teachers College Press, 1965.

Syrett, Harold, *City of Brooklyn, 1865-1898.* New York: Columbia University Press, 1944.

Tauber, Gilbert and Kaplan, Samuel, *The New York City Handbook.* New York: Doubleday and Co., 1968.

Taylor, George Rogers, "The Beginnings of Mass Transportation in Urban America," *The Smithsonian Journal of History,* Part I in vol. 1, no. 2 (summer, 1966), pp. 35-50; Part II in vol. 1., no. 3 (Autumn, 1966), pp. 31-55.

Taylor, George Rogers, *The Transportation Revolution, 1815-1860.* New York: Harper and Row, 1951.

Tri-State Regional Planning Commission. Annual Reports since 1965. *Fuel, Power and Land Use,* 1967. *Direct Freight Transfer,* 1967. *Manhattan Business District Floor Space Trends,* 1967. *Regional Forecast 1985, the Future Size and Needs of the Tri-State Region,* 1967. *Measure of a Region,* 1967. *Regional Development Guide: Technical Perspectives,* 1969. *Managing the Natural Environment,* 1970. *New Communities for the Tri-State Region,* 1973. *Partnership for Waste Management,* 1973. *Outdoor Recreation in a Crowded Region,* 1973. *The Economics of Energy,* 1974. *Dwellings and Neighborhoods,* 1974.

Tunnard, Christopher and Henry Hope Reed, *American Skyline.* Boston: Houghton Mifflin Co., 1953.

Van Burkalow, Anastasia, "New York City's Water Supply: A Study of Interactions," *Geographic Review.* 49 (1959) 369.

Vecoli, Rudolph, *The People of New Jersey.* New York: D. Van Nostrand Company, 1965.

Vernon, Raymond, *Metropolis 1985.* Cambridge: Harvard University Press, 1960.

Walker, James Blaine, *Fifty Years of Rapid Transit, 1864-1917.* New York: Law Printing Company, 1918.

Ward, David, "The Emergence of Central Immigrant Ghettoes in American Cities 1840-1920," *Annals of the Association of American Geographers.* 58 (1968) 343.

———. *Cities and Immigrants, A Geography of Change in Nineteenth Century America.* New York: Oxford University Press, 1971.

Warner, Sam B., *Streetcar Suburbs: The Process of Growth in Boston 1870-1900.* Cambridge: Harvard University Press, 1962.

"The Wealth of Cities." Entire edition of the *Municipal Performance Report.* 1:3 April 1974.

Weiss, Harry B., *Life in Early New Jersey.* New York: D. Van Nostrand Company, 1964.

White, N. and Willensky, E., eds., *AIA Guide to New York City.* New York: Macmillan, 1968.

Widner, Kemble, *The Geology and Geography of New Jersey.* New York: D. Van Nostrand Company, 1964.

Wildes, Harry Emerson, *Twin Rivers: The Raritan and the Passaic.* New York: Rinehart and Co., 1943.

Wilson, Edmund, "A Slave of Two Cities," *The Nation.* June 14, 1922.

Wood, Robert C., *1400 Governments.* Cambridge: Harvard University Press, 1961.

Wu, C. Tsu, *Chinese People and Chinatown in New York City.* Ann Arbor, Michigan: University Microfilms, 1971.